SPIRIT OF THE EAST,

ILLUSTRATED IN A

JOURNAL OF TRAVELS

THROUGH ROUMELI

DURING AN EVENTFUL PERIOD.

BY

D. URQUHART, Esq.

AUTHOR OF
"TURKEY AND ITS RESOURCES," "ENGLAND, FRANCE, RUSSIA,
AND TURKEY," &c.

"Men are not influenced by Facts, but by Opinions respecting Facts."—EPICTETUS.

IN TWO VOLUMES.

VOL. II.

LONDON:

HENRY COLBURN, PUBLISHER,
GREAT MARLBOROUGH STREET.

1838.

CONTENTS

OF

THE SECOND VOLUME.

JOURNAL,

&c. &c.

CHAPTER I.

DESCENT TO THE VALE OF TEMPE — ARRIVAL AT AMBELAKIA.

WHEN our siesta was over, and when the sun had already set behind our lofty horizon, we mounted and proceeded towards Rapsana. After skirting the lake, we turned to the left, over a low hill, and descended into a deep glen, or " lac," opening to the sea. We could not see it; but a sea-scented breeze came winding through the hills. Here we came upon a party of villagers, who had just killed a wild boar. It was with great difficulty that we got away from them, for they insisted on our spending the night at their village, and ran over the bill of fare to which we should be treated. First, there was the boar, appealing directly to our senses with eloquence in ruby tints, and rhetoric in rounded forms; then there were kids, still tender, that had just returned from Olympus;* venison,

* By keeping the flocks very high up, ewing time is delayed.

from a fine deer which they had shot an hour before; moor-fowl, pheasants, golden plovers, wild ducks, from Nizeros; and all that the fold, the barn-yard, or the dairy could bestow, without number or measure. We effected, however, our escape from so fearful an infliction, and, on ascending the steep hill on the opposite side of the lac, we just saw the edge of the moon appearing over Kessova (Ossa), which shewed, by the deep and gloomy shades, the tremendous chasm rent between Ossa and Olympus, where resided of old the Muses, and through which flows the Peneus.

Turning to the left, and descending along the back of a ridge that runs parallel to Tempe, we at length looked out from Thessaly on the sea, and on the Delta of the Peneus, with its waters silvered by the moon, glittering, here and there, through the trees. Turning again towards the poetic vale, we descended on Rapsana, a heap of ruins, but where we were received in most comfortable quarters, and had a supper presented to us, which would not have shamed the bill of fare of the villagers on the road. The night was far advanced, when, as I had to start early next morning, for Ambelakia, the task, and a hard one it always is, of leave-taking came on. Captain Demo declared that the day of my arrival should be kept as a festival at Caria; and I would not have got to bed until it was time to get up, unless I had promised to revisit Olympus, and spend some months there.

" We will go," he said, " and hunt deer and boars, wolves and foxes, shoot pheasants, partridges, and all the tribe of water-fowl that frequent the Nizeros ; we will, now and then, visit the people that live below, in the plains, and *shoot fish* in the Salembria: then you may go, as often as you like, to the summit of Olympus, and hunt all the country over for old stones; but, remember not to forget the potatoes."

All impatience to find myself in the Vale of Tempe, I quitted Rapsana at dawn, and soon after, in scrambling over the crest of a rock, came suddenly in view of the picture which I shall attempt to sketch. Right before me was the towering and conical mass of Ossa. Below was the narrow vale of Tempe, with the greenish stream meandering through the trees, and forming islets in its bed. To the right, the vale opens out, and forms a triangular plain. The side of Ossa on the left, and of Olympus on the right, framed the view, till met, in the perspective, by the roots of a hill which stands in the plain, before the entrance to Tempe. This hill forms the base of the apparently triangular plain; then open out again, in the distance, beyond this hill and the outline of Ossa on one side, and of Olympus on the other, two plains, which again have a triangular aspect, presenting each its apex towards you. In that to the left, and touching almost to Ossa, may be descried Larissa, with its smiling oasis; in that to the right, Tournovo, with the white bed of the Titaressus ; and, beyond these, the indistinct chains of the Pindus meet the horizon. The Peneus comes sweeping round the base of Ossa, amidst rich fields and verdant groves ; and, where it enters the narrow pass, stands the village of Baba, adorned with mosques and cypresses. Where the opposite Ossa is least wild and rugged, and where industrious terraces have restrained the scanty soil in which the vine delights, Ambelakia is stuck, rather than built, and its magnificent-looking mansions appear as if made fast to the rocks. This was immediately in face of the point where I stood, and almost in a line with the summit of Ossa, which towered on high. At Baba, commences the Vale of Tempe; but I could follow it, as it swept to the left, through only a small portion of its course : for the precipices, approaching from either side, made Ossa and Olympus appear to meet, and the vale, where visible between the rocks, looked like the entrance to a vast cavern.

The sight of Tempe produced an effect upon my nerves rather than upon my imagination. I felt my lungs dilate, and my limbs become elastic, as I inhaled its air and trod its steeps. There is no more describing such impressions, than there is producing them by description. I called up no images of the past, I quoted no verses from Pindar or from Lucan, but I felt an enlargement of existence, and an intensity of enjoyment, in looking on the unrivalled landscape spread before me, to each spot of which attached names so proud, and yet so familiar.

No scene, hallowed by antiquity, ever produced on me such an effect as Tempe. The reason may be, that here the genius of man is associated, not with perishable monuments, but with the indestructible grandeur of nature itself, fresh and smiling with all its varieties of life and wayward-ness of effects, as when the bards of old sought inspiration from its aspect, or poured forth adoration at its shrine. Here no cornice has fallen away, no tints have lost their freshness, no rhetoric its flowers: here is nothing to supply, but all to enjoy; no actors swept away to mourn for, no lost language to interpret, no effaced records to restore. Ossa is lofty as it ever was; Olympus majestic still; the plains of Larissa as wide; the waters of Peneus glide still betwixt banks that bear the myrtle and the daphne. Thousands of years have not wasted the hues with which the morning breaks over this land of enchantment, or impaired the grandeur of its setting sun.

It was some part, too, of the effect, to descend on Tempe from Olympus, and with men who might have been the comrades of Theseus.

While descending the rugged cliffs, our attention was suddenly called to Ambelakia, on the opposite side of the chasm, by the reports of musketry. We halted to observe the manner of the fight, and consider who the parties might be. During twenty minutes, along the upper skirts of the burgh, the firing continued, but we could not make out whether it was an attack on the town, or a squabble of the inhabitants between themselves. Captain Demo had sent two men to accompany me. They insisted on returning to Rapsana. I insisted on going on, but told them to return if they liked; and, as people always are ready with their services when certain that their services are not wanted, they declared that they were ready to follow me to the other end of the world, and, that being the case, they had no objection to go as far as Baba. After carefully changing their priming, we proceeded, crossed the Peneus in a punt, and reached Baba. The Aga said that he did not know what the firing meant; but if the spinners above had come by any harm, he would have heard of it by this time. I, therefore, proceeded to climb the sides of Ossa, and, in about twenty minutes, found myself scrambling through the narrow lines of the once celebrated and wealthy, but now bankrupt and sequestered, Ambelakia.

Throughout the whole of this country, the arts of dyeing, weaving, tanning and curing of leather, are domestic avocations; the ingredients, implements, and processes used, are, consequently, subject to continual variation. To my inquiries respecting these matters, the universal answer was, " Inquire at Ambelakia." " You will learn all

that at Ambelakia." Whenever I put questions
respecting the agriculture, administration, and statistics of the country, I was told, "Wait till you
go to Ambelakia; there are men with long heads;
there you will find men who have been brought up
in Europe, and who will inform you of all things."
I arrived, therefore, at this place, not merely filled
with the most exaggerated expectations, but having
suspended my opinions upon all these objects until I should be enlightened by the sages of Ambelakia. Never was disenchantment more complete.
The half-day I spent at Ambelakia first opened my
eyes as to the moral effects which accrue from
sending young Easterns to acquire the manners of
the West, or rather, I should say, to lose every
trace of what is worthy, amiable, and attractive, in
their own.

I now saw the Greek mind in masquerade, and
can conceive all the contempt and aversion with
which it must inspire those who have only seen it
thus attired. What will Greece be when the various influences of Europe will have come to act as
effectively on this new state as they have done on
Ambelakia?

Two days before, the Klephts had carried off
one of the principal proprietors of Ambelakia.
The Aga, with a body of the townsfolks, amounting to fifty or sixty in number, with their long
robes tied up round their middles, mounted on
ponies, mules, and asses, had set forward in pur-

suit. It was the return of this expedition, in
triumph, which was announced by the firing we
had seen and heard from the opposite mountain.
The triumph which they had celebrated was, however, not the recapture of the lost Primate, but the
flight of the captors, who had never ventured to
shew their faces! I was very much amused at
this exhibition of the warlike spirit of the Ambelakiotes. I have before referred to Mr. Dodwell's
attributing the prosperity of Magnesia to the
" number and bravery" of the armed Greeks,
who " set the Turks at defiance." Mr. Beaujour,
in his " Tableau du Commerce de la Grèce," in like
manner refers the wealth and prosperity of Ambelakia to the bravery of the Ambelakiotes, and to the
equal dexterity with which they wielded the shuttle
and the musket! Now, what would we say of a
Turkish traveller, who, after a tour in England, told
his countrymen that a stick of eighteen inches was
found a much more powerful weapon than a musket
and bayonet; and that we had a race of Rustems,
called constables, any one of whom could, single-
handed, beat a whole regiment? And yet the
learned lucubrations of Mr. Beaujour, about the
connexion of the bravery of the Ambelakiotes with
their truly wonderful commercial speculations and
prosperity, or those of Mr. Dodwell respecting the
Zagorites, are not a whit more fantastical than the
supposed inferences of a stranger respecting the
power, in England, of a constable's baton.

At Ambelakia, I was taken to the Serai, as it is called, of one of the primates; spacious and lofty, laid out in the Turkish style, painted in gaudy colours, and ornamented with abundance of gilding, decorations, fretted work, and arabesque. I, of course, expected to see every thing European, whereas every thing was the very antithesis of Europe. Floors raised, floors depressed; rails cutting through rooms; couches spread in corridors; windows from one apartment to another; double rows of windows to all the rooms, and abundance of stained glass; nowhere passages flattening the nose; none of that huddling of box on box, called rooms, as if the rooms had coalesced to drive the house out of doors; nowhere implements for being half seated, called chairs; nowhere raised floors, for getting food on, called tables: but, on every side, airy spaces for circulation; couches for rest, that really seemed belonging to the house, and shewing no daylight between them and the floors; freedom of motion in the centre; invitations to repose around; and, wherever you turned your eyes, the thick-set windows, without intervening objects, presented at once a full view of the magnificence of surrounding nature.

I here found my companion, who had come from Larissa to wait for me, convalescent from the ague, but much alarmed for my safety, and excessively disappointed with, and irritated by, the character of the inhabitants of a place, which he had entered with expectations similar to mine. The difference between this and every other place we had visited, would almost have made us think that we had passed from one world to another. Here were no visits from the principal men to bid us welcome ; none of that delicacy and warmth of feeling which, every where else, made us feel instantaneously at home. When we attempted to see the people of the house, they stared at us, or ran away. The women wrapped handkerchiefs round their faces, and the men quitted the house. Determined on arriving at the bottom of so strange and unwonted a reception, I sallied forth into the street, and, seeing a very handsome house with the door open, walked up stairs and entered the divan khané, where I found several of the natives in consultation. Elsewhere, such a visit would have called forth expressions of welcome, and even of gratitude and thanks: here it was astonishment and embarrassment. I explained to them that I was a stranger, who had been attracted by the fame of Ambelakia and the beauties of Tempe. *They asked me if I had a buyourdi from the Pasha of Larissa ?* I said, amongst the Klephts of Olympus I had not been asked for a buyourdi. They informed me that there was nothing to be seen in Ambelakia, that they had no information to give me, and that our presence might injure and compromise them with the Turks. I could not help expressing my extreme surprise at the reception I

met with, in a place that I had approached with so
much interest, and at the contrast between them
and their compatriots; whilst I expected, in men
who had had so much connexion with Europe,
feelings of a very different character. One of them
replied, " In Europe, are you in the habit of going
and living in the houses of people whom you don't
know, and at the expense of people who don't
know you? What is the meaning of two young
men coming and staying in a village where they
have no business, and in a house where there are
only women?" I quitted them in disgust (after,
however, repeating a good many of the terms I
had learned from Diogenes, who had hit off admirably the character of his compatriots), and, returning to my companion, proposed immediately
quitting the inhospitable place, and trying if we
should be better treated by the Turks at Baba.
It is, perhaps, superfluous to say, that we had not
made forcible entrance, either into the village or
the house, a joint recommendation having been
forwarded from the Greek Archbishop and the
Kehaya Bey, at Larissa, to have this house prepared for our reception.

The proposal to quit the place was no sooner
made than adopted. A difficulty, however, occurred. My faithful Aristotle was the only four-
footed animal the services of which we could
command; we had, therefore, to heap our saddles
and our baggage on his single back, and drive him

before us to Baba. Just as we had made this arrangement, which we had to carry into effect ourselves, for every soul ran from us as if we had been plague-patients, an Albanian ascended the stairs, and swaggering, like a rattling trophy of arms, into the divan khané, where we were seated, sat down and addressed our astonished ears as follows:—
" Brothmakers,* get up and be off." " Whence comes," we inquired, " this civil greeting ?" " I am," he answered, " the Cavash of the Aga ; and the Codga Bashi (the Greek Primate) orders you immediately to quit his house, and go (ἔις τὸ καλλό) about your business." The Cavash made his exit even less ceremoniously, but more expeditiously, than his entry, and never was a flight of stairs cleared in better style. The household first, and then the Ambelakiotes in general, were thunderstruck at this result of their *coup d'état*, and, before Aristotle was laden, the whole women of the establishment, for still the men kept aloof, came about us to beg and implore that we would not leave them. The Cavash was a wild Albanian, a savage, a barbarian, and knew neither our merits nor our greatness, and sued for forgiveness. We said that was a matter now between them and the Pasha. This announcement produced a strange scene of tearful expostulation, and sufficed to disgust us in every way with the churlish, insolent, and cringing

* Tchorbadgi, calk, git.

wretches, of which this community seemed to be composed; an instance, in a small way, of the moral gangrene that takes possession of a trading people when they break down.

We now proceeded downwards, under the silent gaze of the population, which had turned out to witness our retreat. First marched my companion's valet, a Circassian, with a horribly fierce frowning countenance, firmly grasping, and manfully hauling a rope, which was Aristotle's halter; then came Aristotle, his head and neck stretched out horizontally, with a Pelion of baggage piled up upon his Ossa: we followed, each with a lusty stick to stay the baggage and to drive the mule. We returned scowl for scowl to the Ambelakiotes as we passed, and shook the dust from our soles as we cleared the town; and about sunset reached the village of Baba, to claim hospitality and to ask for shelter. The few people we saw stared at us and got out of the way, thinking, no doubt, it was disreputable to be seen in such company. We took refuge in a huckster's shop. The shopkeeper was an Albanian; some allusions to his country opened his heart, and a small room over the shop was cleared out for our reception; and, as my companion returned to Larissa next morning, I remained, for above a week, the solitary tenant of this cell — a hermit in Tempe!

CHAPTER II.

RISE AND FALL OF THE COMMERCIAL MUNICIPALITY OF
AMBELAKIA.

In Turkey, the people, free in principle and feeling,
combine with the Sultan to restrain the power, or
to avenge the oppression of the governors.   In
Europe, the people, *after* they had been reduced to
a state of serfage, and a legalised sacrifice had been
made of their rights, coalesced with the King to over-
throw the feudal aristocracy, who, originally, were
governors, but who had succeeded in converting
authority into possession, and in rendering that
possession permanent, hereditary, and legal.   But
in Turkey the evils have not yet taken root in
her system; they are not sanctioned by prescrip-
tion, epithets, or law; they are marked as aber-
rations, they are reprobated as crimes.   The cultivator of the soil is not a serf; he is not even
a labourer, he is a proprietor.   Here emancipated
slaves have not to fly to a city of refuge, there
to establish, as distinct from their race and national administration a municipal community of

outcasts ; but, with their paternal fields, the whole mass of the population inherits those simple institutions to which — when accidentally they sprung upon her soil — Europe owes her actual progress and her liberties.

On discovering the existence of urban municipalities and commercial corporations in the East, I was naturally led to compare these with the municipal cities and republics of the middle ages, which, in remote corners, or on hitherto neglected shores, burst forth into splendid contrast with the surrounding barbarism, owing their wealth, prosperity, liberty, and intelligence, not to the accidents of origin, soil, or circumstance, but solely to principles of administration.

Do the antecedent pages of history — does the map of the Mediterranean, indicate any peculiarly happy combinations that could promise to Amalphi, Montpellier, Barcelona, or Ancona — places which had no power to make themselves respected; no anterior connexion or habits of business, which are not in the passage of commerce ; not blessed with local fertility, or celebrated for indigenous manufactures — the prosperity that dazzles by its rise, but has not instructed by its decay? Their deserted halls, these tenantless structures, these princely relics of departed wealth, now only record the proneness of man's mind to legislate, and the results of legislation.

With these Ambelakia furnishes the means of

instituting a comparison: its history furnishes the proof that the fundamental rights, which the municipalities of Europe in the middle ages exceptionally obtained or forcibly extorted, are, in the East, common to the whole people, and are the basis of opinion and government. Ambelakia was, perhaps, the spot, amid all the rich recollections of Thessaly, which I visited with the greatest interest; and, but for the lordly mansions that still overlook the Vale of Tempe, the traveller might doubt the reality of a story which appears almost fabulous. I extract from Beaujour's " Tableau du Commerce de la Grèce," published at the commencement of this century, the details he has preserved respecting it, in as far as they were confirmed to me by the information I obtained on the spot.

" Ambelakia, by its activity, appears rather a borough of Holland than a village of Turkey. This village spreads, by its industry, movement, and life, over the surrounding country, and gives birth to an immense commerce, which unites Germany to Greece by a thousand threads. Its population has trebled in fifteen years, and amounts at present (1798) to four thousand, who live in their manufactories, like swarms of bees in their hives.* In this village are unknown both the

---

* But the principal portion of the yarn was home-spun in the surrounding districts, and disposed of to the Ambelakiotes to be dyed.

vices and cares engendered by idleness; the hearts of the Ambelakiotes are pure, and their faces serene; the slavery which blasts the plains watered by the Peneus, and stretching at their feet, has never ascended the sides of Pelion (Ossa); and they govern themselves, like their ancestors, by their protoyeros (primates, elders), and their own magistrates. Twice the Mussulmans of Larissa attempted to scale their rocks, and twice were they repulsed by hands which dropped the shuttle to seize the musket.

" Every arm, even those of the children, is employed in the factories; whilst the men dye the cotton, the women prepare and spin it. There are twenty-four factories, in which, yearly, two thousand five hundred bales of cotton yarn, of one hundred okes each, are dyed (6138 cwts). This yarn finds its way into Germany, and is disposed of at Buda, Vienna, Leipsic, Dresden, Anspach, and Bayreuth. The Ambelakiote merchants had houses of their own in all these places. These houses belonged to distinct associations at Ambelakia. The competition thus established, reduced very considerably the common profits; they proposed, therefore, to unite themselves under one central commercial administration.* Twenty years ago this plan was suggested,

---

* This competition was of a peculiar character; these houses were agents of one factory, and the competition between the agents did not allow the produce of the factory its fair advan-

and in a few years afterwards it was carried into
execution.   The lowest shares in this joint-stock
company were five thousand piastres (between
600*l*. and 700*l*.), and the highest were restricted
to twenty thousand, that the capitalist might not
swallow up all the profits.   The workmen sub-
scribed their little profits, and, uniting in societies,
purchased single shares ; and, besides their capital,
their labour was reckoned in the general amount :
they received their portion of the profits accordingly, and abundance was soon spread through
the whole community.   The dividends were, at
first, restricted to ten per cent, and the surplus
profit was applied to the augmenting of the capital,
which, in two years, was raised from 600,000 to
1,000,000 piastres (120,000*l*.).

" Three directors, under an assumed firm, managed the affairs of the company; but the signature
was also confided to three associates at Vienna,
whence the returns were made.   These two firms
of Ambelakia and Vienna had their correspondents
at Peste, Trieste, Leipsic, Salonique, Constantinople, and Smyrna, to receive their own staple,
effect the return, and to extend the market for the

tages against other factories. The factories had a common administration at home, and it sent its goods to market at its own
expense and risk — combining the profits of merchant, broker,
and manufacturer; as it was carried on by an association of
capital and labour, which equalised the profits so much that
the poorest could wait for a return, to reap the benefits of the
speculation, as well as receive the wages of his labour.

cotton-yarn of Greece. An important part of their trust was to circulate the funds realised, from hand to hand, and from place to place, according to their own circumstances, necessities, and the rates of exchange,"

Thus the company secured to itself both the profits of the speculation and the profit of the banker, which was exceedingly increased by the command and choice which these two capacities gave of time, market, and speculation. When the exchange was favourable, they remitted specie; when unfavourable, they remitted goods ; or they speculated in Salonica, Constantinople, or Smyrna, by purchase of bills, or by the transmission of German goods, according to the fluctuations and demands of the different markets, of which their extensive relations put them immediately in possession, and by which the rapid turning of so large a capital gave them always the means of profiting.

" Never was a society established upon such economical principles ; and never were fewer hands employed in the transaction of such a mass of business. To concentrate all the profits of Ambe-lakia, the correspondents were all Ambelakiots ; and, to divide the profits more equally amongst them, they were obliged to return to Ambelakia, after three years' service; and they had then to serve one year at home, to imbibe afresh the mercantile principles of the company.

" The greatest harmony long reigned in the

association; the directors were disinterested, the
correspondents zealous, and the workmen docile
and laborious. The company's profits increased
every day, on a capital which had rapidly become
immense. Each investment realised a profit of
from sixty to one hundred per cent; all which was
distributed, in just proportions, to capitalists and
workmen, according to capital and industry. The
shares had increased tenfold."

The disturbances which succeeded to this period of unrivalled prosperity, are attributed, by
Beaujour, with that provoking vagueness that
substitutes epithets for causes, to the " surabond-
ance de richesse," to " assemblées tumultueuses,"
to the workmen's quitting the shuttle for the pen,
to the exactions of the rich, and to the insubordination of the inferior, but still wealthy orders. To
us it may, on the contrary, be matter of surprise
such a body could exist, so long and so prospe-
rously, in the absence of judicial authority to
settle, in their origin,' disputes, and litigated interests, which, in the absence of such authority,
could only be decided by violence. The infraction
of an injudicious bye-law gave rise to litigation, by
which the community was split into two factions.
For several years, at an enormous expense, they
went about to Constantinople, Salonica, and
Vienna, transporting witnesses, and mendicating
legal decisions, to reject them when obtained;
and the company separated into as many parts as

there were associations of workmen in the original firm. At this period, the Bank of Vienna, in which their funds were deposited, broke; and, with this misfortune, political events combined to over-shadow the fortunes of Ambelakia, where prosperity, and even hope, were finally extinguished by the commercial revolution produced by the spinning-jennies of England. Turkey now ceased to supply Germany with yarn: she became tributary for this, her staple manufacture, to England. Finally, came the Greek Revolution. This event has reduced, within the same period, to a state of as complete desolation, the other flourishing townships of Magnesia, Pelion, Ossa, and Olympus. Even on the opposite heights of Olympus, across the valley of Tempe, Rapsana, from a thousand wealthy houses, which ten years ago it possessed, is now, without being guilty of either " luxury" or " tumult," reduced to ten widowed hearths. But Beaujour's praise is as little merited as his censure is ill-deserved. " Here," says he, " spring up anew grand and liberal ideas, on a soil devoted for twenty years to slavery; here the ancient Greek character arose in its early energy, amidst the torrents and caverns of Pelion (Ossa); and, to say all in a word, here were *all the talents and virtues* of ancient Greece born again in a corner of modern Turkey."

Had an old commercial emporium ; had a

conveniently situated sea-port, or a provincial chief town, possessing capital, connexions, and influence, extended thus rapidly its commerce and prosperity, it would have been cited, and justly so, as a proof of sound principles of government; of public spirit, intelligence, and honour. What, then, shall we say of the character of the administration that has elevated an unknown, a weak, and insignificant hamlet, to such a level of prosperity? This hamlet has not a single field in its vicinity—had no local industry — had no commercial connexion—no advantage of position — was in the vicinity of no manufacturing movement — was on the track of no transit commerce — was not situated either on a navigable river, or on the sea—had no harbour even in its vicinity — and was accessible by no road, save a goat's path among precipices. Its industry received no impulse from new discoveries, or secrets of chemistry, or combination of mechanical powers: the sole secret of its rise was the excellent adjustment of interests, the free election of its officers, the immediate control of expenditure, and, consequently, the union of interests by the common pressure of burdens, and the union of sympathies by the smooth action of simple machinery. In fact, here might the imagination enrich itself with new combinations and effects; by which, escaping from the dogmatic frivolity of the age, it can enter into, and comprehend the causes, of that wonderful prosperity and administrative science, to which the human race seems to have attained in its earliest days, as indicated in the ruins of Nineveh and of Babylon, and in the institutes of Menu.

Ambelakia supplied industrious Germany, not by the perfection of its machinery, but by the industry of its spindle and distaff. It taught Montpellier the art of dyeing, not from experimental chairs, but because dyeing was with it a domestic and culinary operation, subject to daily observation in every kitchen; and, by the simplicity and honesty, not the science of its system, it reads a lesson to commercial associations, and holds up an example unparalleled in the commercial history of Europe, of a joint stock and labour company ably and economically and successfully administered, in which the interests of industry and capital were equally represented. Yet the system of administration on which all this is ingrafted, and the rights here enjoyed of property, proprietorship, and succession,— foundations of the political structure,—are common to the thousand hamlets of Thessaly, and to the Ottoman Empire. Here is to be sought the root, and found the promise, of the future fruits, the germs of which exist, although they lie inert in the bosom of those primeval institutions which have not yet, in the East, been extirpated by legislation, or trodden down by faction.

Ambelakia, however, is not a solitary instance of the prosperity of united commercial and manufacturing enterprise : Aivali, in Asia, is the counterpart of Ambelakia, in Europe. It owed its origin to the enterprise of a Greek priest, who, at the close of the last century, obtained a firman from the Porte. No sooner was this petty village withdrawn from the authority of the local Governor, and rendered immediately dependent on the Sultan, than the municipal organisation revived in all its purity and vigour. Cultivators, artisans, traders, flocked from the neighbouring country ; the olives of the surrounding plains were converted into soap, and spread, by their vessels, throughout the Archipelago ; their morocco leather rivalled that of Janina ; their silk that of Zagora ; and wealth, rapid in its increase, equal in its distribution, and instruction ardently sought and universally extended, belied here again the libel of European laws and opinion on man's intellect and honesty. " A true creation of commerce and industry," observes M. Balbi,* " this little republic had rapidly become one of the most industrious, most commercial, and best regulated (*policée*) towns of Ottoman Asia. But its numerous manufactories, its tanneries, its oil-mills, its beautiful college, its library, its printing establishment, its fine churches, its

* Abrégé de Géographie, p. 641.

3000 houses, and 36,000 inhabitants, have disappeared during the war of the resurrection of Greece." Such have been the wide-spread and desolating effects of a revolution conceived by philanthropy, consecrated by religion, hailed by freedom, and adopted by diplomacy!

CHAPTER III.

SOJOURN IN THE VALE OF TEMPE.

The time did not pass heavily during my solitary abode in the vale of the Muses. I had thus leisure to arrange and record the impressions I had received in four months of incessant travelling, in the hottest season of the year, and during which I had been ten or twelve hours daily in the saddle. I used to sit and write, and sometimes dine and sleep, on the banks of the Peneus, and bathe in its stream; and regularly, morning and evening, climbed up the rocks, sometimes on the side of Ossa, sometimes on that of Olympus, to enjoy the sunrise and the sunset. Lovely as was the scene, it must have been lovelier in happier days. The shrubs and trees, on many of the elevated parts, had been recently burnt, and a great proportion of the visible parts of both mountains had been, by former burnings (resorted to by the shepherds to obtain tender grass), deprived of their stately forests, which were replaced by a diminutive covering of dwarf oak, oleaster, arbutus, and agnus

castus. The border of the stream had just received so much culture as to deprive it of its wild-
ness; and the stream, diminished, both in size
and rapidity, by the comparative nakedness of the
mountains at the present day, had shrunk in its
sandy bed. What spot in nature could equal this,
if eternal forests still crowned the bolder rocks,
and if a full stream of crystal water still swelled
between banks of verdure and of flowers? The
vale is filled with plane-trees—it is superfluous to
call them beautiful—and in a copse of these was
the spot I generally chose to sit; and there nothing
could equal the effect of seeing a Tartar, or a
party of travellers, dashing by, casting around them
anxious looks, and starting if they chanced to observe me. On the path to Ambelakia, just when
you come upon the rock after leaving Baba, there
is a most beautiful point of view. Baba, its minaret,
and Téké, in the midst of cypresses and fruit-trees,
with a large spreading pine, stands immediately in
the foreground. Close by it you have a glimpse
of the Peneus, overshadowed by plane-trees, the
mountains descending from either side, and the
ruins of Gomphi standing on the last prolongation
of Olympus. Beyond, in the distance, there is
another aspect of the view, which I have formerly
described. But Tempe, to be seen to advantage,
must be seen by moonlight. The gloom of the
frowning precipices is deeper, grander, and more

consonant with the almost unearthly impressions
which such a scene, with night and loneliness, has
the power to evoke.

The pass of Tempe was considered the most
perilous in the whole country. Travellers used to
stop at a stage distance on either side, until they
negotiated for guards with Captain Demo, or with
the Captain of Ossa ; and, even with a numerous
guard, the passage was effected with alarm, not
altogether unfounded. Nine men were shot on
the last day of my sojourn there ; yet I wandered
about in all directions, and at all hours, perfectly
alone, and never thought of danger. I was in a
singular predicament, being treated as a friend by
whatever party I met ; and nothing used to amuse
me more than the constant state of alarm in which
every body stood of every body else, while they
were all very good and peaceable people in their
own way, and required but the services of some
common friend to discover that they were all exceedingly well disposed towards each other. Had
I resided there a month, I think I should have
been in a state to grant *sauf conduits*.

My sojourn in the vale was one continued
dream. The constant excitement of the times, the
incessant watchfulness of the ear for sounds of
strife, the stretching of the eyes to seize each unwonted object, the interest awakened by each arrival, and the imagination unceasingly worked upon

by the name of every spot on which the eye
chanced to fall, produced a state of mind so full of
imagery, so diversified, so vivid, and so incoherent,
that I scarcely believed myself to be awake, and in
the midst of realities.

Wandering, in such a frame of mind, amid such
a scene, I was forcibly struck with the effect of
mythology on the developement of the human intellect, its tendency to raise man from that state
where physical necessity is the sole spur to energy,
and to excite imagination, the pioneer of reason.
What respect for the yet unknown Author of Good
is inculcated in the worship of nature!   What interest awakened in objects thus idealised!   Dryades
in the forests, Naiades in the streams, Genii attached
to every spot, spirits to each person, omens of each
event, knowledge of dark mysteries residing in consecrated groves, divinities upon the mountains, and
the fate of man rehearsed by the stars!   The power
of the Creator, still undistinguished from his works,
was thus venerated in their forms, and adored in
their excellencies.   The ancient mythologist multiplied worship because he had not classified facts.
To us, who have commenced by learning, as children, the constant sequences that have been perceived in the material world, before we have experienced their usefulness, or felt their charms, it is
difficult to return to that fanciful and devotional
frame of mind which perceives those effects with-

out understanding their order. To them, a crystal
or a flower was inexplicable in its beauty; it was,
therefore, the abode of a genius, or the personifi-
cation of a spirit. To us, they are substances,
catalogued by classes and by families, or measured
by angles and degrees. The stars, that shone in
the silent and lonely night, bright, mysterious, and
impressive, could, to their eyes, be destined only to
watch over the fate of men and nations. When
the grander mysteries of their revolutions opened
themselves to the eye of science, astrology sank to
a delirium or a deceit. The sage of old might
wander by night, bewildered by the sight of the
starry firmament, and, in the impossibility of comprehending, he would feel more deeply; the stag-
nation of reason would cause the overflowing of
the soul, and, without advancing in the science of
astronomy, he would return from the contemplation
with a brighter mind, and with purer feelings.
Now, even the child will rehearse to you by rote
the course of the planets and the distances of the
spheres. Flowers, streams, mountains, and stars,
are shrunk to facts, and claim no longer poets for
their priests. Imagination, with inverted torch,
has sunk into the earth, and the universe that lived
in its light has faded away. But, from mythology,
that early union of inquiry and devotion, sprang
the literature which has, in all time, formed the
noblest among the human race; and he who wan-

ders on the banks of the Peneus may still delight
to inhale the atmosphere from which primeval
genius drew its breath.

The village of Baba is one of the early Turkish
settlements of colonists from Iconium. There are
but twenty-five families now remaining, but I understood that there were not less than two Greek
families, refugees from the neighbourhood, living
in every Turkish establishment. But the village
seemed a perfect place of tombs, and scarcely could
I get a glimpse of man, woman, or child. The
houses were all situated within gardens, or enclosed
within mud walls, without any aperture excepting
a door—not that I had scarcely ever occasion to
know that the doors were possessed of the faculty
of opening. The little room I occupied was conveniently placed so as to be sheltered *from* the
cool sea-breeze, that blew through the vale; it
was, therefore, untenable during the day, except
when wet cloths were hung all round, and water
thrown on the matting. There were only two individuals belonging to the village whom I used to
see. One was my Albanian host, who, twice a-day,
made his appearance, with a piece of board in one
hand, and a dish of yaoort and pilaf standing on it,
and a melon in the other, the size of which was
only rivalled by its excellence. The other individual whom, at times, I did get a glimpse of, was
the sole remaining Dervish of the Téké, who, instead of going to bed like other mortals, used to

roost in a tall cypress-tree, that stood in the court of the Téké, and who, evening and morning, was visible as he ascended to, or descended from his perch.

In this Pompeii-looking place, as may be supposed (whatever might have been the state of my wardrobe), I was not very solicitous about my toilet. I made bold to wander about in an old dressing-gown of green silk, a pair of yellow slippers on my feet, and a red cap on my head; and, in consequence of this equipment, a wonderful change took place in my relation with the Babaleans, for I was honoured, much to my surprise, by a visit from the five most important personages in the place : the Aga, the roosting Dervish — a man who let horses — the farrier, and the ferryman. They had all been very much struck with my new costume; and fancied it was one of the recent fashions adopted at Constantinople. After this event, the village assumed quite a different air; the doors were left open; the women and children walked abroad; and I was presented with sundry peskeshes (presents) of tobacco and melons, the two products for which Tempe is now celebrated.

The Aga now gave me more of his company than suited with my present humour or avocations; but he was a learned man, and peculiarly well versed in geography; and his notions were replete with the license which seemed legitimately to belong to the ruler of the vale of the Muses. One day that he was sitting in my little box, with his four inseparable companions, he treated us to his views respecting England, the character of which may be appreciated from the following specimen : " All the salt water in the world belongs to England, and all the fresh water to Turkey; because the fresh water flows through the land, and is only of use to give cattle to drink, and to water fields." " But," observed the Albanian, who was standing leaning against the door-post, " has England, then, no fields nor horses to water ? or do her horses drink sea-water ? " " Man of the mountains," exclaimed the Aga, his convictions and his dignity equally insulted, " don't you know that England has neither fields nor horses ?" The Albanian looked at me ; I said to him, " Why don't you answer the Aga ?" So the Arnout, after a moment's hesitation, and, with the air of an examiner in the schools, looking the Aga full in the face, and twisting his chin, said, " What is England ?" This was a home question, which perfectly perplexed the Aga. He stammered, looked round, but, being left entirely to his own resources, he at length announced England to be " a number — a very great number, of ships — of very large ships." I told him he was an honour to Baba, and ought to have been a Hadgi ;—that is to say, a Hadgi Baba. He had quite hit England off; but he did not seem to be yet aware that we had flocks of fish, as they had flocks of goats; sea-

horses to ride, and sea-calves to milk ; though we
had yet to learn from them the elegant recreation
of shooting fish.*

During my residence here, a dire misfortune fell
upon their heads, and occupied all men's tongues
and thoughts, almost as much as the Protocol had
done to the south. This was a Firman, ordering
contributions to make up the amount of the war
indemnity to be paid to Russia. The district to
which Baba belongs, was assessed at half a million
of piastres : but, as this assessment was to fall exclusively on Mussulman proprietors in easy circumstances, it created an outcry and an irritation
which no words can tell. The amount of the sum
was wholly insignificant as regarded the property
of the country ; but at least three-fourths of that
property was Greek ; and of the remainder, a very
small proportion, indeed, was held by proprietors,
who came under the head of contributors. The
Coniar inhabitants of the plain are all small proprietors, but their property, individually, was below
the amount which rendered them liable to the im-
post ; the consequence naturally was, that the

---

* The inhabitants of Baba suspend a piece of bread over
the stream, just touching it. The small fish gather round to
pick it, and large ones make darts at the small fish. The
sportsman is established in the tree, with his gun pointed on
the spot. His dexterity consists in knowing the ways of the
large fish sufficiently to hit them at the very instant that they
are getting a mouthful of minnows.

principal men suffered severely in their pockets, and were the more exasperated by what they considered injustice in the distribution of the tax. At Baba, it gave rise to many an angry discussion, and the Turks called the Sultan a Greek. The Turkish population bears exclusively the burden of war; they are liable to the conscription, which the Greeks are not; when the Greeks enter the military service, it is of their own free choice; and then, besides emancipation from the poll-tax, which is the equivalent for military service, they receive pay in addition; whereas the Turks only receive pay when they enter the regular service. At the same time, too, a demand came for 1200 young men for the Nizam. It was the first attempt at conscription, and produced a universal ferment. The Turks, therefore, bitterly complained; first, of an act of despotism, which they considered intolerable; and, secondly, of the Greeks being relieved from this call, which made it fall so much more heavily on them. And, in addition to this, there was the contribution towards the indemnity to Russia, which the Greeks were not called on to pay, though, as the Turks affirmed, they had been the cause of the war, and of the success of the Russians.

CHAPTER IV.

CONTRASTS BETWEEN ENGLAND AND TURKEY.

THE remarkable change I had perceived in the
feelings of the inhabitants of Baba towards me,
after I had exchanged a blue jacket for a dressing-
gown, a straw-hat for a red cap, and black boots
for yellow slippers, led me to many reflections on
the weighty principles involved in the distribution
of long cloth, and of calf's leather. I had long
felt that a European's dignity is lost when he gets
beyond the influence of laundresses and of shoe-
blacks. His costume is not made for buffeting the
elements; the square cut of his tight clothes is
not intended to lie down in at night, wrapped in
a capote. The comfort and convenience of having
the neck, arms, and legs bare; the facility of un-
covering and washing them without disturbance of
the dress; the support of a tight belt round the
waist; the freedom of every other part of the body
from all constraints, are advantages of which the

Frank costume is wholly innocent. But in these reside the advantage of any costume.

These were sufficient reasons for laying aside the "snuffers," as the Frank dress is there expressively designated: and the incident which occurred at Baba led me to suspect that more advantages were associated with the change than the mere faculty of being decent without starch, and clean without blacking; and I was thus led to observe a number of contrasts between the habits of the East and the West, which I cannot altogether pass over in silence.

There are members of the community who, enslaved, degraded, and debased, amongst western nations, enjoy, throughout the whole of the East, a degree of comfort and independence, which is a satire upon our so-called free institutions. How far those members of the community whose interests I advocate are deserving of attention, may be inferred from this, that the numbers thus afflicted amount to very nearly the double of the other members of the community, reckoned per head. I refer to the Feet. On the severity of the measures imposed upon our Feet it is needless to dilate, because every one feels where the shoe pinches. Stuffed into black moulds, they are deprived of the common benefits of air, and too often of water, and never permitted to raise themselves from the lowliest grade of existence. But, while

practically conversant with this state of degradation and suffering, we, having no knowledge of
another state of things, fancy that degradation
necessary, and that suffering unavoidable. How
different, however, is the state of Feet in the East.
Admitted to perfect equality of rights with their
brother hands, they there, also, take upon themselves an equal share of duty. No sense is offended at their presence, no aversion excited by
their aspect; placed, with respect, on the great
man's sofa, or handling with dexterity the tools in
the workman's stall, in the full enjoyment of light,
air, and water, and making use of boots and shoes,
instead of being used by them; thus preserving
the original object of these institutions, which, like
so many others, begotten by necessity, have become the parents of despotism. When we hear of
kissing the Foot of an Eastern Monarch, what false
ideas do we not present to ourselves, not only of
human nature, but also of Foot-kind. We imagine
the saluter to be the abject thing that could kiss
the abject and offensive slave we carry in a boot,
and call a Foot. But *the* Foot (as existing in the
East) is a member of no less quality than usefulness; elevated in position, educated with care, and
maintained in elegant ease — *simplex munditiis*.

There the Foot rejoices in a buskin, which, in
common with the covering of the head, and as in
the days of Roman grandeur, denotes the quality

of the man! When the festal henna imparts its
dyes to the rosy fingers, it disdains not to bestow
its purple on the toe; and the artful coquette,
conscious of the power of a pretty Foot, calls attention thereto by dyeing the nail of the third toe,
when she tinges that of the third finger.

No wonder that the distorted and indecent
foot of the West anticipates the aversion which
its presence would call forth, and shrinks from a
display of its ungainly forms. " Cabined, cribbed,
confined," its nature becomes debased, like its
fortunes ; and, shorn of its natural right, as robbed
of its fair proportion, invokes the protecting covering of calf-skin for its hunchback toes, while external grace and lustre compensate, to the helpless
inmates, for the torture of corns, and the terrors of
gout.

This antithesis between the habits of the East
and the West, regarding so fundamental a part of
society, is not the only contrast which it is curious
to observe, or instructive to compare. I shall add
a few more specimens, which may serve as the
nucleus for a museum of Occidental and Oriental
social phenomena. If travellers would commence
collecting specimens, we might obtain data to
guide some future Linnæus of manners in classi-
fying the varieties, arranging, and defining the
characters of these two great human genera.

CONTRASTS.

Europeans commemorate the laying of the foundation stone; Turks celebrate the covering in of the roof.

Among the Turks, a beard is a mark of dignity; with us of negligence.

Shaving the head is, with them, a custom; with us, a punishment.

We take off our gloves before our Sovereign; they cover their hands with their sleeves.

We enter an apartment with our head uncovered; they enter an apartment with the feet uncovered.

With them, the men have their necks and their arms naked; with us, women have their arms and necks naked.

With us, the women parade in gay colours, and the men in sombre; with them, in both cases, it is the reverse.

With us, the men ogle the women; in Turkey, the women ogle the men.

With us, the lady looks shy and bashful; in Turkey, it is the gentleman.

In Europe, a lady cannot visit a gentleman; in Turkey, she can. In Turkey, a gentleman cannot visit a lady; in Europe, he can.

There the ladies always wear trousers, and the gentlemen sometimes petticoats.

With us, the red cap is the symbol of license; with them, it is the hat.

In our rooms the roof is white and the wall is coloured; with them, the wall is white and the roof is coloured.

In Turkey, there are gradations of social rank without privileges; in England, there are privileges without corresponding social distinctions.

With us, social forms and etiquette supersede domestic ties; with them, the etiquette of relationship supersedes that of society.

With us, the schoolmaster appeals to the authority of the parent; with them, the parent has to appeal to the superior authority and responsibility of the schoolmaster.

With us, a student is punished by being " confined to chapel ;" with them, a scholar is punished by being excluded from the mosque.

Their children have the manners of men; our men the manners of children.

Amongst us, masters require characters with their servants; in Turkey, servants inquire into the character of masters.*

We consider dancing a polite recreation; they consider it a disgraceful avocation.

In Turkey, religion restrains the imposition of political taxes; in England, the government imposes taxes for religion.

In England, the religion of the state exacts contributions from sectarians; in Turkey, the re-

* This proceeds from the practice of remuneration by occasional presents, and not by fixed wages.

ligion of the state protects the property of sectarians against government taxes.

An Englishman will be astonished at what he calls the absence of public credit in Turkey; the Turk will be amazed at our national debt.

The first will despise the Turks for having no organisation to facilitate exchange; the Turk will be astounded to perceive, in England, laws to impede the circulation of commerce.

The Turk will wonder how government can be carried on with divided opinions; the Englishman will not believe that, without opposition, independence can exist.

In Turkey, commotion may exist without disaffection; in England, disaffection exists without commotion.

A European, in Turkey, will consider the administration of justice defective; a Turk, in Europe, will consider the principles of law unjust.

The first would esteem property, in Turkey, insecure against violence; the second would consider property, in England, insecure against law.

The first would marvel how, without lawyers, law can be administered; the second would marvel how, with lawyers, justice can be obtained.

The first would be startled at the want of a check upon the central government; the second would be amazed at the absence of control over the local administration.

We cannot conceive immutability in the principles of the state compatible with well-being; they cannot conceive that which is good and just capable of change.

The Englishman will esteem the Turk unhappy because he has no public amusements; the Turk will reckon the man miserable who lacks amusements from home.

The Englishman will look on the Turk as destitute of taste, because he has no pictures; the Turk will consider the Englishman destitute of feeling, from his disregard of nature.

The Turk will be horrified at prostitution and bastardy; the Englishman at polygamy.

The first will be disgusted at our haughty treatment of our inferiors; the second will revolt at the purchase of slaves.

They will reciprocally call each other fanatic in religion—dissolute in morals—uncleanly in habits —unhappy in the developement of their sympathies and their tastes —destitute severally of political freedom — each will consider the other unfit for good society.

The European will term the Turk pompous and sullen; the Turk will call the European flippant and vulgar.

It may therefore be imagined how interesting, friendly, and harmonious must be the intercourse between the two.

The observer who, from a neutral position, marks this mutual recrimination, will perhaps conclude, that when men judge harshly of their fellows, they are nine times wrong in ten.

There is much that is burlesque, but there is not less that is serious in the impressions received, and the conclusions drawn, by the inhabitants of either of these distinct zones of existence, when they visit the other. European travellers have been, in Europe, in contact only with the society *qui vit de ses rentes*, and now they are excluded from that society, and looked down on as inferiors; they are left to shift as best they may, and to draw comparisons. Asiatics belonging to the lower orders, who visit Europe, are generally struck and shocked with the coarseness and indecency, the filthiness, and the addiction to drink and gambling which they find amongst men of their own rank; and they become sensitively alive to the severe line of separation drawn between them and their superiors. Asiatics of a higher rank have their minds more turned to its military and naval power; to its scientific progress, and generally return its enthusiastic admirers. But the European arrives generally with the Western habits of recent times: that is, of having *opinions* upon all subjects.   This is, I should imagine, the greatest change which would strike, in the present state of the world, a Socrates or an Aristippus, were he to reascend from Hades; as man, with opinions on all subjects, is a fearful animal to cast loose on society, if his conclusions are to draw material consequences after them.

But what two Englishmen can be expected to have the same opinion on almost any subject? Yet, what Englishman is to be found who doubts the infallibility of his own, or of those whom, on political subjects, he considers the oracles of his sect or party? The travellers from Great Britain are, like its inhabitants, no longer Englishmen; they are only Whigs, Tories, and Radicals. The previously established opinions of one who visits the East, thus become obstacles to his investigation of the country he visits, or causes of the misapprehension of the facts he sees. And this is so true, that every man who has made some progress in this inquiry, proportionately throws off his sectional character, and feels that he has to commence anew his inquiries into man, manners, and institutions.

If a traveller, arriving in England from a distant land, were desirous to ascertain the opinions of England respecting chemistry, astronomy, mechanics, or geology, he would apply to Faraday, Herschel, Babbage, and Buckland; and every Englishman and every European would tell him he could adopt no better course. But, supposing he wished to know what our most advanced opinions were on the immeasurably important science of politics, to whom would he apply? Say, to Sir Robert Peel—would not the first person he came in contact with probably tell him, that he has precisely pitched upon the person least qualified to

give him correct notions, and that he must go to
Lord Grey ?   The next would warn him equally
against both ; and tell him that Mr. Roebuck was
the sole depositary of political wisdom !   But are
politics less worthy of the title of science than
geology, chemistry, or mechanics ?

Fortunately, in the present day, science is possessed of characters discernible to the inquiring
mind, however ignorant it may be of the subject
matter to which that science is applied ; and, without such characters, science does not exist.   When
the Wernerian and Huttonian schools disputed,
between themselves, every rock and every stratum
of geology, was it not universally felt that geology
had not been reduced to fixed principles ?   The
supposed oppositions were no sooner reconciled, a
common theory was no sooner found to be applicable to the facts before supposed to be contradictory, than every student exclaimed " geology
now *is* a science."

It is the character of science to give, by the
classification of sequences, that meaning to facts
that grammar does to words ; and, as intelligibility
in language indicates the observance of the rules of
grammar, so does the common intelligence of facts
indicate knowledge of them sufficiently extensive
to be accurate, which is science.   Then, and only
then, disciples cease to doubt, and doctors to
disagree.

Politics are not yet a science, because they are

wanting in these characters, either from the deficiency of facts observed, or of powers of mind
equal to so great a task in those who have examined them. How important is it, then, to find
a new field of political inquiry, and new sequences
of facts, which remain distinct from previous associations, and thus bring the mind, in observing
them, to revise and recast its previous convictions.
Turkey presents such a field, and its very weakness
and convulsions facilitate the anatomy of its parts, as
disease in a patient facilitates, and, indeed, affords
the only means of judging of health, and of discovering the means by which it can be restored.

To return to the European traveller. Arrived
in the midst of habits and institutions so completely at variance with those of his own country,
and struck, of course, immediately with all those
things which are worse and inferior to his own
country, whether that inferiority exist in reality or
in his previous opinion respecting excellence, his eyes
naturally revert homewards, with a feeling of satisfaction and exultation; and, from the position on
which he stands, where smaller objects are confounded or lost, he takes a more comprehensive
view than, probably, he has done before, of the
elements of his country's greatness; he reckons
over these fundamental principles one by one, and
then turns again to make application of each to
the country in which he is.

He first, perhaps, appreciates, in England,

the form of government, the settled nature of
the supreme power, and the settled control over
its exercise.   An aristocracy, powerful by the respect of the nation, and not by its privileges ; a
representation of the feelings and interests of the
mass of the community, not less estimable in its
principles than in its action, which opens a field of
distinction and ambition to those who can secure
the respect of their fellow-citizens.   He will then
look at the administration of justice, and he will
perceive judges above suspicion, juries beyond inti-
midation, law above wealth or power, and a citizen
defended in his rights against his government.   He
would then turn to the practical means of strength
and of progress : an enormous revenue at the disposal of the state ; an army filled with the loftiest
aspirations of national honour, perfect in its discipline, and imposing by its numbers ; a navy, the
first in character and in power ; internal means
of communication, the greatest prop of national
prosperity, maintained by a system of roads, canals,
and railroads, which is unequalled ; a banking system, which causes capital to circulate with the
utmost facility ; a press and a post every where in
constant activity, which renders the accumulation
of knowledge and information as easy and as perfect as the circulation of material objects and of
capital.   These will strike him as the elements of
England's greatness ; and, as he feels that England
must descend from her rank amongst nations were

she deprived of these things, so must he consider them as necessary conditions of the well-being, or permanency, of every other state.

Now, in Turkey, he will perceive that they do not exist. He will find the power of the Sovereign, according to his means of judging, unlimited; he will see no permanent aristocracy, no representative chamber, no lawyers, no jury; a slender revenue accruing to the state, and extensive abuses in its collection; no standing army, or, at least, a trifling and recent one, deficient in discipline and in spirit; he will perceive the greatest difficulty in the means of internal transport; no combined banking establishments for the circulation of capital, no posts, no press, no benevolent provision for the poor; and, consequently, he will set down Turkey as a nation in a state of decay, and upon the verge of dissolution.

But, should circumstances lead him to further acquaintance with the material state of this people, he will perceive that many of the objects, and the most essential objects, which are the ends proposed by our own institutions, are there realised, in a remarkable degree, and often to a much greater extent than amongst ourselves. He will perceive an abundance of the necessaries and the comforts of life within the reach of the whole mass of the population. He will be struck by the absence of pauperism, of litigation, and of crime;

and, above all, will he have to remark an absence
of party spirit and political animosity, and universal
habits of submission to a government which, to
him, presents none of the characters which render
a government respectable, and which, moreover,
has no means of causing its authority to be enforced. He will remark, in the absence of all
combination for the facilitating of transport, of a
representative chamber to watch over the interests
of commerce, and of laws for the protection of
native industry; a facility in all commercial trans-
actions, incomprehensible to him who associates
national prosperity with certain forms of government, with special boards and committees, and
with thousands of folios of enactments. The in-
ference is, that there must exist, in Turkey, other
elements of prosperity than those upon which repose the prosperity of England, and, consequently,
that the experience of England, or of any one
country or system, is not sufficient to establish the
laws that regulate human society; and, as he had
seen nothing to lower the importance of those
elementary parts above indicated, of the greatness
of England, he must conclude that, with advantages which Turkey does not possess, England
suffers from evils which Turkey does not know.
He will, therefore, be brought back to the point
from which he ought to have started, and that is,
that much is yet to be learned ; that the dogmas

of party, and the opinion of politicians, are not as yet infallible; and that the mind of man is a more important study, even for a statesman, than forms of government.

CHAPTER V.

EXPEDITION FROM SALONICA IN PURSUIT OF ROBBERS.

Supposing that the reader has seen enough of
Klefts or Armatoles, I will not lead him through
the mountains of Piëra, and beg him to leap over
six weeks from the conclusion of the last chapter,
and to fancy himself, on a bright and sunny Sep-
tember afternoon, which had lost somewhat of the
heat, but none of the brilliancy, of the sun's mid-
summer rays, seated under the shade of a group of
plane-trees that overshadow the tombs in face of
the eastern gate of Salonica.   There, while enjoying, under that elegant canopy of verdure, the
fragrance of a pipe, or of a Nargilleh, and the freshness of the sea-breeze just rising out of the waters,
he will perceive, issuing from the portals of the
ancient walls, a gay and merry group of travellers
passing along the beach, and directing their steps
towards the unfrequented regions of southern
Macedonia.

Foremost of this group is a Surrigée, or

postilion, whose attire seemed composed of an assortment of dirty rags, but adjusted to his person not without an air of sprightliness and grace, and as if an artist had attempted to shew how much that is picturesque can be made out of shreds. A dirty-looking towel is wound round a cap that once had been red; and the ex-embroidery of its fringe dangles on his neck, and sets off the Hindoo features, for he is a gipsy, which it shades. A tight, sleeveless jacket, fitting to the body, and an outer jacket, of which the sleeves fall back from the shoulders, give the exact outline of his chest; and the ample sleeves of his shirt tucked in over his shoulders, leave bare his bronzed and brawny arms and neck; another towel is wrapped tightly round his waist, below which swell an ample pair of dingy trousers, gathered up by short stirrups on his high saddle, and terminating in the ornamental tops that hang over his travelling boots; but while the ornamental remains, the useful had vanished, and the naked toes protrude below from the boots and the shovel-stirrups. The Surrigée always leads the van, holding in his hand the halter of the baggage, or led horse, or horses; after which, immediately comes the Tartar or conductor, whoever he may be, ready to apply the whip to the lagging horse, or refractory postilion, and then follow the gentlemen of the party.

In the present instance, it was not a Tartar

who followed the baggage-horses, but two more
dignified personages, as might be seen by the
silver knobs of their Cavash's staves lying against
the necks of their steeds, the staves having been
run through the fork of the saddle, in the open
space between it and the horse's back.

With the exception of the turban, which had
been replaced by the simple red cap, they wore
the ancient Turkish costume, embroidered vests,
and jackets with open or hanging sleeves, and the
pompous, and not inelegant shalvar; pistols and
yataghan in their belt, a sabre slinging from its red
silk cord over the shoulder; pistols again protrud-
ing from the holsters; a musket slung from the
pommel of the saddle, on one side, and a long
cloth tube, for the pipe, on the other. But the
catalogue of their accoutrement is not yet complete.
Two silver cartridge-boxes were strapped on behind, by a belt round the waist, and from it
depended a small case, containing grease for their
arms, with flint and tow; well-garnished tobacco-
pouches, of embroidered cloth or velvet, dangled
against their thighs; and a brown capote, tightly
made up, was strapped behind the saddle. After
these came something like an Osmanli, mounted
on a gray mule, and beside him rode a Frank, with
meagre, blue cloth cap and jacket, with tight duck
trousers, which, in the absence of straps, were
reefed around the knee; and the cavalcade was

completed by two Greek, and two Turkish attendants. The gray mule *was* " Aristotle," but I was
not " the Frank."

It had been my intention to proceed from
Salonica to Monastir. The road was open; and,
as neither difficulty nor danger of any kind attended the journey, my anxiety to see Monastir
began to diminish. The glimpse I had had of
Mount Athos from Mount Olympus, had directed
my thoughts towards the " Holy Mountain;" and
the accounts which I had heard at Salonica of
the distracted state of that district, and the universal opinion expressed by the *Viri consulares* at
Salonica, of the impracticability of visiting it, gradually led me to the determination of paying it a
visit; and it wanted but the following incident to
determine me to set forward on a pilgrimage to
Agion Oros.

A letter was brought by a Greek boat, from the
captain of some vessel in the neighbourhood, to the
English Consul, stating that it was reported that a
Greek boat, from Mitylene, bound for Salonica, and
having two Englishmen on board, had been captured
by a Greek pirate-boat, in the Gulf of Salonica; that
one of the Englishmen had been murdered, and
the other detained for ransom; and that he actually was at a small island in the Gulf of Mount
Athos, called by the Greeks " Amiliari," and by the
Turks, " Eski Adasi." On this, the Consul required that the Pasha should take steps to ascer-

tain the fact, and to release the Englishman. The Pasha bluntly declared that he did not know how to proceed in the matter; and I no sooner learnt this circumstance, than, supposing the unfortunate travellers to be friends of my own, I determined to proceed without delay, thinking I could easily obtain the deliverance of the survivor, by my " *chatir*"* among the Klephts. This being decided on, the Pasha declared that he would not allow me to go unattended, but a couple of Cavashes should accompany me to Cassandra, where there was an influential Greek Captain; and that he and the Turkish Governor should be directed to take such steps as I judged advisable; and that boats and men should be placed at my disposal. It was but a few hours after the arrival of the intelligence, that the cavalcade above described issued from the gate of Salonica. The Frank who accompanied me was a merchant who had business at Cassandra, and who availed himself of this opportunity of proceeding thither.

The district I was now proceeding to visit was one which scarcely yielded in interest to Thessaly or to Olympus itself: not less unfrequented, for many years, by travellers; and offering, in its natu-

---

* This word is untranslateable. Its meaning will appear subsequently, as far, at least, as it is intelligible to Europeans; that is, to people among whom there is more than one standard of opinion; and who have, consequently, lost the play and interest of individual character.

ral beauty, in its singular geographical conforma-
tion, and in the history and the mode of existence
of two of the most extraordinary communities
throughout the whole of the East, interesting and
attractive subjects of investigation. This region
had been selected both by Athens and by Sparta
for important colonial establishments; and here,
on more than one occasion, was the fate of the
Peloponnesus decided. Hence was drawn the ore
of those beautiful Macedonian coins which embellish the cabinet of the *virtuoso*, and without which
the battles of the Granicus or Arbela never would
have been won, nor a Grecian fleet have navigated
the Indus, nor an Aristotle classified the natural
history of central Asia. Here were to be sought
the scoria from the long cold furnaces of Pagæ;
here the groves long silent of Stagyra; here, after
thirty centuries, were to be sought or seen the
still doubted track of the fleets of Xerxes. But
objects of more immediate interest were not wanting. The monastic rule of Athos claimed the
attention of whoever took interest in all the extensive combinations associated with the Greek faith
and name; and the political institutions of the flourishing communities termed the Mademo Choria,
were calculated to rivet the attention of every
inquirer into the state and prospects of the
Ottoman Empire, or, indeed, of the science of
government.

Here, too, were to be seen the effects produced

by the Greek insurrection on provinces so far removed from its original focus.   Mount Athos, in
immediate contact, through that powerful clerical
organisation, with Greece on one side, and Russia
on the other, hurried the surrounding countries
into a sudden and desperate revolt, while no immediate oppression could justify the act, and no
chance of success could excuse the actors.   The
prosperous communities of the Mademo Choria
saw their exaggerated expectations extinguished,
together with their real prosperity; their hitherto
peaceful boroughs became heaps of ashes.   For
ten years, Chalcidice and its three promontories
had been a prey to the Klepht on land, and the
Pirate afloat; and, at the present moment, the
same scenes of anarchy and disorder were there
enacted, to which a term had been so recently
placed in the provinces of the west.   .

We were to sleep, the first night of our journey,
at Battis, a village ten miles from Salonica.   The
country all around, from the shore to the hills on
the north, seemed dreary and barren; the grass
and shrubs were seared to sandy yellow; and the
soil itself was light-coloured and sandy clay.
About two miles from Salonica there was a hill of
brilliant verdure, covered with vineyards.   Beyond
this, along the shelving hills that extended northward from the gulf, or that stretched before us
into the headland of Caarbournou, forming an extensive and broken amphitheatre, were to be dis-

tinguished but three Tchifliks, or farm-establish-
ments, one single good-looking house, and a village
to the left of the road, to which the eye was
attracted by a coppice of cypress-trees, and a
minaret in decay.

Seven miles from Salonica, we entered a narrow
plain, the shore of which forms the inner angle,
or bight, of the Gulf of Salonica, and through it
creeps the Shabreas.   It is three miles across, and
sweeps up, for about fifteen miles, to the north-
east, towards the mountains of Chalcidice, exposing
throughout its whole extent an unbroken waste of
withered herbs.   The only proofs of its being
available for the abode of men were two farm-
offices, one cottage near the road, and, in the far
distance, upon the sides of the hills, one village
and a hamlet.   Yet it is but nine years since the
prospect that I now looked upon was designated
" the villages" !

As we wound our way round the shore of the
little plain, I was amused to see enormous buffaloes lying chewing the cud in the sea, their awkward heads alone appearing above the water, their
noses turned to the sea-breeze, and the rippling
waves breaking over them.   As we ascended the
long low hill that forms the eastern side of the
plain of the Shabreas, we looked back on the white
walls and minarets of Salonica, with shipping riding
before it.   There was nothing picturesque in the
sweeping lines of the bare downs and hills, but

yet, whether from the strangeness of the prospect, or the lenslike effects of the evening atmosphere, there was something very pleasing, — something scenic and dreamlike. No sooner, however, had we ascended the hilly ground, than, as usual, we found that cultivation which had disappeared from the plains. We were here sheltered from the blighting sight of the high road; and vineyards, and fields of cotton, Indian corn, and sesame smiled around.

In the once considerable village of Battis there were not twenty houses roofed ; they were, however, busy building, their quarry being old Hellenic blocks; and, to my horror, I saw the fragments of a statue piled in a limekiln by the hands of Greeks.*

The peasantry here presented a striking contrast with those of Thessaly, with hale frames and cheerful countenances, and elegantly attired in white jackets and kirtles like those of the Albanians, but without their enormous width; their

* It is generally supposed that Mussulmans mutilate and deface ancient structures. Mr. Michaud says, that "*posterity* will learn with amazement, that to the Turks we are indebted for the conservation of the two noblest relics of religion and the arts." Mr. Michaud's contemporaries have as much to learn, in this respect, as their posterity. There is a saying of Mahomet to this effect: let the man be a reprobate who sells a slave, who injures a fruit-bearing tree, and who makes lime from chiselled marble.

turbans, belts, and other portions of their dress, which is all white, elaborately broidered in square borders, like those of shawls. This village is entirely Greek. This description would not apply to the Turkish peasant, whom I have found, in almost all parts of Macedonia, decidedly inferior to the Greek. Generally speaking, the Greek peasant degenerates in Asia, the Turkish, in Europe;—that is, where they come in contact, both loses his value;—so the Turk in contact with Europeans, and the Europeans among the Turks. The two systems, when in juxta-position, and not under the control of a mind that grasps both, are mutually destructive of each other. The moral character of both is lost, owing, I imagine, to the confusion respecting external signs, or conventional sounds, by which feelings are conveyed from man to man: a difference of language, when manners and ideas are the same, matters little; but, with different manners, ideas, and languages, men must fail in coming to a mutual understanding ; ill-will and hatred are the result of intercourse without reci-procal sympathy and respect.

. As the sun set, my supper was brought to me in one of those simple but delightful Kiosks, which is a mere flooring of planks, with a ledge all round to lean against, raised in some commanding posi-tion, from six to fifteen feet, on stakes, sheltered by a roofing of thatch, and reached by a ladder.

Here I sat, and saw the sun go down behind

Olympus, casting its broad shadows along the
Thermaïc wave; and when the rays ceased to
shine on the white battlements of Thessalonica,
they rose from summit to summit of the mountains of Mygdonia, whose loftiest crest still shone
with evening beams, which had set for Salonica
twenty minutes before. As the sun went down,
the sea-breeze freshened, and it became even more
than pleasantly cool. I had been, all the morning,
broiling under the sun, in making my hurried preparations for departure, and the sudden change
and chill of the atmosphere as suddenly brought
home to me the idea of a reckoning with time, and
the scoring up, as of a thing gone by, of another
year, whose flight had slipped away unobserved.
My days, hours, and even minutes, had been so
fully occupied since the last sap had begun to rise,
that I never had had time to think about time; and
his course, protracted as it might have seemed from
the extent of ground which I had gone over — the
interest and the variety of the objects which had
occupied my attention, seemed, when considered
as time, to have been so short as scarcely to
exceed the measurement of a month or fortnight.
But now the sudden chill that made me draw my
cloak around me, reminded me that a whole revolution of the seasons had been nearly completed,
and that a new cipher would soon be required to
designate the age of the world. There is something so expansive of existence in the association

of thoughts with things, of the internal mind with
external nature, that one may dwell with gratitude
as well as pleasure on the spots which have called
forth such associations; and it is with such a feeling
that I recur to this platform at the village of Battis,
where, on looking around on the vines despoiled of
their blushing burden—on the leaves, delicately
tinged with autumnal hues, I turned to examine
and review my own internal being; and while
feeling the chill of approaching winter without, I
listened from within to regrets for opportunities
and hours alike irrevocable, and to make resolves,
perhaps not less vain, for the time to come.

This village had formerly belonged to Yousuf
Pasha, by the confiscation of whose property it has
now passed into the hands of government, which
receives one-tenth of the gross produce. Each
male adult has to pay thirty piastres, or about ten
shillings, karatch; and each family fifty piastres,
for what is called agalik, or the expenses of local
government. But besides this, contributions have
been arbitrarily raised, in consequence of the necessities or the disorders of the times, amounting
to thirty piastres per fire for each three months,
which will give nearly two pounds per family
a-year; the poorer families paying less, and the
richer families paying more. The people said,
they had nothing to complain of as to their contributions and taxes, but that they were sorely
oppressed by the Greek Klephts, and by the

passage of Albanian Agas, and also by a debt
which had formerly been contracted by the community for the purpose of constructing an aque-
duct for the irrigation of their fields. This debt
was 2000*l.*, at an interest of twenty per cent:
the village had contracted for it just before the
breaking out of the Greek revolution, when it
amounted to 280 houses, and they reckoned upon
its being discharged in. eighteen months; but in
the interval the insurrection of Mount Athos took
place, and their village was the first sacrifice that
fell. It had remained for several years entirely
deserted: sixty families had now returned; they
would long ago have returned, and many more
would return now, but for this debt, which still, of
course, weighs upon the community, though the
interest, during the last ten years, has been disallowed by the court of Salonica, and the depreciation of the currency has greatly reduced the
original debt. Indeed, but for this depreciation
of the currency, the great proportion of the
country, which was devastated in consequence of
sharing in the Greek revolution, would now be a
desert.

From Battis to Cardia is ten miles. The road
lay over an undulating country;* low brows, close

* This undulating surface is formed by a stratum of rock, of
granular and tuffolike limestone, interspersed with a few pectine
and terrebratulæ, the moulds of the shells having been filled in
with quartz. This layer is from three to ten feet thick; below

to us, generally formed the horizon to the left; to the right, over or between them, we had always a sight of the gulf, and Olympus rising on its opposite shore, apparently in two majestic masses. Further down could just be distinguished Ossa and Pelion, through the exhalations of the sultry day. The country now became barren and dreary; former cultivation had displaced the forests; the recent burnings of the shepherds had destroyed the underwood, and the season of the year had defaced the verdure of the lowly grass. On our left we passed Adalu, a Turkish Yuruck village of thirty families. They had also undergone the common lot of the district to which they belonged. After the Greek insurrection, their village had been given, with the others, to the flames; but they had soon returned, and were now in the same condition as that in which they were before the insurrection.

Cardia is a tchiftlic or farm, of Achmet Bey, of Salonica. It is an enclosure of 120 paces square,

it there is another layer of limestone, of the same thickness, but more compact, and filled with triturated shells. Under this, there are several very thin layers of clay, marl, and masses of broken shells; under this, there is yellow sand, without shells. This formation (above the sand) varies from ten to twenty feet in thickness. And in the direction of the watercourses, where the sand has been washed away from below, long narrow slips of the stratum have fallen in, and left the sections standing on either side, like walls on both sides of a road.

surrounded with cottages, granaries, stables, &c., though now they were nearly all in ruins. Before the insurrection they worked ten yoke of cattle, of four oxen each; they have now but four, of two oxen each. The system of farming is neither that of the French metayer* nor of English rent. Sometimes the farmer furnishes work, cattle, implements, and seed; sometimes the landlord furnishes one or all of these; but whoever furnishes the various portions of cattle or of labour, receives the regular proportion of the net proceeds which is allotted to each branch of the expenditure. Thus, in the present instance, Achmet Bey furnished every thing: then it will be supposed that the labourers were hired labourers, and the director of the farm an overseer. But it was not so; the farmer and the labourers had twenty-two parts of the net proceeds of every hundred, which they distributed between themselves, giving seven portions to the farmer, at whose charge was the entertainment of guests; and reserving fifteen for the labourers, distributed according to the amount of labour which each family could furnish. The mode of distribution is as follows: — The produce is divided into masses of 110 measures, the odd ten measures are set aside as seed for the forthcoming year; ten are then set aside for the Spahilik (the

---

* Derived from the Greek terms and practice, implying partition of profits between farmer and landlord.

tenth contributed for military service)—in the present instance Achmet Bey was himself the Spahi; ten for Zabitlik or Agalik (local expenditure); twenty-two for labour; which leaves fifty-eight of the hundred and ten for profit. If the stock had belonged to the farmers, thirty-five more would have gone to them, which would have left twenty-three per cent of the produce of the farm as rent. The overseer told me that, after all expenses were paid, the proprietor benefited to the amount of ten pounds for each pair of oxen.

Wherever, throughout the East, you do get a glimpse of the foundations, you are struck with the solidity and durability of the materials. Whatever may be the prevailing ignorance — however backward may be the most essential science and practice of agriculture — however much we may lament the rudeness of their implements—the absence of improved means of transport—still, what do they not possess in that constant association of the interest of man and man—nowhere labour dependant upon hire, and nowhere the well-being of the community independent of that of its members. Fortunately, here are no laws to interfere with man's interest, or his industry; and therefore the Easterns have no philosophers reasoning upon the evils, moral, social, and political, which such laws have produced.

The Kehaya of the farm inquired very anxiously about our mode of making butter and cheese,

which I took considerable pains to make him understand; and he pressed me to return next year, to
see what progress he should have made.

The butter and cheese is, almost throughout
the whole of the East, wretched, in consequence of
the use of the milk of sheep and goats, which it is
necessary to heat or boil to cause the cream to rise;
and sometimes even they render the milk sour to
obtain butter, and it is generally from the milk so
manipulated that they make their cheese. Our
mode of making butter from cream thrown up by
cold milk originates in our early practice of using
cow's milk, which Eastern nations have not done—
from, I believe, a reason peculiar to the cattle of the
East, which will be understood by residents in India.
To this practice is to be ascribed the excellence of
our butter, and perhaps to that the peculiarity in
England of a distinct character in the morning and
evening meal, which is spreading to other lands
with the use of butter.

This was a festal-day — the fête of the Agia
Lechousa; and though there was not a sufficient
crowd for people to be merry or boisterous, they
were all dressed out as if intending to be so; and
regretted very much that they were not at Salonica,
where the peasantry assemble on this day from all
the country around, and go about in their various and
gay costumes, dancing and singing as their fellows
in England do, or used to do, on the first of May.
But no rural joys, or simple sports, can survive the

obliteration of the national costume of a peasantry; and if ever the peasants of Cardia put on cloth trousers and gingham petticoats, they will leave the dancing on Agia Lechousa to chimney-sweeps (the only original dressers now in England), or to those who would be chimney-sweeps—if there were coal measures in Roumeli.

The women's costume is every where varying: here they wore little cylinders on their heads, which are composed of a paste-board mould, the upper part filled with dough, and the lower with cotton; over this is tied a white handkerchief, that falls over the shoulders: by no means an uncomely accompaniment to a pretty face.

We spent the greater portion of the day at Cardia. It was evening before we set out for Soufular, a village only three miles distant. The prospect was now more open, shelving down to the sea, and extending northward to the hills, once celebrated for their rich ores, and amongst which are situated the 360 villages known under the name of Mademo Choria, and Sidero Karps. But still nothing met the eye but yellow barrenness, where not a vestige, a tree, or a broken rock, interfered with the smoothness of the undulating surface, until we came in sight of the village of Soufular, and there we saw three large square towers, one ruined (Metochi, or farms belonging to the monasteries), standing at a little distance from each other on the bare plain between us and the sea. There did not appear to be a shrub or a wall in the vicinity—they stood alone like relics of a former age. The landscape was a singular combination of broad unmixed colours: the yellow land spread below and around us—beyond it lay the deep blue sea—behind arose brown hills, with gray hills in the misty distance across the Gulf. There were no details whatever to fill up the ground, or to break the outlines—there were no tints to mingle or embellish the colours: the landscape looked like a table of inlaid marbles.

Soon after leaving Cardia, as we turned the crest of a hill, we suddenly came on a group of nine peasants in a circle, locked arm-in-arm, and dancing, or rather leaping together, to the sound of a bagpipe, the musician standing in the centre. On this landscape, which looked so like a study of the old Florentine school, these gaily attired peasantry dancing on the hill-side seemed a group of Perugino's Muses, just leapt from the canvass. At Soufular we stopped to take our evening meal, which we did under a mulberry-tree, to the light of slips of resinous fir placed to burn upon an iron tripod; and, while my companions lay down to snatch an hour's rest till the moon had risen, I enjoyed an hour's *tête-à-tête* with my note-book. But I shall never take up my position again under mulberry-trees, in the neighbourhood of a cottage. There is a small insect which has an equal predilection for two-footed animals, whether they be

plumis or *implumis,* which makes the place where
the poultry roost a dangerous neighbourhood. Four
hours after sunset we were again *en route,* with a
brilliant full moon, and in two hours found ourselves on the site of Potidæa, now called Porta,
which gives entrance by a narrow isthmus to the
peninsula formerly called Pallenæ, and now Cassandra. A rampart, with turrets, stretches from shore
to shore; and by the moonlight we could distinguish the rectangular chiselling of the Hellenic
blocks, that once defended this flourishing and
warlike city. The Aga got out of bed to receive
us : coffee was ordered, and first presented to my
Cavashes, whom, with my growing knowledge of
etiquette, I had been able hitherto to keep in their
places. I got up, left the Kiosk, and had coffee prepared for me and served in the open court : the Aga
soon came and sat below me, and was there served
by my servant. When afterwards the Cavashes came
for their Backshish, I gave them none.

After entering the peninsula, and threading our
way for three hours through brushwood, and a
straggling forest of young fir, we reached an eminence whence clear land and cultivated fields spread
before us, and the Toronaïc Gulf broke upon us.
The morning star hung over the high land of the
promontory of Sithonia ; the cone of Mount Athos
could mistily be distinguished immediately under
the star, between the dark outline of Sithonia and
the red streak of the Eastern horizon, the warm

tints of which were repeated on the polished surface
of the intervening Gulf. The fore-ground, and the
forests of Pallene on the right, were touched with
silvery light from the coldly bright moon behind
us, which blanched before the breaking day, but
struggled still with its crimson beams.

CHAPTER VI.

CASSANDRA.

I ARRIVED at Atheto as the sun rose, and found the whole place in motion. An expedition was just starting against the robbers of the mainland, headed by the father of Captain Anastasi, to whom my letters from the Pasha were addressed. Amidst the indignation that prevailed against the Klephts, and the excitement of the enterprise in which the whole population was interested, the additional grievance of which I bore the intelligence, and for which I came to claim redress, was hailed as an accession of strength, and I was invited to join the expedition. This would certainly have been as good a means as any for obtaining a clue to the detained Englishman, while affording me an opportunity which I might not meet with again for visiting the remainder of Chalcidice and Mount Athos. I therefore gladly accepted the invitation, and we all repaired to the elevated Kiosk in front of the Captain's house, to talk the matter over. But when I looked down upon the lakelike Gulf, tran-

quil as a sleeping child, and on the prospect from
the low plain of Olynthus to the shelving hills and
headlands of Pallene, running out beyond each
other in parallel lines, fringed with forests, and
falling each in succession, by little precipices, into
the Gulf—I was rivetted by the soft beauty of the
morning view, and by its shadowy halo of ancient
glories; and, yielding to the emotions that stole
over me, my head declined on the cushion of the
Kiosk, and I fell—fast asleep.   No doubt the
night's ride contributed to this effect, no less than
the past glories of Chalcidice, or the present beauties of the Gulf of Cassandra.   When I awoke,
silence reigned around; the noisy Palekars were
already on the distant hills; in the village not a
soul was to be seen—not a sound to be heard; the
sun reigned in a cloudless sky, and not a breath of
air disputed the empire of calm over the wide expanse of waters.   I broke through this solemn
stillness of nature, and this repose of Atheto, by
calling aloud for water and for breakfast.

Having thus, by my own remissness, lost an
opportunity which I had decided on taking advantage of, I commenced, like my countrymen, to
put forward a public motive to justify my private
negligence.   Nothing, I reflected, was more unworthy of an independent mind than association
with party.   A party man—is he not one who
adopts the opinion of ten millions of his fellow-
citizens, and reprobates the opinion of as many

more ? The first is servility—the second, monstrous presumption, and the party man is thus at once base and overbearing; and that, because he has not the common sense to perceive that, when masses of men have before them the same facts, they can only disagree because their common faculty of judgment has been impaired, and the opinions of all parties must, under such circumstances, be incorrect.

I had had the good fortune, among that honourable class of men called Klephts and bandits, to have hitherto stood well with all parties, although ranged with none: was I not therefore very lucky in having escaped committing myself to either party, by joining this expedition? The independent position I still maintained, might it not be more conducive to the relief of my friend, caverned in the Pirate's isle, than the muskets of thirty Armatoles? Having satisfied my mind on this point, I proceeded to detail, more circumstantially, to Captain Anastasi, the business about which I had come, and to inquire into his opinions respecting the steps that ought to be taken. He suggested our adjourning to the Turkish Aga's, and thither we accordingly repaired.

The Cavashes were called; one was sent to announce our approach, and one preceded us, as we leisurely wended our way; the Captain walked beside me; immediately behind came my body-guard and interpreter Hadji, whom I beg particularly to introduce to the reader, and with whom I trust he will become better acquainted by and by; the tail was formed by the Turkish attendants of the Cavashes, and a dozen of Captain Anastasi's men. As we proceeded, the villagers turned out respectfully before their doors, or dismounted from their horses; and before we arrived at the Aga's Konak, I had become wonderfully satisfied with the whole village of Atheto. Here I am, thought I, charged with an important mission, bearing a letter from the viceroy of the province, surrounded by the executive authority and force of the district; and, of course, I expected to find the Aga waiting at his door. We came presently in sight of the Konak; no Aga was to be seen, no guards drawn out; unobserved and unannounced we walked up the ladder, to a not very elegant Kiosk, where his governorship, a little brown-faced and insignificant individual, lay reclining at his length on the sofa, in defiance of all Eastern decorum. He barely noticed the Captain, and cast a glance, which scarcely condescended to be contemptuous, on " *the Frank.*" We sat down, nevertheless: he then turned a pair of small black eyes upon us, and had not a word to say, even about our health. The Captain presently exposed the cause of our visit, to which he may have listened, but to which he vouchsafed no reply. My letter was handed to him, which he in turn handed to a Gramanaticos, telling us we might return in the evening, as he was then suffering from the ague. As we left the Konak, the Captain, evidently incensed at our reception, told me that he, the Aga, was the greatest villain unhung; that he was no Turk, but a Christian renegade; that he drove all sorts of trades—lent money on usury—bought the produce to sell it again, combining the insolence of office with the sharpness of a broker, and that he believed him in league with the pirates; that he was irritated by my interference respecting the robbers, but more particularly by the arrival in the Peninsula of a rival and competitor, in the person of the merchant who accompanied me.

The conference which we had during the evening, justified the opinions and suspicions of Captain Anastasi. The Aga commenced by informing me, that the letter I had brought was only a letter of introduction for myself; and as for the affair of the robbery I had spoken about, that it would require three months to make the requisite inquiries. Captain Anastasi here interposed, and said that he could, within a single hour, despatch a couple of boats round into the Gulf of Mount Athos, while he should send to his father to strike down on the Isthmus; so that it would be impossible for the bandits to escape either by sea or land. The Aga listened till he had done, then answered as follows:—" Christian! don't you see that it is *you* that the Frank accuses of having robbed and murdered his countrymen? And he says, the watch you wear is a robbed watch."

I was struck mute by the audacious villany; the Captain gave one glance at a truly English chain and bunch of gold seals which hung from his breast, and by which, no doubt, hung a tale; and then another of scrutiny at me; satisfied by my look of astonishment and indignation, he quietly got up and observed, with a coolness by no means comforting, "Aga! mount your horse and ride away, without bidding us good bye! If you sleep this night in this Konak, you will need no Capote to keep off the ague shivers." And so saying he stalked forth, and I followed. He turned round and said, with equal placidity as before, "I am going to make a bonfire of Atheto to-night; I am going to impale that lying renegade. I have two boats, they will hold all my men, and there will be room for you if you like." After thanking him for his generous offer, I proceeded to urge various reasons for passing the night without taking the trouble of impaling the Aga or burning the town; but it was not till after I had examined the watch, been told at what shop he had bought it at Salonica, and declared it to be in no ways, even like to an English watch (it had " J." or " G. Grant" written on the dial), that I got the illumination and the impaling postponed.

The Aga, apparently more exasperated than

intimidated, although he was destitute of the slightest means of defence, sent for the Cavashes; and, without consulting me, they were despatched to Salonica. He then sent for my servant Hadji, and asked him if his master knew that he (the Aga) had Anatolian blood in his veins? Did I imagine that I was come there to insult him, or did I trust to the empty threats of Captain Anastasi, who would pay dearly for his insolence?—that if I remained quiet I might stay as long as I liked at Atheto, and that good quarters would be given me; but he was Voivode there, and knew how robbers were to be treated;—that the other Frank, who came to look after bees'-wax and cotton, must quit immediately, otherwise he would have us both bastinadoed. On the receipt of this message, I instantly went back to the Aga's Conack; and, walking in with my firman in one hand, and a stout stick in the other, I seated myself at the top of the room. My servant would not interpret, but I knew the Aga spoke Greek, so I took the opportunity, without infringement of decorum, of shewing my knowledge of the details of his administration. The result of this step was, that the Aga, passing from insolence to meanness, declared that Hadji had told me a string of falsehoods, and that he had the greatest possible respect and regard for me.

We ascertained next day, that the supposed "Englishmen" had been Maltese or Ionians;

though, indeed, the ubiquious **Mr. Wolf's** miraculous escape from pirates, about the same place and time, leaving all his worldly possessions in their hands, might have been the foundation of the report of the capture of an Englishman. I therefore resolved on spending some days at Atheto, and visiting in detail the Peninsula, thinking I should be no further molested by the Aga; but, on starting for this expedition with the Salonica merchant, who in reality was going to look after " the bees'-wax and cotton" of the villages, the Aga sent to stop us. I rode up to his Conack; he stood on the staircase outside of his house; he ordered me to dismount, and then called out to his people to seize me; they shewed no disposition to venture on that duty; he vociferated; they one by one disappeared, and he re-entered, as if to order them out again: finding no practical obstacle placed to my departure, I rejoined the party which had waited at a little distance, and we proceeded to explore the Peninsula, and shaped our course to the south-west: but, I anticipate.

I spent very pleasantly, and not without profit, the three days I remained at Atheto. I obtained the following details respecting the Peninsula of Cassandra. Before the Greek insurrection, it contained 700 families—600 of small proprietors, and 100 families of farmers, on the Chiftlics or Metochia of the monasteries of Athos; they had then 500 yokes of oxen, which averaged five heads of cattle to each yoke. In estimating the number of cattle in these countries, it is essential to ascertain the number of cattle which are reckoned to a yoke; these vary according to the circumstances of the farmer, and of the country, but the numbers are far more materially affected by the structure of the plough. These are of three kinds: the first is the Grecian plough, the plough of Triptolemus, which preserves the original character of the implement—a branch with a double fork—the branch made fast to the horns of the oxen, and scraping the soil with its inverted prong. With this plough never more than one pair of oxen is used, though peasants in easy circumstances keep three cattle as belonging to one yoke; and the more so, as many of the municipal imposts are apportioned to the number of yokes.

The second plough is the Bulgarian, having a share exactly like our deep-soil ploughs, which cuts deep into the earth, and turns it well over; but the wing is spread so far out—sometimes eighteen inches, and the angle of the share is so obtuse, that the greatest efforts are required to drag it through the ground; and the furrow, instead of turning over on its edge, is thrown the whole width of the share from its original position. A large plough of this description, in deep soil, will sometimes require seven pair of buffaloes and oxen, with three or four men. Whenever, therefore, there are four or more oxen to a yoke, the plough used is some variety of the Bulgarian plough, which would be an excellent plough if the wing lay closer to the stock: with this trifling alteration, triple the work might be done by the same cattle.

The third plough is a sort of hoe reversed, and dragged by two shafts to a single ox: this I have seen in the higher parts of Macedonia, but it is now only used in the culture of the abrupt sides of hills. This is, I believe, the original Sclavonic plough.

The Peninsula was thus inhabited by 700 families, who were proprietors of 2500 head of oxen, besides cows and horses, and flocks of sheep and goats, to the amount of from 20 to 30,000. The wealth, in equality, distribution, and amount, of this population, thus surpassed that of any similar community of Western Europe. It enjoyed civil, religious, and municipal rights, actually unknown to the nations of the West.

Such was the condition of the Peninsula when news arrived of an insurrection in Moldavia, closely followed by intelligence of a rising of the Greeks in Constantinople itself: then came rumours of the march of a Russian army—then reached them the echoes of " Genos " and " Eleutheria," from the Peloponnesus and continental Greece. " What did we know," said the Primate, " about such things ? We thought the end of the world had come: we could only consult the monks of the Mountain: it was only from them that we could know what was doing elsewhere; and they told us that the

Ottoman Government was overthrown, and if we did not make haste to revolt we should be considered as men without souls and without faith, and might be even punished as traitors. We consequently had a public meeting, and it was unanimously decided that we should revolt, and the whole assembly shouted—' Let us revolt' (*na apanastisomen*). After this, all the people collected cried out—' Let us revolt;' and the Primates went to the Turkish Aga, and we told him that we were going to revolt." The remonstrance of the Aga might, perhaps, be rendered in their own language; but it is not translatable in its eloquent *naïveté* This proving ineffectual, and the Aga himself being overpowered and confounded by the rhetoric of the monk who acted as interlocutor, and who shewed, by unanswerable arguments, that Turkey was already overthrown—arguments which have become perfect in Athos by constant use for the last 300 years—the Aga finally declared that he too " would revolt:" at least, that he would not quit them.

Priests were now sent to Odessa and to Greece to proclaim the decision of Cassandra, and to suggest the best mode of turning to account the ammunition, provisions, artillery, men of war, &c. &c. &c., that, of course, would be sent to their assistance.

During several months they were left, unheeded by their friends, and unmolested by their foes; but over this external calm and apparent repose stole

fearful hours of self-examination and reproach —
emissary after emissary was sent both to the north
and the south. Magnesia and Cara Veria, in Macedonia, had revolted, but no extensive region north
of Acarnania and Thermopylæ had joined the insurrection; and soon dark foreboding stole to the
heart, and words of fear escaped from the lips of
the agitated community of Cassandra. They now
despatched their Aga to sue for mercy and forgiveness; but the blood-thirsty Abul Abut had not forgotten them, and his vengeance, though delayed, was not
the less sure : he at length marched at the head of
3000 men. The youth of Cassandra assembled on
the neck of the Isthmus, where they had a very
defensible position, and where, at least, terms might
have been obtained; but, although they were well
armed, they were not supplied with that compound
which has become, in these latter days, the spirit of
the battle, and the alchemy of power. Abul Abut
was, however, delayed a few days in making preparations to force the entrenchments of the Peninsula, for which it was necessary to send to Salonica
for guns. In this moment of fearful suspense, the
glad news was spread from mouth to mouth of the
arrival of real and tangible succour from the Emperor of all the Russias. Two of the emissaries
had returned; they were conducted by the Primates
of Atheto to the camp behind the wall of the Isthmus, and displayed, before the expectant eyes of
the devoted band, the tokens of sympathy and the

amount of succour which they had brought; and these were—reader, faint not!—three cotton flags from Hydra;—a piece of the executed Patriarch's pontifical robe, with two barrels of gunpowder from Odessa.

Abul Abut entered the Peninsula that night. Three hundred men, taken in arms, became food for the cimeter's devouring tooth — two hundred families had already escaped, or now found means of escape — the houses of the fugitives were razed or burnt—two or three Turkish soldiers were quartered on each remaining family; and, when the Turks departed from the exhausted land, the bandit and pirate completed the destruction that insurrection and subjugation had only begun. The distracted peasantry flying from this doomed region, it was left wholly untenanted for two years; and thus finally was crowned with success in the Peninsula of Cassandra, that demon policy which, since 1770, has reflectively based its action on such scenes as these.

The sack of Cassandra quelled the insurrectionary spirit in Thessaly and Macedonia, and was soon followed by similar vengeance taken on Magnesia and Cara Veria. Here, for the first time, the Turks sold Greeks as slaves, looking on them as no longer subjects of the Porte. This circumstance contributed, powerfully, to the exasperation in Europe against the Turks, and consequently ma-

tured the policy of which one cycle was completed
by the treaty of the 6th July.

It is strange that, in all that has been written
about Greece, a parallel has never been drawn
between the intervention of the triple alliance and
that of the Romans. Between these events there
are coincidences of the most remarkable description; for instance, Philip, by the sack of Olynthus
(three miles from Potidæa), and the sale of its inhabitants as slaves, struck terror into the neighbouring regions, and reduced the insurrections in
Magnesia and Northern Thessaly. This act of
cruelty was represented by the Ælotians to the
Romans, and further excited them against Philip.
These ravages became, subsequently, the chief
grounds of debate; Philip declaring he would make
no compensation beyond sending plants and gar-
deners. Then came the battle of Cynocephale,
and the proclamation of the independence of Greece,
at the Isthmian games — the battle of Navarino,
and the assertion of the independence of Greece by
the allies. Then the establishment of a Greek
tyrant at Argos, supported against his country by
his country's protectors. The Greeks of old at first
attempted, as recently, by the most constitutional
means, to enlighten their protectors, and to restrain their tyrant; and, strange to say, assembled
for that purpose in the same village, as insignificant
then as it is now. Deputies from all Greece were

assembled at Calauria (Poros), in a species of representative assembly—Strabo calls it Αμφικτυονία τις. Precisely such was the first open opposition to Capodistrias;—then followed the assassination of Nabis, at Argos—of Capodistrias, at Nauplia. The Romans then assumed possession of the country, but without interfering with commerce or industry, the election of municipal officers, &c.: they imposed no financial system of their own — laid no debt on the people, and burdened the state with no representation for which it was inadequate. Greece consequently sunk only by slow degrees, and lived on for centuries. The allies have given to Greece the forms of independence ; address it with lofty expressions; but its commerce is interfered with — its immemorial institutions are rooted up — its real freedom is gone : pauperism — diversity of opinion — distinct and hostile interests between class and class — severity of punishments — inefficiency of law — troops — swarms of public functionaries, and all the other circumstances, moral and political, of western state-economy, are fallen upon her : besides this, extravagance of habits, and embarrassment of affairs, which place before her the alternative of bankruptcy or foreign bondage, neither of which she will probably escape.

But to return to Cassandra. About three years ago, Omir Vrionis, pasha of Salonica, receiving numerous applications from the refugees scattered over Greece and Macedonia, took measures for re-establishing them in Cassandra. Two hundred families were collected. The Pasha told them that it would be of no use to give them Turks to protect them, for that, in the actual state of land and sea, would lead to the destruction of both; but desired them to select, from among the Klephts, a Captain who should protect them by his " Chatir."

This Captain, with 30 or 40 men, would of course be wholly unable to protect the shores of so extensive a Peninsula. The security expected from the arrangement lay in the respect of the other Klephts for the " bread" of one who had been their comrade. The inhabitants chose Captain Anastasi, but he had joined the Greeks; nevertheless, a buyourdi was addressed to him by the Pasha, with letters from the Primates and the Archbishop of Salonica. On the joint demand of the Primates and Archbishop, a firman was issued by the Porte, naming Anastasi Captain of Cassandra, and emancipating him and his followers from all taxes; and a contract was entered into between him and the Primates of the district, stipulating the amount of his allowance and the pay of his men, legalized by the seal of the Cadi of Salonica. I mention these details in illustration of the habits of the people, and of the system of the administration.

Since that period, Cassandra had enjoyed uninterrupted tranquillity. The fields were coming again into cultivation—the houses rising from their ruins. Individuals and whole families, deemed lost, were daily re-appearing, and the only source of anxiety or alarm was the exhibition of some royal *penchants* on the part of Captain Anastasi. To place a check on these, the people bethought themselves of petitioning the Pasha for the re-investiture of their former Aga, who was also a proprietor in the district. The Pasha took the hint, but neglected the recommendation, and sent them, a few months before my arrival, the dastardly renegade already described, but who had the merit of being the Pasha's brother-in-law.

CHAPTER VII.

THE HELEN OF CASSANDRA.

AT Atheto I was the guest of the Primate. He had lost two sons in the insurrection, and had carried two daughters with him in his flight to Greece: one alone survived, a girl of eighteen, who, in spite of my remonstrances, suffered no one else to present coffee, or to pour water over my hands before and after meals. It is only the shallow vanity of a painter or a poet that can attempt to describe beauty; and if glowing rhyme and tinted pencil fail in the unequal task, what can avail prose without license, and words without colour? I will not, therefore, attempt to describe this maiden, and will only say that she was eighteen, and a Greek. Blooming she was not; a shadow of care, and a tinge of suffering, not yet quite pencilled upon the outward form, could be traced through a fixedness of eye-feature, which might be the natural result of the alarms midst which her youth had ripened and her beauty bloomed; but which suited ill with her sprightly attire, and the strings of shining coin that encircled her forehead, and the plates of gold that heaved upon her bosom. Except the formal salutation in presenting refreshment, I did not hear a sentence fall from the lips of this mysterious daughter of the isles. Still, though unspeaking, was she ever watchful and sedulous in her matronly charge of hospitable duties. The Klephts and Pirates were, principally, the objects of my inquiries, and more especially the band which had captured the boat from Mitylene. When the conversation took place at her father's, Aglaë used to approach and listen with an abstracted air; and on one occasion, when we were talking of the facility with which they might be circumvented and cut off, my eyes accidentally fell upon her, and she stood a perfect image of horror. Her mind is agitated, I thought, with the recollection of some hairbreadth escape from these savage men in their wrath.

The morning of my departure I was surprised, on awaking, to see a young man lying at his full length on the sill of a door which opened into my room. He got up and walked away, and I asked no questions. Presently the door opened, and Aglaë's morning face shed its pure, soft, neræid sweetness, on my chamber. I now suspected that the young man had been placed there as a guardian of the Gynæceum. Such a thing in any Eastern land, unfamiliarized with Europeans, would be incredible, and this was sinking one to the level of a

Frank; I therefore took occasion to request an explanation of the father.   After a short pause, he he said, " I am a very miserable man; we have all been miserable, and my misery is no more than that of the rest: but it is longer and deeper, and it has come when others rejoice, and it springs from that which I expected to have been the source of the happiness of my old age."   He here paused; a vague sense of apprehension and curiosity took possession of me: was Aglaë the source of her father's misery—of what guilt could she bear the impress—of what crime the sear?   The old man continued—" I had hoped you would not have observed that young man; he is not of my blood, but he is of my family, and he has made a vow to sleep every night before my daughter's door."   He then related, at some length, the story which, in fewer words, I shall repeat.

On the revolt of Cassandra, the Primate of Atheto, with his wife and daughters, had fled to Greece, and taken up their abode with a Primate of Talanti, in the Gulf of Volo.   Great affection had grown up between the two families.   The Primate of Talanti had two sons; the elder of them was betrothed to Aglaë, who had reached the age of fourteen; her betrothed was only four years older. But soon after the waves of devastation flowed and ebbed over the plains of Phocis and Bœotia.   Talanti became, successively, the prey of Greeks and Turks, and the refugees of Atheto had again to fly

from the smoking ruins of their adopted home.
Their host, with his family, had directed his steps
to the West, while Aglaë and her father found
means to escape to Salonica, and had subsequently
returned thence to Atheto. The two families being
now entirely separated, my host thought of annulling his daughter's engagement, and finding for her
a more suitable match amongst the Primates of the
neighbourhood. His friend of Talanti was of the
same opinion, his sons having entered the service
in Greece, where now their fortunes were to be
pushed. The young couple, however, were by no
means of the same opinion; and the father, probably, was not the best historian to record the
stealthy tokens of affection, and the vows of constancy, that found their way across the Egean wave.
When he opened to his daughter this resolution,
she fixed her eyes upon him, and said, " Father,
you gave my hand, and you told me to give my
heart, and I did as you desired: you now take
back my hand, but a heart once given cannot be
taken back." The father thought, as fathers sometimes do, that time would mature her judgment,
and soften her regrets. Two years had passed by,
while he was congratulating himself that Aglaë was
forgetting her swain of Talanti. At length, however, his choice had been made, and a day of so-
called merriment was fixed, when the chosen suitor
was to be formally introduced to his expected
bride, and when a new betrothed was to " crown "

the widowed virgin and the unwon mistress. The
future son-in-law had just arrived from Polygiro,
escorted by his friends, and the Primates and the
neighbours, assembled from all the country around,
were seated in the Kiosk of Captain Anastasi, on the
cliff which overlooks the landing-place, when a
mystico was descried making its way over the still
waters with splashing oars, and waving from the
peak of its fourth latine yard a Greek ensign. It
pulled straight for Atheto, and, as it approached,
they saw it filled with armed men. So frail a craft
did not come alone, or in the face of the sun, for
evil or in hate: they are Helenes from afar, or
Klephts from Scopelos, who have come to fill a
bumper to the lily of Cassandra, and to tread
a measure on the betrothal night of Aglaë. The
guests rushed down to the beach to welcome the
strangers, and — they were Greeks — to ask the
news. The keel of the mystico ploughed the sand
of the beach—a single youth leapt into the water—
he was followed by another — the mystico was
shoved off, and directed her course towards the
opposite Peninsula of Sithonia. The people on
the shore, astonished at a proceeding so unwonted
and abrupt, crowded round the two young men,
inquiring whence they came, whither they were
going, and what they sought. The eldest replied,
" We are your guests, and we have come to make
merry at the betrothal of Aglaë." The bridegroom
elect welcomed and conducted them to the village,

and presented to his astounded father-in-law the betrothed of his daughter.

There was no merriment that night at Atheto; the Church and Priest for once stepped forward to protect the crossed in love; and the hearts that quaked with fear, the night before, had now ceased to beat with the tortures of alarm, though they scarcely yet ventured to swell with the palpitation of hope. Aglaë's heart had triumphed over her father's will, but still his pride was to be appeased. The term of a year's probation had been fixed upon to prove her lover; and he and his brother, during the whole of that time, had laboured in the old man's fields, and taken the place of the sons he had lost. It wanted only a few but long days to fulfil this period of apprenticeship, when the renegade Aga arrived in the village. He slept the first night at the house of the Primate; Aglaë had presented to him the first cup of coffee he had drunk in Atheto; a powerful potion it had been, for it had disordered his heart or his senses. It was but darkly that were hinted to me the wiles which had been used, the threats which had been employed, or the brilliant offers which had subsequently been resorted to, to obtain the wedded hand of this Helen of Cassandra. But, unlike the Helen of yore, blandishments and wealth had been treated with equal disdain as wiles and menaces; but disappointments were gusts of wind to the flame of the Anatolian. A small detachment having been sent

from Salonica, he ventured on a bolder course,
and had his rival seized and dragged before him,
charged with some crime.   The young Greek met
the charge with scorn, and his judge with defiance.
The Aga seized a balta, or small metal hatchet,
intended as an emblem of power, but not as an
executioner's instrument.   The Greek, as he sprang
on the Aga, was laid hold on by the guards, and in
the struggle his side was gashed from the back of
the arm-pit down the ribs, by the balta of the
Governor.   In this state he was conveyed to a sort
of cage or prison, which the Aga had had made in the
lower part of his Conack.   The Conack was soon
surrounded by an infuriated mob, and would have
been immediately razed to the ground, had it not
been for the presence of the newly arrived Turkish
soldiers, who, from the barricadoed windows, prepared
to repel violence with force.   The people now retreated beyond musket range, and commenced preparing for action the houses that overlooked the
Conack.   Captain Anastasi, however, succeeded in
restoring tranquillity ;   and the Turkish soldiers, on
being informed of the real state of the case, became
no less indignant than the Greeks ;   but they were
afraid of taking part openly against the Aga, whom
they dreaded, not only in consequence of his official
position, but also from his connexion with the
Pasha, who was married to his sister; and, as the
young Greek, though severely wounded, had neither bones nor limbs injured, they planned a simu-

lated escape; and Captain Anastasi prepared a boat to convey him to Greece. But the young man, once at liberty, refused to quit the country: he would not leave the land of his Aglaë; and, besides, he now had his new debt of blood to repay. He joined the bandits — he was numbered among the very party that had captured the boat from Mitylene, in pursuit of whom I had undertaken this journey; and to compass whose destruction our daily meetings were held in the house of the Primate, and in the presence of Aglaë!

My host, on perceiving the conduct of the Aga to me, had anticipated the possibility of my getting him removed. I need not say that I warmly enlisted in this service; the result of my endeavours will appear in due time.

The young man who had slept at Aglaë's door was the brother of her betrothed.

CHAPTER VIII.

ANTIQUARIAN RESEARCHES AT ATHETO AND OLYNTHUS —
FEAST OF ROBBERS AND ROBBED—INFLUENCE OF SCHOOLS
—MANUFACTURES OF CHALCIDICE—SCHEMES OF THE AR-
MATOLES.

I HAD scarcely concluded the extraction of the
various details I was desirous to obtain respecting
the insurrection in the Peninsula, and in the
course of which I had learned so much to prepossess
me in favour of their former Governor, when an
Osmanli entered the room, and saluted me with
" Selam Aleikum!"*   This was the first time that
such a sound had struck upon my ear, as addressed to myself, and could not fail to awaken
curiosity and interest with respect to my visitor;
my anticipations were not disappointed, nor my interest diminished, when I learnt that the stranger
was Hassan Aga, the former Governor of Cas-

---

* " Peace be with us!" This salutation, with the accom-
panying external sign of laying the hand on the heart, or carrying it to the lips and forehead, is never, in Turkey, given by a
Mussulman to an individual professing another creed.

sandra : from that moment he never quitted me till I was again without the gates of Cassandra.

There are scattered around Atheto well-chiselled remnants of Hellenic strength and splendour. There were also indications of its having been selected for a Venetian settlement; as what spot of strength and importance has not been ? I was taken by the Palicars to see the entrance of a subterranean passage, which they said communicated with the centre of the Peninsula. There was a low entrance between two perpendicular hewn stones, just large enough for a person to squeeze himself through on all-fours. No one, they said, had ever ventured to enter; and they related to me the mishap of two young men who had entered a similar passage on the other shore, and who had returned bereft of their reason. The entrance had been closed to prevent similar accidents. I sent for a light, to see how far I could penetrate; and Hassan Aga, after attempting, with the rest, to dissuade, declared he would accompany me. I led the van, and he brought up the rear; and, after crawling in for three yards, we found ourselves in an open space like a large oven: it was the top part of a Roman arch, filled up with earth and rubbish; this was all. We now bethought ourselves how to turn to account, for our own amusement, the superstitious dread of the folks without. Blowing out our lights (for we had each a candle), we crept close to the orifice, round which the Palikars were assembled;

and, during half an hour, and for a long time after they thought us finally and irrecoverably lost, we had that gratification that ghosts are said to enjoy who sit beside their graves, and hear all their virtues and their merits discussed by the dear, dear friends they have left behind. As for me, I was a stranger, and there was little to be expected, except in so far as it was advantageous to ascertain the real thoughts of the guardians of Atheto respecting the pursuit and capture of the Klephts. Poor Hassan Aga was the sufferer; and he might have learned something worth knowing, if he had not known it already, respecting the views of the Greek Palikars, on the many important subjects connected with the Voyvodalic of Cassandra. At length one of the party observed, that though we had been in the earth so long, still we might return; that a stone or two might be so placed as to prevent other people from tempting Providence by entering such places; that the Frank knew a great deal too much about Klephts in general, and about them in particular, and that he was just as well where he now was as any where else; that Hassan Aga was no friend to them; and that since he and the Frank had become such great friends, and since the Frank had been insulted by the reigning Aga, something might be brewing between the two, which was much better under than above ground; that, after all, if they never did return, it would only be a couple of heretics and infidels the less.

This might be a good joke to them, but it was no joke at all to us; so, without announcement, we hastened to present ourselves before them. They were immediately talking on all other subjects, devoutly crossed themselves, congratulated us on our return to the world and sun, and asked what treasures we had found. We answered, " Nothing, nothing! — a low narrow passage filled with mud, dirt, and stones — thank God, we are back again;" I endeavouring, all the while, to appear anxious to lead them away in one direction, while Hassan Aga pretended to sidle away in another, shewing that he was concealing from observation a heap of rubbish gathered up in the folds of his binish. " Oh, ho!" they exclaimed, "you have found a treasure, have you?" running after Hassan Aga, and pulling him, apparently in jest, but with a keen eye, the while, to business. I stepped out to rescue; Hassan Aga clenched his folds, with the air of a man prepared to die for his pelf. The Palikars now began to grow serious, when Hassan Aga stepped forward, spread open his skirt, looked around upon them, let the rubbish fall, and said, with the look and tone of a man that does not jest, " There, — that's the dirt that you have eaten! We have heard every syllable that you have uttered." The Palikars, to use the favourite metaphor of Clarissa Harlowe, were " struck all of a heap."

From Valtos to Furca, and from Furca to Calandria, is exactly the same distance as from

Atheto to Valtos, that is three miles and a quarter; and they lie in the same direction, so that these four villages run diagonically across the Peninsula, on a line extending ten miles. Close to the latter, on a headland, still termed Posidio, are the remains of an ancient city; which, of course must be Posidium. Here I had heard of another subterranean passage, but not being again inclined to run the risk of being buried before that operation had become necessary, I did not explore its hidden wonders.

After completing my researches in the Peninsula of Cassandra, I again returned to Atheto, to bid adieu to Captain Anastasi and the Primate; not forgetting Aglaë, who, in consequence of my quarrel with the Aga, looked upon me as her protector, and surprised me by running and seizing my hand to kiss it, which compliment the Turkish feelings, which were gradually growing over me, prevented me from returning, as it might be supposed, such a distinction, authorised or claimed.

Without asking the Aga's permission, I departed alone with Hadji, Captain Anastasi having sent before to request the Turkish Aga at Porta to give me as many guards as he judged advisable; for I had now determined on making the best of my way through the villages of Chalcidice, and then to Mount Athos; the country being considered more secure, both in consequence of the rumours spread of English vessels having been sent to pursue the pirates on the coast, and of the expedition of Captain Anastasi's father on the mainland.

We left Atheto at noon, and retraced our steps to Porta; and, just before reaching it, turned off to the right to visit a Metochi, or fortified farm of the monks of Athos. There I found masons at work; and in the court-yard stood a couple of one-pair wheeled carts, neatly and firmly put together, with a sleek, shining-skinned mule, harnessed to each. This was a novel and a pleasing sight, and spoke volumes for the worldly wisdom of the monastic fraternity whom I was on my way to visit. In this place, there were a good many columns split and broken by fire. The substantial table of the refectory, which probably once had been a hospitable board, still stands. It is formed of the granite lids of Sarcophagi, which, no doubt, had afforded grounds for many a convivial jest, as well as for the display of Hellenics.

The Isthmus is a low and narrow neck, about 1000 paces in width. It is fortified by a thick stone-and-lime wall, strengthened by square turrets, some of which have been converted into dwelling-houses. There is one larger than the rest, between a house and a bastion, looking upon the Gulf of Salonica. It is surrounded by a wall and ditch, and approached by a drawbridge; close to the gate · is a dwarf ill-favoured fortress, with imitations of bastion, curtain, ditch, &c. Such are the remains

of Potidæa, with a marsh marking the spot where
its port has been.

From Porta it is little more than an hour north
to Agia Mama. The village is hid among trees,
but on a rising ground behind it appeared four
white towers, connected by mud walls, formerly the
farm-yard of Youssouf Pasha, now the residence
of the Aga. To the right, along the shore of the
Toronaïc Gulf, the land is low and flat, with a
marshy smell. It is covered with an efflorescence of
salt ; but under Agia Mama, where the shore turns
to the east, and the level ground is more extensive,
it wears a green and smiling aspect, and a single
magnificent ash towers in the centre, over the
humbler mulberry, olive, and fig-trees—the only
survivor of a goodly race that ten years ago embellished the prospect, and overshadowed the
plain.

I struck off from the road among some small
hills that lay on the left hand, to look for remnants
of days of yore, and came upon the ruined tower of
one of the Metochi, which are scattered over the
whole country, and which attest the extended possessions of the monasteries of Athos, as also the
industry of its monks. When I entered this ruin,
resembling a bastion rather than a farm, myriads of
ravens arose, like a black cloud, darkening the air,
and deafening me with their croaking. The top of
every wall, every ledge, and cornice in the building,

was covered with their nests. The rustling of their wings was like the noise of a storm suddenly falling on the water. These towers are structures of thirty to forty feet square, by fifty or sixty, or even more, in height, generally without windows, but crenelated all round; they are arched within; and the platform on the summit is paved. On this stands a dwelling-house, generally of wood. There is a small door below, in one of the sides; and a staircase runs round within. A small watch-tower projects over the door, closed on all sides, but open below; so that from it the inmates may look, or fire down on the door. Around, or at one side, there is a square of offices, with houses, for the work people, well and neatly built and arched. Precisely similar to these are the towers of the Dere Beys, on the north and east of Asiatic Turkey. Similar towers are also to be seen in Naxos, belonging to the old Venetian families; but these are always entered by a drawbridge.

On arriving at Agia Mama, I visited all the wells where remnants of antiquity are generally to be found, and at each saw fragments of columns and of cornices. At one, four columns were laid across, and let in to each other like logs of wood: two ruined churches also exhibited numerous remnants of ancient temples; all which, especially those of granite, had been severely damaged by fire, and recorded in their splinters the " we will revolt " of Cassandra. These stones had a voice to relate their story; but

how many human victims, not less innocent than
these, have left no record behind of the reality of
human sufferings, that sprung from causes which
they could no more fathom or trace than they
could the depths of the ocean, or the path of the
hurricane! In traversing these regions, it is no
uncommon thing to see sufferers from chronic
complaints, chiefly women and girls, in the last
stages of exhaustion, but not bedridden, wandering
about like spectres. They generally attribute their
malady to some sudden panic; and an inquiry into
the state of a hectic emaciated girl, crouching by
a stranger hearth, and receiving the bread of charity
that in this land even indigence can bestow, is sure
to lead to some event of the last ten years, and to
date from the night when her father's house was
burnt, when her brothers were killed, or when her
lover fell a corpse at her feet!

The numerous remains at Agia Mama, together
with its position, left no doubt as to its being the
ancient Olynthus. I saw some broken inscriptions
on sepulchral stones; and, near the entrance of
the village, an altar standing upright, though half
buried. I procured from a cottage a pickaxe and
a shovel, but could get no one to assist me in clear-
ing away the soil. The reason for their backwardness was, that when the Turks entered the place
after the insurrection, they set about oversetting
this stone, when suddenly, the sky being perfectly
clear, a gust of wind arose, so violent as to lift the

tiles from the houses. The Turks, astonished, de-
sisted, and instantly it fell calm again. On hearing
this report, I seized the pickaxe; and no wind coming to the rescue of the rubbish, I was proceeding
in my labour unassisted, in the middle of a numerous
circle of spectators, when a Priest stepped forward
and begged to be permitted to share in the adventure; because, he said, he saw my star was bright.
I replied, " Whoever *does*," if I may so Saxonise the
Greek, ἐνεργει, " has a bright star," and offered him
the shovel; upon which the whole population set
to scraping the soil into their clothes, and carrying
it away. The learned reader will not fail here to
call to mind the Caliph Omar at Jerusalem. I must
so far deviate from the rule I have been forced to
lay down against antiquities of all kinds, as to record
the inscription thus laid bare:

ΑΙΛΙΑΝΟΣΗΕΙΚΩΝ
ΟΑΡΚΙΣΥΝΑΓΙΩΓΟΣ
ΘΕΟΤΗΡΩΟΣΚΑΙΤΟ
ΚΟΛΛ ΟΝΒΑΙΒΙΩ
ΑΝΤΩΝΙΩΑΝΕΣΤΙΣΕΝ
ΤΟΝΒΩΜΟΝ
ΤΟΝΔΕ ΙΝΑΚΑΑΝΕ
ΣΤΙΣΕΤΑΜΒΡΟΣΑΥΤΟ
ΑΖΙΔΑΡΗΣ.

I went to the square enclosure, with the white
towers before-mentioned, and found the Aga was
still in the fields. His Vekil was sitting at the
gate. Knowing me to be a Frank, he scarcely

condescended to notice me; and one or two civil
speeches did not advance me any thing. I had sat
down on the bench beside him: my first thought
was to get up, and ask hospitality at one of the
cottages; my second was to demand, on the spot
where I was, that hospitality as a right, which they
seemed little inclined to grant me as a favour. I
therefore ordered my servant to take my things to
the Aga's own oda, or apartment, and began myself to move in the same direction. The Vekil was
immediately brought to that most embarrassing
diplomatic position of asking questions, and making
protests: I merely signified to him that I was the
Aga's Musafir. The instantaneous change in my
position was exceedingly amusing, and I was enjoying all the delight which a man feels in making a
discovery which is advantageous as well as interesting, when the Aga returned, welcomed me most
kindly, and called for supper. My host, who had,
at a former period, been governor of the mining
district, gave me a great deal of very interesting
conversation respecting the statistics of this province, its former administration, &c. He made me
take a list of the men in the different villages whom
I ought to see; pored with delight over my map,
and traced out the track by which I should combine most convenience with most objects of interest;
and sent for two Greeks from the village to accompany me, next morning, in my search after the
ancient harbour of Olynthus, and the remains of

Mecyberna, on the coast. The Vekil came to beg pardon for the reception he had given me, and excused himself by saying that he had taken me only for a Frank. When I assured him that I was *only* a Frank, a strife seemed excited between his credulity and his scepticism: he took his eyes from me, cast them on the floor, then on the walls, and looked very stupid.

Next morning, after an unavailing search for the ancient harbour of Olynthus, and the very satisfactory discovery of the ancient Mecyberna, at the distance of three miles from Agia Mama, in a heap of stones now called Molibo Pyrgo; I was led a wild-goose chase of several hours among the hills northward, in search of a ruin called Palaia Porta, which proved to be but a natural fissure in the rock; and towards evening reached the borough of Polygiro, situated amongst barren hills about ten miles north from the bottom of the Gulf, but overlooking a beautiful and broken glen, through which a mountain-brook pursues its noisy way, amid vineyards, poplars, mulberry, fig, and walnut-trees. Polygiro being one of the chief of the association of villages which farmed the gold and silver mines of Chalcidice, I determined to remain here a couple of days, to make inquiries into the interesting circumstances connected with this community. The Aga of Agia Mama had given me a letter to one of the Greek Primates, and warned me not to go near the Aga, whom he described as a wild beast of an Arnaout.

My reception here was somewhat different from
that at Ambelakia: I was met as if I had been one
of the family returning from a long pilgrimage, and
a large party had, in anticipation of my arrival,
been assembled to supper. The loudest ejacula-
tions of welcome proceeded from the lips of the
great hunter of men himself—the father of Captain
Anastasi.

During supper, the old Armatole related his
various exploits since his departure from Atheto;
but which I could not find to amount to more than
five good suppers eaten at Polygiro, with as many
dinners, minus one, which had been despatched by
the way at Agia Mama: he, nevertheless, was constantly comparing himself either to Capodistrias
or to Orpheus. My surprise was scarcely less great
at the coupling of these two individuals in one yoke,
than at the points of resemblance of each, or both,
with Captain Anastasi senior. I was enlightened,
however, in this respect, and found that the Armatole was the link between them; for he, like Orpheus,
collected wild men together with a whistle; and,
like Capodistrias, he reduced robbers to submission,
because he was a greater rogue than any of them.
The ingenuity and the frankness of this explanation
produced thunders of applause and peals of laughter
from all the guests. A very interesting subject of
discussion was then brought on the tapis — the pil-
lage and burning of the town, a few years before—in
which drama the whole of the guests had figured,

Palicars and townsfolks, though not on the same side.
One of those present had formerly robbed the master
of the house. They now sat down together, drank
together, and passed their arms through each other
as they held their cups to their mouths. They then
lovingly embraced and called each other " cousin."
In the midst of the conviviality a sudden alarm was
given : the father of Captain Anastasi looked big and
diplomatic—men came and whispered—men whispered and went away—the room and the house
was soon filled with Pistols and with Bardolphs;
their portly and convivial master at length condescended to inform me that it was all nothing;
which opinion, indeed, I had not ceased to entertain
from the time the whispering had commenced.

Next morning, being Sunday, I was up betimes
to attend the matins, which commenced before
daylight. I have found it a most advantageous
practice to make the place of worship and the
school-room the first objects of visit. This at once
opens to the stranger the hearts of the strangers
amongst whom he has fallen—associates him, in some
degree, with the objects they revere; but in a much
greater degree, as regards the school-room, with
those things with which they desire to become acquainted; and this more especially as connected
with the character of a European, from the disposition of all Eastern populations to look to the West
for instruction. While the stranger thus at once
possesses himself of the readiest access to men's

confidence, he finds himself at once placed in a
position to influence them; and, while his first
intercourse is established through the Priest (the
Imam), the Schoolmaster (the Hodga), the circumstances of his visit are related by the schoolboys
at each fireside of the hamlet. The church and the
school-room are, moreover, the quickest means of
coming in contact with the people — an object of
no inconsiderable importance, as every traveller
must know who has considered the people of a
country as a *more* important object of inquiry than
the stones which sheltered or defended the genera-
tions that existed there a couple of thousand years
before. But these objects I had not in view in
attending morning service in the church of Polygiro.
If at that time I had had such views, my journal
and my journey might have presented a different
interest: I merely went to see the splendid dresses,
for the manufacture and wearing of which this district is alike celebrated. I was, however, disappointed; but, on my return, the wife of my host
redeemed the honour of the dyers, weavers, milli-
ners, and embroiderers of Polygiro, by displaying to
me a wardrobe, which exceeded my expectations.
The stuff appeared to be cloth of silk—for the silk
was untwisted, and thickly wove: it had thus the
softness of wool, and the brilliancy of silk. The
pliancy of the stuff made the folds fall as free and
graceful as those of shawl, while the weight of the
material gave them statuelike boldness and solidity.

I could not help thinking our silk manufactures were very backward. How much do they not lose by the twisting, or, to use the expressive sea-phrase, the hard laying of the silk thread? Cotton and other substances of short fibre acquire their sole strength by being twisted: but the silk comes from the worm, and afterwards from the reeling vat, in one continuous thread: by twisting, it does not gain strength, while it loses softness; and, if much twisted, from the unequal tension of the parts of the thread, it is not susceptible of being washed.

Now that I am on the subject, I may venture a remark with respect to the cotton manufacture. The machinery performing the different processes of spinning are, indeed, monuments of human ingenuity, and of the progress—I was almost going to say perfection—of mechanics. But what can be said of that barbarous, savage thing, called the devil? Can no means be found for adjusting the fibre, save tearing asunder and destroying the staple? For a long time it has been supposed that the superior fineness of the thread of India, which our machinery could not rival, was owing to the saliva with which the hand-spinners moistened their fingers, or to some peculiar excellence in the cotton of Dacca. Its fineness is owing to the absence of machinery. There is no tormentor-devil, or carding-rollers; and the fibre is adjusted before spinning, without being torn asunder, by strong vibrations of catgut. This has been the common

practice of all countries, until the application in
England of mechanical powers to spinning. We
have facilitated immensely the operation of twisting;
but as yet we have not overcome the difficulty of
imitating the operation of *bowing;* and we have
recourse to the expedient of tearing asunder the
fibre to make it more equable, which, consequently,
requires that the thread should be hard laid to
keep it together.   It is this practice of twisting hard
which, with other processes, has passed from the
manufacture of cotton to that of silk; but with silk
there is no necessity for twisting, and there is no
advantage thence derivable as regards tension.

It may appear high treason to call the elementary portion of the manufacture, both of silk and
cotton, as performed in England, barbarous.   But
let whoever denies the proposition open his eyes;
let him compare the stuffs, the tints, the combinations of colours of the East and the West, and his
wonder will be how the manufactures of England
can compete with the productions of those countries, and how indeed England herself can be great
amongst them by her manufacturing capacity.   Of
course the question lies in cheapness, not in quality;
but does not this seem but meagre grounds for
such national pretensions? When one looks over a
cabinet of the productions of China, knowing such
to be the manufactures of one-half of the population
of the earth united under a single chief, and then
when one hears that a small island in the northern

sea, great only by its commerce and its manufactures, threatens and overawes this mighty empire
with two or three frigates, must not the doubt
come over any mind unbranded by doctrines, un-
harnessed to words, that the commerce of England
may have as much to do with our greatness, as
the satins, porcelain, and japan of China with its
weakness?

My hostess's select and gala wardrobe consisted
of four dresses of this silk cloth, which, she said,
answered for the four seasons of the year. The
sleeves and the skirt were ornamented with a deep
border of elaborate embroidery, generally in square
figures, very complicated, and resembling the borders of Cashmere shawls; round the neck, and in
front, were narrower stripes of the same. The
embroidery is in silk thread; the colours are all
fast, and most beautiful. These dresses wash
without injury to form or colour, and last for gene-
rations. The four dresses in question were of the
following colours,—umber brown, light blue, crimson, and yellow; the general tints of the borders
varying to match. I need not add that the whole
materials were of home produce, and the work
domestic manufacture.*

I was this day present at an assembly held for
the purpose of allotting the Government tax upon

* In washing silk, and also shawls, they do not use soap,
but a yellow crumbling root, which may be seen in the shops of
almost every village.

silk by the Primates and the inhabitants, which was satisfactorily dispatched in about a couple of hours. The produce amounted to between 6 and 7000 lbs. of silk.   The rate of the tax was as follows:—a grower that produces sixteen okes or less, pays at the rate of one in six; a proprietor of thirty okes or more, pays at the rate of one in three; between ten and thirty okes, the rate is one in four and a-half.   There seemed not to be the remotest backwardness in stating the amount of produce; and, as the adjustment appeared to me quite simple and easy, I do not feel called upon to account for its not being the reverse.

When I returned home, I found the father of Captain Anastasi, who told me he had come to consult me about his proceedings against the rob-bers.   " I am very uncertain," he said, " as to my own situation.   The Pasha promises me the cap-tainship of the whole country, if I can clear it of robbers; but, when I have taken them, will he not demand them from me?   Now I can only clear the country by my 'Chatir.'   Nothing is easier than to make the bands that now range the mountains as docile as the men you now see about me; but I can only do so by the faith I would have plighted, and they would have accepted.   But if, when I get them into my power, the Pasha demands any of them, either I must fall out with the Pasha, or become an object of contempt to my own people; and I therefore cannot proceed against the robbers till the Pasha gives me his word that he will not require that any of them should be given up. This he will not listen to : and then he orders me to clear the country ; and these fools of Primates, notwithstanding all their fine speeches, are just as bad as he is ; I have therefore a great mind to turn Klepht myself. They now are going to send their contribution of silk to Salonica, which amounts in value to 20,000 piastres. They won't allow any of my men to escort it ; and they have collected eighty peasants, armed with muskets, no better than sheep. This want of confidence is an affront ; and my men are all mad at the insult that has been put upon them. The only thing that restrains me is the apprehension of what might be done to my son at Cassandra ; and that is a point upon which I would be glad to have your advice." I was excessively gratified by this mark of confidence of the old Klepht, into whose mind the idea of the possibility of my betraying him never seemed to have entered. I, therefore, solemnly enjoined him to let the silk go unmolested, which opinion he forthwith went to propound to his men, as if it had been an oracular response. I did not fail to stipulate, that if ever he did turn Klepht, whoever bore a token from me should pass uninjured.

CHAPTER IX.

MINING MUNICIPALITIES OF CHALCIDICE.*

CHALCIDICE, which, although not a portion of
Greece Proper, played so important a part in her
ancient history, and has left so many illustrations
of the colonial policy, diplomacy, and foreign relations of Athens and Sparta, has, in later times,
merited attention for administrative combinations
of a most remarkable nature.

This district owed its emancipation, most probably, to the obligation imposed upon it, of working
the mines which it contains, and remitting a stipulated portion to Constantinople. Belon, who
visited it in 1568, and who has left us so minute a
description of the manner of working the mines,
and of its state at that period, makes no mention
of such institutions as those which I observed there,
but that I am not surprised at, as I had travelled

---

* See " Turkey and its Resources," chap. iv.

for years in the East before I suspected even the existence of any principle whatever in the administration of these countries.   He gives us, however, a different distribution of the proceeds of the mines than that which existed at a subsequent period. When he visited them, private speculators extracted the ore, refined and coined the metal, and sent it in that state to Constantinople.   The state received a third of the proceeds, which amounted to from eighteen to thirty thousand ducats monthly. The collection of this large revenue, from between five and six hundred furnaces scattered over the mountains, must have required a considerable number of agents, whose office presented great temptations and little control.   By the relaxation of the energy of the Porte, this mode of collection must have become inefficient; and the Fisc, awakened by the sensible decrease of revenue, no doubt bethought itself of some expedient for correcting the abuse, and adopted that of compounding with the neighbouring villages to take and work the mines, on payment of a certain portion of the profits.

Such has been the progress of the legislation of the mines under the Roman Empire.   First, the Government received a tax on the produce.   As the severity of control became weaker, the treasury was more and more defrauded; it had then recourse to farming the mines; but as corruption increased, the next step, before their final abandon-

ment, was the allotting of them to the inhabitants
of the neighbouring villages, which gave rise, under
the lower empire, to the class of peasants denomi-
nated " adscripti glebæ et metallis." *

* The condition of these people was not that of serfs, or
slaves, but a certain portion of labour was compulsory. They
did not work for individual masters who had rights over them, but
they laboured under the direction of elective officers, to perform
a given task for the benefit of the state. They were not fixed
to the soil; but they could not quit, unless they could gua-
rantee to the community their share of the common burdens.
Their right of property in their lands was unquestioned, as
the right to dispose of them, but on condition of their obligations
being undertaken by the purchasers. They were allowed to
regulate among themselves their time and services, to meet the
additional burdens imposed on them in consequence of their
possession of the mines. These conditions became intolerable
when the fixed imposts were levied, without regard to the pro-
ductiveness of the mines, or the decrease of the inhabitants.
Similar to this is the actual state of the peasantry.

Subsequently to the insurrection, identical causes led, in
one night, to the total dispersion of two villages. Under the
empire, bodies of miners simultaneously abandoned their homes.
Under Valens, the miners of Dacia, to the number, I believe, of
30,000, deserted to the Goths. (The Dacian mines have been
discovered and opened by a gentleman who accompanied me in
a subsequent tour, and exceed all known mines in the structure
of adits and corridors.) Our jurisconsults, reasoning from
analogies of the day, have, I conceive, mistaken the legal and
social position of the " Adscripti glebæ."—The identity of their
position, with that of the Raya of Turkey, will be perceived
by consulting Amm. XXXI. 1. 567. See, also, the Codex
Theodosianus, de Metallis, lib. vi. sect. ix. et lib. xv.
passim.

It would be very interesting positively to ascertain the manner of the establishment of this little federation. Supposing it to have originated as I have just said, it proves the simplicity with which administration can be carried on, when physical force cannot be employed to enforce and cover legislative errors, and when men apply the same common sense to government that they do to their private affairs. It is both curious and instructing to see the raya population of a Turkish province sitting down to discuss and to decide on what form of administration they should adopt. The constitution they formed would have done honour, not to the people, but to the learned of any country of Europe. A firman, for a stipulated sum, granted them immunity from all services, &c., defined the limits of their authority, and constituted them·a corporate body. 550 lbs. of silver was the tribute paid, just before the Greek revolution; the federation consisted of twelve burghs, and 360 subordinated villages. Such firmans, strange as it may appear, are perfectly in accordance with the principles of the Turkish government, which recognises in its agents no control over any man or body of men who are not criminal, and who have paid their local taxes; the criminal can only be legally punished by the decision of the Cadi, and not by the Pasha: for non-payment property is attachable, but neither person, nor lands, nor implements.

On accepting this charge, they naturally had to

alter the system of working the mines, as the tribute to be paid to government was the ore extracted; so that the contribution of each individual, became labour for the extracting of that ore. So under the Roman empire, on a similar change of the administration of the mines, *corvée*, on account of the community, came to be substituted for hired labour, on account of capitalists, and for slave labour, on account of the state.

Their treaty with the Porte bound them to obedience to the Madem Emin, the only Turkish authority; and, indeed, the only Turk that could reside in their district, in matters of civil and correctional police, but stipulated entire emancipation from all interference with their internal administration. The payment of the stipulated quantity of metal, discharged them from all other Government imposts, and from spahilic (contribution to the militia cavalry); and for their caratch, or poll-tax, the community compounded with the collector of the Pachalic; but the district and the Turkish Governor were rendered independent, both of the Pacha and the Mekkiameh (judicatory) of Salonique. As for their internal administration, that of each village was, of course, the municipal system prevailing throughout the country. The general representative system adopted in the mining districts, was perhaps an imitation of the monastic administration of Mount Athos. A central committee was formed of deputies from the twelve boroughs. Each subject of discussion was debated by the different municipalities separately. If the whole committee did not agree, the members returned again to the municipal bodies to re-argue the question, as it was necessary for them to be unanimous* upon every measure. To secure this unanimity, no decision was considered valid without the seal of the committee; and that seal was formed of twelve co-partments, one of which

* It was curious to observe, at the election of members of the assembly of Argos, how deeply implanted in the minds of the Greeks was the ancient principle of the members being mandatories of their constituents. The vote of the members was looked on as the vote of the district. It is true, Capodistrias sought to convert this feeling into a tool for party purposes; but it never originated in his suggestions. The fears of the people were aroused by the most insidious means; their virtues and their vices were alike worked on; they were led to suspect treachery from their members, and a coalition of the primates and capetani against the central government; so that they drew up, in some places, the conditions according to which they empowered the members to vote, and *declared they would ratify* no decision in opposition to these instructions. In some cases they even threatened to burn the houses of their deputies, and hang them themselves, if they betrayed their trust. Does not this forcibly recall the deputies carrying their instructions to the Amphictyonic assembly; making their report on their return; depositing copies of the acts; accounting for their votes; to make which valid the ratification was necessary of the γερουσία and the ἐκκλησία of the constituent city?[1]

---

[1] See Æschines, *passim*.

was intrusted to each borough ; and all the portions had to be united before the seal could be used.   What I have so often repeated respecting the effect of direct taxation, will sufficiently shew that there was nothing unreasonable in the requiring perfect unanimity in all their decisions, so long as the municipal officers were freely elected, and subject to public responsibility.   The unanimity required in the decisions of the committee is con-

When Capodistrias' government had raised a loud and universal cry for the maintenance of the constitution, and afterwards for a national assembly, these words might be supposed mere Shibboleths of faction, or terms borrowed from Europe.   Two answers were given to the president, which, even if invented, suffice to prove the intelligence of the people on these points. The president asked an illiterate Greek why he had signed a petition for the maintenance of the constitution, and what he meant by the words.   The peasant answered, with ready indignation, " We mean and invoke the covenant, which teaches us our duty to you ; and you, your duty to us !"   Not long before the termination of his unhappy career, he went into Maina, where disaffection was strongest.   At a meeting with some of the chiefs, he protested that he was willing to adhere to the acts of the congress of Argos, but they persisted in demanding the convocation of a national congress.   He petulantly asked, what use there could be for a national congress, if he adhered to the decrees of the last ? one of them replied, " When Moses, having received the law from God, broke that law, he had to appear before God again, and to receive anew the laws he had broken. You, who are neither our conqueror nor our hereditary chief, possess your power by the constitution you received from the people : you have broken that constitution ; you must come to the people to have it restored to you."

clusive as to the purity of election, without which such unanimity never could have existed, so as to have allowed the seal to be used at all.*

Each of the twelve boroughs had attached to it a certain number of villages, represented in the corporations on which they depended. But here, as elsewhere, the absence of all formality in the operation of the system ; the absence of all familiarity with names and principles; the absence of all idea of rights and prerogatives in the people, render the inquiry difficult and obscure.

But, whatever were the principles of its administration, this was essentially a mining joint-stock company, and might be supposed to be indebted for its prosperity solely to the success of the speculation, for which alone it was primarily established. It was bound in a heavy sum to the government, as rent for mines, which it was not likely could ever be worked with advantage, under the management of a committee of little farmers. The speculation naturally turned out a most unfortunate one ; and, for several years previous to the Revolution, the mines had ceased to be worked at all; yet, so chary were they of the institutions granted on this condition, that no supplications were made to Constantinople to be relieved from its burdens, when they were attended with no profit; nay, Spanish

* Amongst the islands, it was customary to have the common seal formed of as many co-partments as there were burghs in the island.

dollars were yearly bought, and melted down, and sent to the mint, as if just extracted from the mines. They asked no exception on account of their poverty; claimed no remission on account of their exhaustion; but anxiously contributed the required amount, in the wonted form, to check all inquiry, and to take away all pretence for annulling a contract which, as a speculation, had been so unfortunate, but which had been so inestimable in granting them the free exercise of their own administrative intelligence, which gave them, in unshackled industry, and in the undisturbed possession of their exuberant soil, greater treasures than in its hidden veins.

CHAPTER X.

DISCUSSION WITH A GOVERNOR—CRUIZING BEES—RAVANIKIA
—BIVOUACK—GOMATI—EUROPEAN MANNERS—SHRIVEL-
LED PRIEST—SPLENDID PROSPECTS—TANACHUS.

CAPTAIN ANASTASI, senior, and the Primates both
coincided in dissuading me from continuing my
rambles amongst the mountains northward ; but
imagined the country would be clear and free from
danger after my visit to Mount Athos, if I went
directly thither. The former refused to give me
guards from his men, as that might rather endanger
than protect me ; but said that the Aga would give
me, as the other Aga had done, a couple of
armed peasants, who were the best protection, for
two reasons—that the Klephts generally respected
them ; and that they were sure to give advice, if
any thing happened, by running away.

The accounts I had heard of the great man of
Polygiro, gave me little inclination to pay him a
visit ; and the picture that had been drawn of him at
a distance, was more than confirmed by the reports

on the spot.   He seemed to be a specimen of all
that is bad, in the circumstances and the times;
and, beyond this, was revengeful and cruel.   The
sober tranquillity of the every day's existence of an
Eastern, the affection and respect so strongly cha-
racterising every household, give a patriarchal tone
and simplicity to their minds, which may be ruffled
and exhausted when driven by circumstances out
of its natural tenour, which may give way to the
cravings of the lust of power and of pelf, but which
never settles down into cruelty.   The Turk's crimes,
when aroused, are those of the beast of prey,
—violence, with an object.   They are never those
of the monkey or the inquisitor, — they never do
damage for mischief's sake, or—on principle.

Having, therefore, sent my firman and bujourdi
to the Aga, with a request for two armed peasants
to accompany me to Ravanichia at dawn next
morning, I received a very civil message in reply.
The Aga welcomed me to Polygiro; and was surprised that I had not paid him a visit; and that the
men should be waiting me, at dawn, at my Konak.
Dawn broke, and the sun rose, but the guards
appeared not; and, after waiting about four hours,
ready to start; and, after two or three ineffectual
messages, I determined at last to face the wild
beast in his den.   I found him seated on a bench,
on the shaded side of his house, with a large troop
of Albanians around him.   He was a fat, coarse,
and dirty-looking Albanian; and, as I had fully

made up my mind for a squall, I saluted him with
the greatest civility and meekness. He answered by
a gurgling noise in the throat ; on which I stepped
up to the bench, and seated myself beside him.
This monster of indecency never once inquired
after my health ; in fact, for some time, he left me
entirely to the enjoyment of the prospect, not even
interfering with my meditations by the offer of a
cup of coffee.   When a sufficient time had elapsed
to shew that he had inquiries neither ready nor in
preparation, I addressed myself to him with extreme humility, to ascertain whether it was his
pleasure that the guards should be furnished to me ;
I had by this time learned, that if a Turk renders
himself culpable of acts or conduct palpably inde-
corous, you have him completely in your hands. " I
should like to know," said he, turning round upon
me with a look full of contempt and of anger, and
moving about his chin as if it had been a pendulum,
" what it is brings you wandering about our villages ?"   " Only," I answered carelessly, " to see
how the Agas conduct themselves." The vibrations
of his chin instantly stopped ; some very sudden and
inexplicable change took place in his mind ; and
his broad countenance was turned from me to his
grammaticos, or scribe, who looked at me, then at
him, then at me again, and observed, " Oh, the
Franks write journals, — that is what he means."
"Yes," I said, " the Franks write by the post to
Salonica and Constantinople ; and in both those

places they might be amused with the question of
the Aga of Polygiro." The Aga now seemed to
have made up his mind that if I was not one of
those government inquisitors, sometimes sent
through the provinces to inquire into the conduct
of governors, that I was something quite as bad :
and, affecting an air of indifference, he asked me,
" What Agas I had hitherto found good, and what
Agas I had found bad ?" I said, " It was a hard
thing to choose between them." " Are we then," he
rejoined, " good people, or are we bad people ?"
" You are both good people, and you are bad people."
" How is that ?" " You yourselves are of one
opinion; the people you govern are of another."
" But," said he, " you have travelled a great way
to see us; surely, you have some notion of your
own on the subject." " Then," I answered, " with
these ruins around you, and with the thirty men
you have got caged in your cellars, you surely don't
require a stranger from so great a distance to tell you
what you are ?" An indignant ejaculation burst from
one of the Albanians, but it was instantly drowned
by the others. " Let us hear him! let us hear
him!" they exclaimed, " he knows all the worlds
(ολλὰς τὰς δύνιας); and he knows us better than we
do ourselves." " But," continued the Aga, " if this
place is in ruins it is their own doing; why did
they revolt?" " You," I said, " are the masters ;
and if the subjects revolt, of course, it is your fault.
But, at all events, there is no one who talks now

of revolt; and there is no excuse for violence or
injustice." "Since you are so very compassionate
for the Rayas, have you not got any money to dis-
tribute amongst them ?." "If I paid for your rob-
beries to-day, perhaps you would ask me to be
hanged for your murders to-morrow ?" "If it
is me you mean," exclaimed one of the bystanders,
"I want nobody to be hung for me; and to whoever demands my head there is my answer;" and
thus saying, he pushed his middle finger into the
muzzle of his pistol, and then drew it sharply out,
so as to make it clack. "But," said the Aga,
anxious to bring the conversation to a more ami-
cable tone, without appearing to avoid the question,
"have you no bad men in your country ?" "Oh,
a great many !" "What do you do with them,
then?" "That is a point upon which we are very
backward. An Aga with us cannot go even into a
sheepfold to take a lamb to roast. I am, therefore,
anxious to enlighten our Agas with your experience. You have tried many expedients ?"
"Yes," he said, with great simplicity, "I have tried
every thing with the dogs, but they only become
worse and worse." "What ?" I said, "your splendid
prison without effect ? your falacca of no use ?
Will you take a piece of advice from me ?" Having
expressed his readiness to be guided by my counsel,
I recommended that the inhabitants of his Konak,
and of the prison below it, should change places.
Some of the bystanders murmured; but some

laughed outright. The Aga knit his brows, and
held his tongue. The learned grammaticos came,
however, to his relief, by relating the fable of the
man, his son, and the ass, which proof of his learning and discrimination appeared [highly satisfactory
to the Aga and the majority of the bystanders.
His triumph was, however, of short duration. I
explained the fable, by pointing out that the drift
of the grammaticos was this, that the Aga had
tried all sorts of absurdities; and that he should
now return to the original intention of nature,
which was that the man should ride on the back of
the ass; that is, that the Greeks in the Chapsi,
or prison, should be translated to the Aga's Konak,
and the inhabitants of the Konak should be trans-
ferred to the Chapsi. Finding my interpretation
succeed, I immediately proposed that the grammaticos should himself be imprisoned, as the most
incorrigible vagabond in the village. A hearty
assent was echoed to the assertion and the proposition; and those nearest him began to set
themselves to work as if it had been seriously intended to commit the man of the pen. Good will
being now restored, the Aga asked me if I were
sent to travel about the country by the English
government, to see how they could best take possession of it? I told him, " I did not think that
England, if she wanted to take possession of the
country, required to send travellers; for that,
thanks to the Chapsi and the falacca, if she wanted

to take possession of it, she had only to send a serjeant and ten men."

I have quoted this conversation partly as a curiosity in itself, but partly also to shew the indirect mode by which business in the East is transacted. I went to the Aga, for the purpose of getting a couple of peasants to accompany me to the next village: the reader will observe that not a word had passed upon that subject, and yet I left the presence escorted by eight guards—half of them Turks!

Thus accompanied, I descended from Polygiro ` to the south; and, wandering about in search of ruins, was led among burnt shrubs, and over broken and difficult ground, to what must have been the enclosure of a city in the very lowest ages. I remarked here very rich iron ore. In three hours, I reached Roumelia, a small, but very beautiful village, on the edge of a small and rich plain. Here we were to rest a few hours; and I wandered alone into the fields and gardens, and was charmed with the sight of a blue streamlet, glittering among the trees. I was so audacious as to trespass upon a garden, by leaping over an enclosure, when I was accosted by two young men, the most magnificent looking youths I ever set eyes upon. They were Greek peasants, their costume of snow-white cotton, embroidered on the borders, as was also the pendent extremity of the scarf they wore as a turban. Instead of an insolent or churlish rebuke, I was presented by them with a delicious water-melon. After some conversation, one of them went and brought me a sweet melon. They told me of a magnificent ruin, not above two miles off, and pointed out its situation, on a conelike hill that rose on the other side of the plain; and volunteered their services to accompany me thither, and I fancied this might be Chalcis. After crossing the valley, we entered the bed of a mountain-torrent; and, after passing through a narrow gorge and turning to the left, the cone, crowned by the ruins, stood before me, insulated from the surrounding hills by a symmetrical torrent on either side. We scrambled up through brushwood and wild olives; the walls were thick, and formed of unhewn stone; the gate by which we entered was in the Hellenic style, but the walls were merely flat fragments of schist, piled on each other; and, what tended still further to destroy the illusion of their antiquity, was finding that they were in some places plastered with lime.

From Roumelia to Niket, a village situated at the north-east angle of the Toronaic gulf, is three or four hours. After following the vale already described nearly to the gulf, you cross the hill that bounds it, running north and south; and, in proceeding along the shore, you meet and cross fifteen ridges, like waves, lower than the first, and running like it, north and south, from the mountains to the gulf, and forming along its shores a succession of cliffs and coves. At first they are barren, then covered with brushwood, then with small trees; which, in the vicinity of Niket, become forests of lofty fir. Fire has been set to them in all directions, but they have not proved very inflammable. In one place you may see the remnants of a clump of a dozen that have consumed each other; in another place a solitary black stump; here the trunk burnt, and the top green, there one half of a tree consumed, and the other smiling in verdure; and every where bright green mingled with yellow and brown, as if it had been a meeting of spring and autumn.

A general order had lately been issued to set fire to all the forests; a Turkish nostrum for the cure of robbers, of which the country people complain very much; as they make a great deal by their honey; and they prefer the chance of sharing a hive or two with the Klephts, to the certainty of being left without any. The bees of this part of the world have a fanciful taste; and are, moreover, both lazy and filthy bees; for, instead of culling its dulcet store from the calix of a bell heather, or the blossoms of wild thyme and marjorum, they content themselves with swinishly catching the excrement of a little insect, of the kermes kind, that feeds on the succulent sprouts of the fir. The hives are very numerous; they produce several swarms in a year,—I do not venture to say how many; and, as the inhuman practice of stifling these little creatures has not been as yet introduced, by civilisation, into the East, the Malthusian principle is altogether neglected in their propagation. Pasturage for bees becomes thus as important an object as pasturage for any other domestic animals: but the limits by which such property is fixed being more easily transgressed, and the trespassers less easily pounded, the rights therein involved are open to much litigation; which, in the absence of lawyers, is not profitable to any one. Some of the bee-feeders have thence devised a very ingenious method, by which to extend the field of their industry, and the amount of their profits, by constructing little yachts, in which the swarms cruize about in the adjoining gulfs of classical renown—the Strymonic, Syngitic, Toronaïc, and Thermaïc; rifling the sweets of their respective coasts, and exhibiting that superiority over their continental neighbours which is always assumed by a maritime people.

The village of Niket is scattered over a chasm worked in a hill of sand, which rests against a rock of the most singular character and appearance: it is shining and sparkling schist, or slate, crumbling easily away, cut out into grotesque and extravagant forms; and is sometimes white, and sometimes light blue. The skirt of the wood comes over the edge of the hill behind; and a few trees stand upon flat spots, in the declivities to which they

seem to have slipped down. The ruins, or the remains of 280 houses, are fancifully placed around
on the steep sides, or on the terraces, or are concealed by orchards in the bottom of the chasm.
On the side of the hill, in a small enclosure which
once surrounded the church, stand seven white
marble columns, huddled together. The enclosure
itself is nearly undermined, and below it a column
hangs suspended across the road, having been
caught and sustained by bushes on either side.
No hewn stones or marbles smaller than the shafts
of the columns were to be seen; these having been
covered by the mouldering soil.

I sat down amid the columns to watch the
magnified disc of the sun as it disappeared behind
the western horizon; and saw stretched out before
me the singular country I had lately traversed.
The light and shadows brought out the towers at
Porta, and the white turrets of the Tchitik of
Agia Mama. I tried to fancy that I looked
upon the hostile battlements of Olynthus and
Potidæa. The long dark peninsula of Pallene
seemed suspended in air by a slender band; for
the sea assumed the deep brown tints of the sky.
Thick volumes of smoke rose from Potidæa; and,
driven by a northerly breeze, hung like a dark pall
over the Isthmus. Pelion, Ossa, and Olympus,
were thrown forward, especially the last, like gigantic and moving shadows. From this point, and

on such an evening, must the machinery of the
battle of the gods have been conceived.

It was a short hour from Roumelia to Agia
Nicola, a village on the neck of land which con-
nects the promontory of Sithonia with the main:
it is, therefore, in the centre of this cluster of promontories and gulfs; and it looks down at once
on the Toronaïc Gulf to the right, and on the Syngitic Gulf to the left. To the angle of this latter
it is about a mile and a half; and, perceiving in
the very bight a large rock covered with fortifications, and connected by a bridge or causeway with
the main land, I went down to visit it, and found
a tower and a fortress, of massive stone and mortar.
Along the adjoining shore may be perceived, under
water, a row of hewn stone, and the foundation of
an ancient pier; and, consequently, this has been
the site of an ancient city. I now turned northward; and, after five hours' march through a wild
and beautiful country, where the pasturing deer
stood and looked at us as we passed, we reached
Ravanikia. Its little upland plain seems to have
been a lake, so perfectly level is its surface, though
the hills around are excessively broken and rugged.
This plain is covered with all the trees that adorn
the garden and orchard, the mountain and the
forest. Here are mingled the almond and the
oak, the olive and the fir; walnut, chestnut, fig,
and cherry-trees, flourish under the shade of the

lordly platanus. Among these are scattered cultivated fields, and wild vines clustered among the
branches. But fire had recently made tremendous
havoc; and, more than once, the white ashes and
smoking embers lay across the path.

Arriving early in the day at Ravanikia, I spent
the afternoon very agreeably with the primates,
who were occupied in settling their poll-tax. The
twelve boroughs of the Mademo Choria had to
pay 40,000 piastres between them. This had to
be divided by 1200, the number of khans* of
which the district was composed; but, since the
insurrection of Cassandra, they had not only to
bear up against all the ills which had immediately
followed that event, but against the long continuance of disorder which had resulted from the
disturbance of their administrative relations. The
district possessed 1200 khans, but there were now
only 770 capable of paying taxes; and it was according to this double reduction that the sum of
40,000 piastres had to be apportioned. They first

* This village formerly contained 200 families, it was
reckoned at 120 khans; the khans alone being taxed. In
other places a certain number of families, for instance, eight
day-labourers' families, three tradesmen's families, or one primate's, are estimated as a khan, and taxed accordingly. This is
altogether a local and municipal subdivision. Where the administration was entirely municipal, as in the Mademo Choria,
instead of forming lots of families into khans, they contented
themselves with excepting the poorer from taxation.

divided it by 1200, to obtain the general distribution amongst the villages; and made use of the scale of 770 in each village separately.

The next day was devoted to a triple search after ruins, geology, and the picturesque. It had been my intention to strike across to Stagyra, and then to return along the coast to the promontory of Mount Athos; but, after a whole day consumed in search of apertures of mines, and losing my way, notwithstanding the peasant guardians that accompanied me, we got sight towards sunset of the gulfs to the south, and found ourselves at no greater distance than seven or eight miles from Ravanikia. I, therefore, resolved on bivouacking; and a more enchanting spot, a more splendid prospect, a more heavenly sky, or a sunset of greater power and beauty, could not have been found, if the earth had been searched from east to west, and the loveliest hour from spring to autumn gathered from the year.

In a night's bivouack in the open air, one of the most interesting episodes is making the fire—not your fires made with a few logs of wood, but of whole trees. There was a fallen tree a little way off from the spot which we had selected, with which I should have been perfectly satisfied, but not so my companions; they turned their destructive eyes upon an enormous platanus, in the trunk of which (measuring seven yards round) a cavity presented a ready-made fire-place. They were soon

dispersed, collecting dry boughs and building up a
pyre around the devoted Chenar. The Esca, or
Amadou, caught the spark from the flint and steel;
it was then wrapped in the middle of a handful of
dry grass, which, swung rapidly round by the extended arm, gave forth, first, wreaths of smoke,
then a crackling flame; and, in a few minutes, the
platanus was enveloped in smoke. We had proceeded thus far, when, perceiving some passengers
on a path hard by, we sent to reconnoitre. It was
a monk returning from one of the Metochia, or
farms of Agion Oros, with two or three mules, one
of them laden with wine. After a short parley, he
consented to stay and spend the night with us;
and a most important addition he was to the *soirée*,
for he was full of jests and merriment, and quite a
Mathews in his way.

Our provisions were black bread in abundance,
and a few eggs, which my servant had stowed
with forethought and with care. The fire we had
kindled soon became too hot for us; and we found
a supplementary hearth necessary for roasting the
eggs. Commend me to a Palicar for that operation. The ashes are first raked, and their bed is
made, but not too hot; they are covered, uncovered, turned, and ever and anon taken out to be
whirled about like a teetotum; the increased facility
of the revolutions indicating the increased consis-
tency of the substance within. The monk contributed to our repast wine, more remarkable in

abundance than in quality, and caviar. The country around afforded abundance of mushrooms, which we roasted, and snails, which we scorched. Though it was fast-day, the Greeks satisfied their consciences, as regarded the snails, by affirming that they were animals without blood. As the night darkened, the burning tree became a very beautiful and exhilarating object; and when at length it fell, with a crash, and rolled downwards for many yards, supporting itself on its reversed and flaming limbs, my guards leaped up in ecstasy, and discharged their muskets and their pistols, and called aloud for the Romaika, which the sprightly monk did not disdain to lead. My Mexican hammock, which I always carried with me, was, at length, hung between the branches of another platanus; and I looked down on the merry group, till the last sank to sleep, wrapped in his capote, with his feet to the fire, and till the last flicker had fled from the smoking stump of the mountain patriarch, who had a few hours before exulted in the green leaves of a single spring, and the strength and dignity of a hundred winters.

It will be long ere that evening is effaced from my memory, or the beauty with which the next morning broke, or the splendour with which the sun arose, and what a theatre for light and darkness, shadow and colour, to display their powers. Where elsewhere on the surface of the earth can be found such variety condensed in so small a

space, multiplying, magnifying, and changing all
around, without vacancy as without superfluity?
But these are not things susceptible of description;
these are enjoyments which must not only be felt
to be understood, but be laboured for, to be felt.
What would be the repose of such a scene, without
the fatigue of the road, or the softness of such a
twilight, without the glare of the day?

Descending towards the shore, I reached
Gomati at noon. Every spot seems more beautiful than the last; this place surpasses all that
I have hitherto seen. The village is scattered
among fruit-trees and gardens, in the middle of a
narrow and steep valley, with abrupt and wooded
sides. This valley, as it descends to the south,
spreads into a circular basin, hemmed in by low
and rounded hills; beyond them, in the misty distance, spreads the sea and rises the broken cone of
Athos. In the centre of the village and of the
valley, there is a circular mound of earth, the
summit encircled by a band of oaks, the trunks
incline outwards from the steepness of the sides,
and the branches hang like festoons around; in
the centre of this coronet of verdure, stands a cy-
press like a plume.

I went to breakfast with the Bouluk Bashi,
the Albanian chief of a few irregular troops. He
was shivering with a fit of the ague; but that did
not discharge him from his hospitable duties.
While I was with him, his brother, who was an

officer in the regular troops, and whom he had not
seen for years, arrived from Monastir. The Bouluk Bashi seemed very much moved on hearing of
his brother's arrival. Every thing here was in the
extreme old style; and he himself was dressed in
a splendid Albanian costume. The brother entered in a light blue surtout and trousers. The
Bouluk Bashi attempted to throw himself into his
brother's arms, but the new Nizzam motioned him
back, and extended his hand to be kissed. The
retainers of the Bouluk Bashi were each, in turn,
in the same way repulsed, and had each to kiss the
hand of this representative of European manners
and civilisation. The gentleman in the blue frock
and trousers no sooner understood that I was a
European, than he came patronizingly to sit beside
me, shook hands with me (the last time I ever
shook hands with an Eastern), and began, in sundry
ways, to exhibit his contempt for his brother, his
costume, his ideas, and his feelings, in a manner
that most thoroughly disgusted me; and expelled,
at once and for ever, all my previous notions about
civilising the Turks.

When I returned to where my things had
been deposited, I found the woman of the house
in a great state of distraction about her husband,
who, that morning, had been sent for by the Bouluk Bashi, and not having returned, she appre-
hended he had been put in prison. She sat
crouching in a corner, and when I attempted to

say something encouraging to her, she replied,
" Go see the fine cow I am going to sell, to buy a
handkerchief, that my husband and I may dance
together !" *

Gomati formerly consisted of 230 houses;
there are now but 130, of which, seventy are
exempt from taxation. They have abundance of
mulberry-trees, but from the destruction of the
buildings, and the distracted state of the country
ever since the insurrection, they have not yet sufficiently recovered to have the means of rearing
silk-worms ; this year, however, they have recom-
menced.

The exemption from taxation of the poorer
families, is not in consequence of legislative enactments ; the village being left to its own discretion
as to the mode of taxation, does not make poor-
laws out of philanthropy, but, from the most
interested motives, adjusts taxation so as to prevent the existence of paupers ; and the consequent
tone and feeling of the place is such, that accidental destitution easily finds relief.

In passing through this village, I was struck
with the sight of a stiff and shrivelled corpse,
clothed and seated in a chair, laid slanting against
a wall, so that the feet were in the air, and the
head was bent down upon the breast. While I
stood looking at it, I was startled by a jerking

* In dancing, they hold the ends of a handkerchief; the
sense implied, is destitution and wretchedness.

motion in the right arm, and then seeing two black
and vivid eyes straining to catch my attention.
This was a human and a living being, which had
existed in this shrivelled and motionless state for
28 years; flesh seemed to have disappeared from
his bones; the skin had shrunk and was almost
black: I have seen mummies that appeared in a
better state of preservation.   The joints were all
fixed, with the exception of the right shoulder and
the jaws.   This freedom of the shoulders amounts,
however, only to three inches of a see-saw movement of the fore arm, and he keeps working it
backwards and forwards, as he says, *for exercise;*
his hands are closed; all his joints doubled up;
the pelvis is as a pivot; and the only change of
attitude is resting his back against the wall, or his
feet on the floor; in bed, he lies upon one side
only.   He says, he first began to have his joints
contracted twenty-eight years ago; he had succes-
sions of boils upon them, and one after the other
they became immovable.   During the last two or
three years, he has experienced little change for
the worse, and he hopes he will preserve what he
calls the use of his right hand, to the grave.   He
is forty-five years old, and was a Priest.   When he
saw me start, on perceiving the living eye in what
I took to be a corpse, he laughed heartily; his
tongue and teeth, he said, were better than those
of walking men; and his large clear eyes had a
brilliancy not very common in health.   I told him

he might very soon make his fortune in London;
he replied, he was very well pleased with his own
village, and did not want to lose in travelling any
of the time he had yet to live.

From Gomati, I descended through the valley
into the basin below, which had once been entirely
occupied with gardens, and the onions of which
used to be transported in great quantities to the
maritime islands. It is now a useless but a blooming and luxuriant waste. Two hours and a half
brought us to a brow overlooking the Strymonic
Gulf—the last of the succession of gulfs and promontories of this commingling of land and sea—
where a new prospect opens at every step, composed of dark foregrounds, with light and airy distances; stupendous mountains, seen through softest
glens; a country now a waste, now covered with
forests; the land sometimes gray and yellow, sometimes dark green; the rocks, here dark brown, there
of shining white. Here are thickly scattered records and ruins of all races and of all ages: here
are recalled the heroic days of Man, the middle
ages of Europe: here might be remembered, on
the same fields, the glory of a Brasidas and of a
Contarini, of a Dragut and a Doria, of a Robert
and a Mahmoud. Before me were the scenes of
monastic penance and the trophies of imperial su-
perstition; around me were traces, so mingled as
scarcely to be distinguished, of peaceful industry,
of anarchy, of political wisdom, and of blood-stained

oppression; while I exulted in the solitariness of
my own reflections and the consciousness that not
a living soul, in the extensive regions exposed to
my view, communed with the genius of the spot, or
lived in the life of its recollections. At my feet
lay the track of the canal through which the fleets
of Xerxes had proudly steered; the mountains of
Magnesia and Pieria still embellished the western
distance; Pangeus, and the mountains of Macedonia and Thrace, spread to the north and east;
the Toronaic Gulf is concealed by the high land of
Sithonia; the Thermaïc is visible; the Strymonic
and Singitic are spread on either side of the isthmus below. On a rock, projecting into the Eastern
Sea, stood Acanthus. Beyond the low and narrow
neck, the promontory rises and swells into rugged
and wooded hills, appearing over each other and
forming a throne for the monarch of the spot,
where he sits alone in sublime majesty, towering
from the ocean to the heavens, and forming, with
its Chersonese, but one insulated mass, traced
against the water or the sky, and only touching
the earth by the isthmus at my feet.

The country I have passed through is primi-
tive, gneiss schist, mica schist; between St. Nicola
and Ravanikia, schist, alternating between formations of marble and quartz rock—stratification very
perpendicular and inclining generally to the East.
Looking down towards Acanthus, the hills seemed
of sand; but they were of rounded and mouldering

granite—the feldspath being decomposed where
exposed to the air. The structure of the rocks of
the peninsula of Athos is the same; but it is a
distinct group, totally separated from the rocks of
the main land by the low and narrow isthmus.
On its western shore they approach so close as
just to leave the space that has been occupied by
the canal.

At Acanthus (the name of the present village
on its site is Ozeros), there are heaps of large
hewn granite blocks; two churches—one of them
ruined—are ornamented in a most singular manner with human bones and skulls, placed in small
baskets, which are hung from the eaves and set up
in every aperture. Towards the sea, at the eastern-
most point below the castle wall, appears a portion of the ancient battlement, very broad, and
not, as in general, filled in the centre with small
stones, but through and through composed of
large blocks. There are, all about the place, numbers of subterranean reservoirs for storing grain.
A small hole, like the mouth of a well, faced with
stones, opens into a round cavity, lined with clay*
—this has probably been an ancient practice. In
the centre of the isthmus, a low long ridge of
friable lime-stone rises and runs towards the hills
on the north. On the extremity of this ridge
there are Hellenic ruins—probably of Sance. To

* Such is, at present, the practice in the East Indies.

the north of the canal, at a short distance from its western mouth, stands a ruined Metochi, chiefly built of hewn granite blocks; of course, the remnants of an ancient city. I had the satisfaction of clearly tracing the line of the canal from one gulf to the other; the isthmus was of a faded yellow colour, but a green streak marks the line of the canal as it approaches either extremity. On the western side, stagnant water and rushes stretch for several hundred paces. The isthmus does not appear above a hundred feet in height, and there is a continuous depression of from twenty to thirty feet in the line which the canal has followed.

I left Ozeros for the Holy Mountain, early in the morning, with an escort of four armed peasants. Great alarm prevailed in all directions respecting the robbers, but more especially at this point, where they had been guilty of frightful atrocities, and had, by attacking on several occasions the peasantry, aroused the feelings of the people against them. A superior officer had been here, a couple of days before, to inspect the district; and though accompanied by an escort of thirty men, he had not ventured to proceed by land. The Aga endeavoured to dissuade me from prosecuting my journey further, and, at all events, insisted on my going to Caries by boat. My object being to see the country, and, moreover, being by no means apprehensive of the bandits, and rather inclined to meet than to avoid them, I persisted in my intention,

and started as already stated. This day, however,
I was destined to share in an adventure, in no
ordinary degree alarming; and now I cannot but
congratulate myself on the decision which threw
me into difficulties and danger, but which opened
up to me most interesting trains of thought. As in
Europe, the manners of all countries are the same
(when you look at them from the East, the trivial
differences that do exist become scarcely worthy
of observation), it becomes impossible for us to
estimate the value of custom and manner. I have
found it, therefore, an exceedingly difficult task to
render intelligible the character and importance of
details connected with a subject which itself is
unappreciated by my readers; but I had, myself,
at the period of which I am writing, the same
difficulties to contend with in my own mind, in
applying myself to the study of these details. The
incident which occurred to me in the course of
this day, and in which I owed my life to the little
knowledge I had then acquired of Eastern manners,
was a new era for me, and made me feel by what
means the minds of those men, with whom I had
to deal, could be led. These considerations have
induced me to enter minutely into the circumstances connected with this event.

CHAPTER XI.

CAPTURE BY BANDITS.

WE had not proceeded more than an hour, when we stopped to drink at a fountain, before engaging in the passes which are termed the Gates. Here the guards I had got at Ozeros left me, saying they had orders to turn back, as we were now almost in sight of the Koulia, a post that guards the entrance of the isthmus; and they had shewn such symptoms of cowardice, that I was glad to be rid of them. As we sat on our horses, drinking at the fountains, we laughed heartily at the haste of their retreat; my Greek servant Hadji, who wore my arms and looked more like a Cavash than a Rayah, pointed at them with disdain, and asked contemptuously, if such men were worthy of liberty. Inspired by the words, he began to sing Riga's song; our protecting genius inspired the tones, for they arrested the triggers of levelled guns that marked and singled us out at the very moment, and we continued our journey without a suspicion of the fate we had so narrowly escaped. We had left the fountain about fifteen minutes, and I was fifty paces a-head, winding round the side of a steep and wooded hill, in a narrow path, which jutted over a deep dell on the left, and had a bank and depending trees overhanging it on the right, when I was arrested by a loud shriek, followed by sounds that boded no good. I saw through the trees the crowding of men, white fustanells and arms— caught at last by the Klephts! Whether or not escape was practicable, it did not enter into my mind to inquire; resistance was out of the question; but, in the confidence which extensive practice among them had given me, I felt only incensed at the outrage, and reckoned on instant submission; I, therefore, turned and galloped towards them. I was certainly led into another train of reflection, when I saw a couple turn at me, holding their muskets levelled; I held up my hands, unarmed, but they made a rush on both sides, vociferating imprecations, and distorting their faces into the most hideous and exasperating grimaces: at the moment, I saw only two besides. Considering the stake, the game seemed worth a throw; but the priming, six months old, of weapons I never expected to have to use, successively refused their service, and I was struck senseless to the ground. The next thing I recollect, was a blow on the back, as I was raised on my knees, which is generally preparatory to the act of decollation. How I escaped this, I had not sufficiently recovered

my senses to know; but I well recollect an object
which aroused me, though it may appear compara-
tively trifling; this was a ball of strong twine, which
one of them was measuring out hastily, with his
extended arm. Recovering, at this sight, my senses
and my limbs, and finding myself loose, I leaped
up, and stood prepared with a stout stick to do
what might be practicable, to prevent myself from
being bound.   My companions in misfortune were
on their knees, calling out "Amaun! Amaun!"
and with streaming eyes held up their joined hands
to have them bound.   The bandits had no wish to
be pushed to extremities in the vicinity of the
guard-house, and with the guards that had left me
at no very great distance; so they listened to me,
and left me alone.   The others were quickly bound
in silence; one of the party, the only very ferocious one of the set, turned to me with the cord ;
I offered him my breast to strike; his yatagan was
in an instant bare; when a youth, of slender and
even elegant air and appearance, and who had
been looking at me, pushed him back. The others
then approached, and told me to go quietly, and
that I should not be bound.   I told them (this
seemed to me the only way to produce an effect),
that I was perfectly resolved not to move a step,
unless, not only relieved from all insult, but treated
with respect: " nor will I stir, from this spot," I
continued, " unless that man" (pointing to one
who seemed the chief), " whose countenance I will

trust, gives me his word that the wretch who has insulted me shall not be allowed to approach me while I remain unarmed." Not only was the promise given, but my mule was brought to me; and I even insisted that my harmless pistols should be replaced in the holsters. We now plunged into the depths of the wood; I had, therefore, immediately again to dismount; but the point was gained, and, after about an hour's most fatiguing run, arrived at an elevated spot, whence we could command a view of the sea on either side, as well as of every access to the isthmus.

It was now most essential for me to improve rapidly the position I had established among them, and on my way I had anxiously considered how that was to be done. What I had more particularly to fear was, that having seized an Englishman, they would dread pursuit by the English cruizers that were in those seas, which the Turks would cut off their retreat by land; they might, therefore, seek to retard pursuit and prevent detection, by despatching me there, and effacing every trace of the party. My plan, therefore, was first to conciliate their respect to myself; and secondly, to convince them that I sympathised with them in their wrongs, and that Europeans were inclined to use their best endeavours to relieve them from oppression. But amongst them was that savage Albanian, who was evidently intent on my destruction, and who had twice so nearly effected it, and with whom these considerations would be of no avail. I, therefore, determined upon keeping no terms with him; which, indeed, offered me two advantages, that of keeping up the character I had assumed, and the chance of effecting a division amongst them, and conciliating the Greeks by abuse of Albanians.   On arriving at the spot where we were to halt, I directed that my servant should be unbound, that he might unlade the baggage and spread my carpet.   After a moment's hesitation, without any remark, this was done.   I took the opportunity of reproaching him for his dastardly conduct: I might, I said, have overlooked his not using his arms in my absence and against Greeks, but that his imploring for his life made him so despicable in my eyes, that from that hour I should consider him no longer my servant.   He was, at the moment, filling my pipe; I snatched it from him, and, turning to the young man who had before saved me, I told him that he should fill it, for I was sure he never would disgrace the arms he wore, or the master he served.   It was caught with alacrity, and more than one jackomaki (flint and steel) was pulled out to strike a light.   Emboldened by this first success, which was most critical, I found immediately a number of little wants, which, one after another, employed them all in serving me; while poor Hadji, who in his terror, first for the Klephti, and next in his amazement at me, had stood rooted to the spot where I took the

pipe from him, kept whispering instructions and
directions to the Palicars, as to how I ought to be
served; so that, had he been up to his part, he
could not have played it more dexterously.

The Klephts were only six; they had been ten
at the fountain, where they first intended attacking
us, upon seeing us part company from the four
guards. The captain and three men had followed
these, to despatch them, if their companions,
within their hearing, had to make use of their fire-
arms. We were four—a guide, a muleteer (both
unarmed), my servant, and I.

When I was comfortably arranged on my
carpet, with coffee and pipe, I seized the moment,
before the Palicars sat down, to tell them to be
seated. The Albanian, all this time looking on
with no less surprise than dissatisfaction, at length
came forward and said, " This is all nonsense, we
are robbers, and you are our prey; your coffee is
ours, your money is ours, and your blood is ours:
τοῦ κλέφτι καθένα τοῦ χρεωσὰ (every one is in debt to
the robber.) I am sultan here; I am king of
England here; and you pretend to treat us as if
you were a Pasha!" I vouchsafed him neither
regard nor answer; but, turning to the Greeks, I
exclaimed with great warmth, for I am sure I felt
it, " What is there in that Hellenic blood, that so
distinguishes its race from the barbarians that defile its soil ?" A movement was made, to repress
the violence of the Skipetar. He called them

fools, and was called in return a brute by my
young friend; a schism *was* established. The only
one I could however yet reckon on my side was
the youngest, and least influential; but even this,
what an acquisition in such circumstances!   The
others were inclined, I thought, in my favour; but
the Albanian kept constantly handling his weapons,
and looking at me, as if he wanted neither the consent nor the assistance of his comrades.   The absent
party, and the captain, if I could hold out till their
return, would of course turn the scale.   They now
left me with two, while the others went to consult;
and these two were again relieved by others.
Hadji was called and re-called, and examined and
cross-examined.   The point they seemed most
anxious to ascertain was my being an Englishman;
had I turned out a German, a Frenchman, or a
Russian, my fate would have been instantly sealed.
The baggage was visited, all the better parts of the
habiliments of my attendants were gradually abstracted; and I was requested, but respectfully, to
deliver up what I had in my pockets, excusing
themselves by saying nothing less would satisfy the
Albanian.   During this time I was not unemployed,
finding out the history of each, the cause of his
being driven to the woods; and I found each most
anxious by himself to impress upon me the belief
that wrong had reduced them to so wretched an
alternative; and that now, but for the others, he
would be glad to see me released.   This gave me

an opportunity of sympathising with each. I took an opportunity, during these hours of mortal suspense, to interrogate the lad who had proved my friend. He was a native, he said, of free Greece, and had come to Atheto because betrothed there to a maid, who had attracted the eye of the Aga of Cassandra. He had related to me the persecution that had driven him to the woods; when I supplied the name of his Aglaë, his amazement knew no bounds. I had now my story to tell him; and in five minutes we were sworn brothers. Vasili now set about the work of my liberation in earnest; and declared that he was ready to risk his life to save mine.

He soon returned from the select committee held at a little distance, to tell me that the prevailing opinion was, that I should be released, on paying 50,000 piastres. "But where, Vasili," said I, "am I to find 50,000 aspres?" "Oh!" he replied, "they well know a paper with your seal is as good as gold." "And will they release me on giving them such a paper?" "That will depend on the captain."

The subject was then discussed by the whole assembly; and it was settled, under the condition of the captain's approval, that I should send Hadji for 10,000 piastres to Salonica, and should remain with them until his return with the money; and that my head should answer for his discretion.

At length the captain was descried, and Vasili

ran to meet him, to prepossess him in my favour. His reception was now my grand stroke; and I whispered to Hadji, instructing him as to minute details. What I had heard of their chief, led me to admit favourable expectations; and I prepared my words, looks, and gestures, with the utmost solicitude. As the new comers broke through the thick boughs into the open space we occupied, they were evidently struck with our relative positions, and the respect which seemed to restrain their comrades; for by this time none of them ventured to sit down. As the Captain approached, I rose not, stirred not, looked not even towards him; till, having come close up, he saluted me, by making the temenaz, which I returned, with a slight motion, and then indicated the corner of my carpet; he seated himself exactly on the designated spot. In a couple of seconds I turned my eyes gravely upon him, and to remind him fully of the yoke to which he had been broken, repeated in Turkish the ordinary salutation, which he returned in the humblest manner. Coffee had been prepared; I now called for it, and Hadji took care that a proper interval should intervene between the presenting of my cup and his. The few minutes that thus elapsed appeared most irksome to the Captain, who looked like a sober and homely farmer; the new comers spoke not, but turned wondering eyes on me, and inquiring looks at the others, who seemed rather ashamed of themselves; while to me these mo-

ments were of more intense anxiety than any
former period. I now held so many strings in my
hands, that it was no longer a matter of impulse,
but of calculation, and that too of the minutest
points; while the slightest indication of plan or
design would have destroyed all. My heart
throbbed, so that it shook me. When the coffee-
cups were taken away (and in Turkey, coffee is
always despatched before business is commenced),
and after two or three long and deep whiffs—changing my manner entirely, I turned abruptly round and,
with warmth, addressed him to this effect:

"I have long known the Greeks—I have long
admired their character, and pitied their misfor-
tunes; I have wandered over every mountain, from
Makronows to Trickeri—from Zitza now to Agion
Oros; I have eaten calamboki with the black
Rayah, Mgithra with the Vlach, and roasted kids
with the Klepht; I have been ever received as a
friend, and parted with as a brother. I would, but
for this day, have carried these impressions with me
to Europe; but you have taught me to do the
Turks justice! I have gone to seek out and visit
the Armatoles of Olympus, and the Klephts of Thessaly, thinking that amongst these men, who were
too proud to submit to the tyranny of a Turk, I
should see the true descendants of the Hellenes.
Had I feared you, I could now have been accompanied by guards, that would have set you at defiance;
but, on the contrary, had I known where you

were, I should have come to visit you alone; expecting more hospitality at your hands than I do from these monasteries. But it seems you make war, not on your oppressors and the Turks, but upon mankind and Christians. And how are you so mad as to lay your hands on me, the well-wisher of your race—an Englishman; for whom vengeance will be sought, both by his countrymen and the Turks; and one who has shared the hospitality of all the Capitani around you? However," I added, " I can in part excuse your men; they knew me not,—my capture originated in a mistake, which I see you both regret and are ashamed of; and I must say, the subsequent conduct of most of them has gone far to efface the impressions of their first violence."

The Captain's reply fully justified this appeal to their nationality; for he commenced by attempting a justification.

" The boys (τα παιδια) will tell you, that though I am not a young man, I am no old robber. Not very long ago I had houses, lands, and children. Why should I have been a robber? For what I am now, those who drove me to it must bear the blame; and if these allow me some authority over them, it is not for my Tufenk's sake, but by memory of some kindness I once shewed to this band. Look at those men, some of them barefoot, with clothes of strings rather than cloth, with empty tobacco bags, and empty stomachs; what makes them lead such a life, and what restraint can you place on men who live so? What care they for life; and why should they? Does the injury they do to others bring any good to them? And what serves the feasting of a night, and the plunder of a day, when they can carry nothing with them against a week's cold, rain, or hunger? Speak not, then, to such men of your English ships, nor of Turkish gibbets; but tell them that one is come from Europe, who will tell again how their name is disgraced; how they are driven like oxen in the fields, or hunted like bears in the mountain. Speak to them but words of consolation and kindness, and they will lay their heads on the ground, and put your foot on them. But you know what we are. We have injured you; we know what injury you may do us. We are not all of one mind; we are as many captains as men, and fewer men than opinions. I held the plough with these hands: it was the Turks put this musket in its place; this now must find me food."

The discourse which followed it would be too long to relate. They afterward retired a little way back into the wood, to consult; not even leaving a guard over me. I felt relieved, until the length and loudness of the discussion again awakened my apprehensions. However, they were of short duration; for presently Vasili came running, and kissed my hand, telling me that all was arranged; he was followed by the rest, who clamorously

surrounded me, telling me they had determined on
making me their captain.   I, without the slightest
indication of satisfaction or surprise,—without a
betraying word of thanks,—asked whether they
allowed me a voice in the matter, and whether
they thought the picture they had drawn of their
life was so very attractive? This was quite an
unexpected difficulty, to come from one whose life
was in their hands; but as in their new frame of
mind they had lost sight of the connexion, I took
care to lead them as far away from it as possible.
They now set about persuading me that the whole
country was distracted by the Turks and by the
robbers; that the present oppression was like the
knife reaching the joint; that the Turks had no
strength, and the whole country would turn Klephti
if they could be respectable; and that the Klephti
would unite among themselves, and protect the
people if they had a chief; that during the last insurrection if they had had a chief on whom they
could have depended, and to whom they could
have looked, the Turks would have as easily con-
quered the moon, as re-conquered their country;
that now, if it was known that an English Bey
Zadeh, was their leader, they could collect 500 men
in three days, carry some fort, which would be the
signal for the rising of the whole country. "Where,"
said they, "is there a man to oppose us? The
Grand Vizir cannot garrison even Monastir:
25,000 armed Greeks occupy the mountains round

Thessaly, from Volo to Tempe, and to Mezzovo. The Tagmatas of the free Greeks stretch from Thermopylæ to Dgumerca. The Albanians are up; the Bosnians are up; Scodra has 30,000 Ghegues in arms; the Servians are our brothers. The Turks will not fight for the Nizzam; and here, from Salonica to Cavalla, in three days a Turk would not be left. The harvests are got in: we could lay our hands at once on immense stores of grain and provisions; and the vintage is just commencing. Never was such a moment, and no point is so favourable, to take the Grand Vizir in the rear; to encourage the Greeks and Albanians to the west, and unite them at length; and then we shall have the cutting off of the hasné (treasure), now on its way from Constantinople to the army."

Dread, doubt, and confusion, at that time, throughout the Ottoman Empire, pervaded men's minds and opinions. This incident served but to confirm the conclusions at which I had already arrived. I felt that a soldier of daring, and a man of energy, might have changed the face of the East, if statesman enough to seize the leading points. I was convinced, also, that the name of Englishman alone might instantaneously have given importance to such a gathering; and led to rally round it sections, interests, and races, which scarcely any other watchword could call together. These views I frankly entered into with these men. I pointed to them what qualities and qualifications were requisite in the chief of so desperate an undertaking: where there was no alternative,—no middle position between destruction and success; and where success would almost be miraculous. That if such a man could be found to lead such a movement, it might perhaps succeed, not otherwise; that such men were found once only in ten centuries; but that, whether it succeeded or failed, there would be a curse on the projectors. They gradually became thoughtful, mournful, and subdued; and thus this strange vision flitted by.

Strange to say, the Albanian was now my warmest partisan; we talked over " Alvanitia," Veli Bey, and Arslan Bey, with whom I found he had been at Milies; and we thus were old friends. He now had a great deal to tell his companions about me; and summed all up by saying that I ought to have been an Albanian.

After the Grand Divan was over, they proposed sending to a flock of the monks to fetch a sheep; but, though it was near sunset, I preferred making for the nearest monastery, seven or eight miles off. Our " plunder" (plachika) was brought out: whatever was mine was punctually restored; and amongst these were silver and gold articles. I made them a present, after finding that nothing was missing, of my money and a telescope: my baggage-horse was laden, my mule brought to me,—one held the bridle, another the stirrup; and they accompanied me down to the road. They then pressed round me, to shake hands; and, as this was an exceptional case, I did shake hands with them. The Captain said, " We trust implicitly in you; we have exacted no promise from you, that you would not cause search to be made for us. When you speak of us, I am sure it will be to plead our cause; when you think of us, it will not be with anger." I assured them of the gratification I should feel, not only in preventing search being made for them; but in contributing to their pardon and restoration to their homes. Our parting was more like the severing of affectionate friends than of robbers from their prey; and I had left them some fifty paces, when the Albanian shouted after me, " If you have any friends coming this way, just give them a buyourdi (note), and we will take care that no one hurts them."

When we found ourselves again alone, our very mules seemed to step out, to put as much space as possible between us and the Klephts. Our first impression was that of wonder at the reality of our escape, the next was the recollection of the wanton cruelties, from which even the monks were not exempt; one poor wretch had at this place, a few days before, been ransomed by the monastery, and was sent back — without nose, lips, or ears!

We hurried on, without exchanging a word, until we were long out of both ear and musket-shot. At length we made a halt, when Hadji

dismounted; and, running up to me, shewed me,
with the most extravagant demonstrations of joy, a
small black thing, exclaiming, " This has saved us,
and I have saved it !"   A bit of holy wood (wood
of the cross), within an envelope of wax-cloth, to
save it from the wet, was the object thus displayed.
Hadji told me that, from the moment of his capture, all his fears had not been in the least about
himself, but about the holy wood: before he was
stripped, he had confided it privately to Vasili;
and nothing now could exceed his joy, at its being
restored to him, which restoration had been our
deliverance.   Here he devoutly kissed it.   I entreated to be allowed to look at it, to which he at
length consented.   I unfolded the wax-cloth,—
three several coverings of paper and silk ; I then
got to some cotton in the middle : " There it is,"
said he, " in the cotton; but it is not a very large
bit."   " No, Hadji," I said, " it cannot be very
large; for I can neither feel nor see it."   The holy
wood had vanished !

Being better mounted, I hurried on, thinking
the monastery could not be distant, nor doubting
that I could mistake the way,   It soon became
pitch dark ; and, amidst the impenetrable gloom of
the woods, my animal picked its way.   I heard
the waves surging on my left,—sometimes close to
me, sometimes far below ; and their sheets of
phosphoric light shewed afar the line of the breaker-
marked coast.   I had now got a considerable way

before the rest, and was doubtful whether I should still go on, when a dog rushed at me, and set up a fearful yelling. Presently I was hailed by several voices: I answered not. At last the singing of a Turkish ball* rang in my ear, and several shots followed. I started a-head; and, after spurring on about a mile, finding I was not pursued, and fearing I had lost my way, I halted, dismounted, and drove my mule into a thicket, a little off the path. I had not been long thus secured, when I heard shouting in the distance; and soon recognised Hadji's voice. I therefore emerged from my place of retreat, related with exultation my escape from this second band, and inquired how they had avoided them. I was answered by a most " un-Oriental roar of laughter." The men who had so bravely discharged their muskets were not Klephts, but guards. I had passed before they had heard me; and, not answering or stopping when challenged, they were about to pursue when Hadji came up, and told them who I was. I thought it, nevertheless, a hard case to be seized by the thieves for an honest man, and shot at by the honest men for a thief.

* The lead tail is not cut from the ball: to this the cartridge is tied, so that the ball sings through the air.

CHAPTER XII.

MOUNT ATHOS.

WE toiled on a little further, but still no signs of
the monastery could we perceive; it seemed to fly
before our weary steps.   At length we came to a
metochi, or one of those tower-farms which I have
described.   Alas! we found it was untenanted, all
save a barn, where there were some cattle; and
the still warm place, where a man had been lying,
who had been frightened away at our approach.
Hunger was clamorous for proceeding, but Fatigue
insisted on remaining, and gained his point; so I
laid me down to rest for a few hours on the straw
of the vanished shepherd, in a sarcophagus, that
served as the basin to a dry fountain.

We approached the monastery of Chelendari as
the sun rose.   It was a grand and imposing building, the first of the kind I had seen; and struck
me exceedingly.   A road led to it, terraced and
sweeping, supported by parapets; gardens, rows of
trees, and cypresses were spread around, with many
other interesting objects, for which at the moment

I had very little attention to spare. On arriving, I was ushered into the dormitory of the temporary Abbot, who was just awakening from his morning nap; after salutations, and ordering coffee and sweetmeats (for it is against the rules of Eastern hospitality to inquire who the stranger is, or whence he comes, till he has been refreshed), I startled his ideas of decorum, by telling him that the coffee and sweetmeats would come better after something more substantial; and the sooner that came, the more acceptable it would be. As I perceived the Goumenos was astonished, not less at my morning appetite than at my hardihood, I explained to him briefly that I was a traveller; who, for the last six-and-thirty hours had had hard work, and nothing to eat.

My breakfast was a frugal one, but it was Friday; which, with its meagre companion, Wednesday, are not the show-days of a Greek refectory. During this time, the noise of the robbery had spread through the convent; Hadji had the fathers and servants collected round him, while he enacted the scene of the day before. He had no sooner concluded, than they came trooping up to the Abbot's chamber, to inspect the hero of the eventful tale. The Abbot seemed at first offended, thinking it was a hoax; and when, at length, assured that it was really fact, he crossed himself over and over again, opened a pair of large eyes upon me, and said, " Have you been half an hour

with me, and not told me of this?" Then mut-
tered to himself, " Well, this does account for such
an early appetite!" Hadji was called up, to repeat
his story; which went swimmingly on till he came
to the wonderful effects of his holy wood from
Jerusalem. He had evidently, in his first version,
attributed the honour and glory of our preservation
to the relic, and not to me; and now, before me,
all his ingenuity could not reconcile the previous
hypothesis with the simple facts of the case. He
would fain have passed this over in silence, but
there was no escape for him; the monks all cried
out, " The holy wood! the holy wood! Tell the
Abbot about the holy wood!" Generously I stepped
to his rescue, and related how he had assured
me that, at the moment the packet, intended to
contain the holy wood, had been restored to him,
an instantaneous change had been effected on the
Klephts,—all thoughts of blood vanished,—every
idea of ransom even was set aside; and then it
was that the marvellous thought struck them, of
making me their captain. Hadji's countenance
was now white again, and looked upon me a world
of thanks.

  This convent is Sclavonic, most of the monks
are Bulgarians: the Abbot was actually on a tour
in Russia; and the monk who filled his place had
just returned from Moscow.

  After a few hours rest, I left Chelendari, and
shortly afterwards, I suppose from a change of

wind, we were nearly suffocated by a forest-belt, that was in flames: it was with difficulty we extricated ourselves, for we knew not which way to turn; the conflagration was parallel to the road, which a slight ridge had hidden from us while we were to windward of it; the wind changing, blew the smoke and flame over us. We could not get off the road, from the dense thorns and thickets that covered the country, and rapidly spread the flames; which now crackled furiously, and seemed to envelope us on all sides. By pushing on, we escaped, however, with the fright, a little roasting, and a complete blackening, and repaired to the convent of Simeon, which soon received us; wondering at the fertility in adventure of the Holy Mountain.

Simeon is a cenobite monastery; that is, where all things are in common. I was very much interested by the Abbot; and regretted that my arrangements did not allow me at least a day to spend with him. The simplicity and elegance of this man's manner and address, his attractive and instructive conversation, prepossessed me strongly in his favour. I subsequently learnt, in helplessness and in suffering, to appreciate his truly charitable and Christian spirit.

In the evening I arrived at Vathopedi, situated on a little bay on the east of the Peninsula, encircled by walls and turrets so disproportioned to its extent, that it looked like Cybele's crown. As

I crossed the gateway, the toll of the large bell for vespers shook the building, and startled me by a long unaccustomed sound. From the impression then made on myself, I can imagine that the bells of Athos alone would be enough to consecrate the spot to the sound-loving Greeks, whose rights are elsewhere shorn of this loved distinction;* thence have the monks of Athos been designated the " Lords of the Bell." This is the largest and most interesting of the monasteries; and, as I was at present pushing on to ascend the Mountain, I determined on staying here two days on my return, to examine the library and a manuscript history of the mountain that was shewn to me. The church is internally a light, airy, and lofty building, composed of two oval halls, opening into each other, adorned with enormous pillars of porphyry, with pavements, columns, and ornaments of jasper, verd-antique, and variegated marbles.

Here I found a Turkish Binbashi, whom I had formerly known, and who was making a *tournée, by boat*, to report on the state of the roads. He was a large coarse man, with a face at all times nearly as red as his fez; but when he heard of my mishap, which he seemed to consider no less as a personal insult than as a disgrace to his administra-

* Mahomet the Second prohibited the use of bells at Constantinople, because they were annoying to the other populations. He suffered the bells to remain at the Princes' Islands, because exclusively inhabited by Greeks.

tion, that face grew redder still; he stormed and raged, abused all the female relations of the Klephts, threatened hanging and impaling, and was only soothed by the thoughts of a heavy fine on the monasteries. Hadji was again called upon for his story, with which he entertained us while we supped. But this time the poor holy wood was entirely forgotten; so I reminded him several times of the facts which I had admitted and related on his testimony. I observed, that the Binbashi, not knowing the power of holy wood, might be much edified by the relation. Hadji could not understand at all what I meant, so I was constrained, as at the convent, to relate how the restoration of the holy wood had helped us in our hour of need. The Abbot, who was supping with us, nodded his head as I went on, and considered it perfectly a common occurrence. " But," said the Binbashi, " it would have been better for the holy wood to have saved you from getting into the danger at all." " But," I continued, " the holy wood was never returned at all." " What!" vociferated the Goumenos to Hadji. Hadji's eyes dropped on the ground; his face was black; the Abbot's yellow; the Binbashi's sides were long, and fearfully shaken.

It may appear surprising that my servant, a Christian, should be designated by the Turkish religious title of Hadji — a pilgrim; a title, too, so much prized, and often so dearly earned. But

what is more surprising is, that Christians and Mussulmans may earn that title together, performing
the same ceremonies in the same places, and these
places sanctified by the recollections of Christ and
the traditions of the Gospel. The great Hadjilik,
or Mecca, is forbidden to all but Mussulmans; but
to those who are debarred from the performance
of this ceremony, enjoined on all the disciples of
Mahomet, the minor Hadjilik of Jerusalem is open.
It is not, however, a mere visit to Jerusalem or
Mecca which gives the title of Hadji; it is the
participation in certain ceremonies that are performed at either place once a-year. At Jerusalem,
this ceremony is performed by Mussulmans and
Christians in common. After various prefatory observances in the respective places of worship of the
different sects within the walls of Jerusalem, those
who aspire to the honour of the Hadj assemble
in the afternoon of the day before Easter, at a
place of common rendezvous, three miles from
Jerusalem; thence the caravan, composed of Turks,
Arabs, Courds, Bedouins, Greeks, Armenians, &c.,
proceeds to Jericho. Thence it again departs with
great pomp, and attended by a numerous escort,
three hours after sunset, so as to arrive at the
banks of the Jordan by break of day, and to plunge
in the waters of purification at the earliest dawn of
Easter. The tract of country between Jericho and
the Jordan is covered with a grass not above six
or eight inches in height, but exceedingly inflam-

mable, giving a bright light; it is always dry and like tinder at this season of the year; the caravan is preceded and followed by men with torches, who set this grass on fire; it then burns on both sides along their path, producing the most singular and splendid effect. Strange stories are told of the saints, who have furnished this district with a plant so admirably adapted to give splendour to this nightly pilgrimage of devotion. Strange stories are also told of the furious storms, and the torrents of rain, that impious Giouls have aroused in the welkin to quench the flame that guided the pilgrim on his pious way. Such a storm overtook the caravan with which my faithful Hadji went a sinner, and returned a saint. The burning grass was at one moment almost extinguished before the anxious eyes of the benighted crowd, when, by Hadji's account, he fortunately bethought himself of the very bit of sacred wood that had rendered us so lately such an important service.

Next morning, we went on to the village of Caries. Here sits the governing committee of the Monasteries; here the fair is held, and the Aga Bostandji, from Constantinople, resides. It is a strange place—there is a Tcharshi of shops, houses, and gardens, without a woman, a child, a hen, or a pig; and, besides the moustachioed monks, no other character to be seen than huge tom-cats, seated cross-legged at every door. The approach

to it is by a most delightful path, with hedges, and
stiles, and gates.   It is seated inland, but looks over
the sea, and the pretty little bay of the Convent of
Iviro to the East.   All around, the ground is
broken into singular and beautiful confusion, as
it descends to the shore, or rises to the hills;
completely covered with orchards of fruit-trees and
hazel, and, the loftier parts, with forests of walnuts
and chestnuts, sometimes planted in rows.   Some
small monasteries are scattered around; and peep-
ing through the forests, or perched on the rocks,
are hundreds of chapels, habitations of single
monks, and cells of the solitaries.   To the south, in
the clear sky, sits on its throne of rocks, the Holy
Mountain.   But who could describe the effects of
light mist, and clouds, as they mingled on that majestic summit? Gauzy vapours, now hanging in mid-
air, stretched in parallel lines, at morning dawn, in
perfect stillness ; sometimes it stood like a column,
supporting a roof of clouds, and sometimes, like
new mountains, they were heaped upon it; sometimes, I have seen a single mass of cloud lingering
on its gray peak, sheltering itself to leeward from
the sea-breeze, like the " meteor standard" of an
Eastern Andes, waving o'er the clime of the sun
and the realm of the muse.

Shortly after my arrival, the whole place was
filled with dismay and alarm; the tocsin was sound-
ing, and the population thronging the streets with
axes and other implements.   There was fire in the

vicinity and to windward ; without my late experience, I should have found it difficult to understand
the alarm and activity so suddenly called forth.
The fire, by prompt measures, was soon got under.
I paid a couple of visits to the convent of Iviro ;
which is entitled from the Turkish name of
Georgia, where it has a Metochi and dependencies. It preserves many traditions and portraits
of chiefs and warriors of that race, who have been
its benefactors, and who have bequeathed · to it
their riches and their bones. The Didascalos, an
infirm and venerable old man, deeply versed in this
traditionary lore, was delighted to find an attentive
listener. I requested him to arrange my trip to
the summit of the mountain, so as to pass by the
cells or caverns of some of the severer or more
remarkable ascetics, and expressed my great
anxiety to see and converse with them. After
a little reflection, he said, " I think I can satisfy
your curiosity, without going to the Mountain.
On the rock above this monastery, a Solitary has,
for the last twenty years, occupied a little cell, and
we consider him the most remarkable individual in
the Peninsula ; it is not impossible that he may
receive you. His name and parentage no one
knows ; but he is supposed to be one of the independent princes who have been expelled by the progress of the Russian arms. He maintains, with the
utmost strictness, the ascetic discipline ; eats but of
black bread, and at long intervals ; and has no inter-

course with any one, save once in three months
with his brother, who is also an ascetic, and lives
on a rock in the sea on the other side; yet does he
appear to be mild and timid as a child; and though,
of course, no one of us intrudes upon his seclusion,
yet, I am sure, he would not shut his door against
a stranger."

This account interested me so much, that I
determined, without loss of time, to penetrate, if
possible, into his cell. One of the monks accompanied me, and we soon arrived at a little square
enclosure, on the top of the rock, where a small
chapel and cell, and space for a grave, were surrounded by a wall of six or seven feet in height.

We tapped gently at the door, and waited;
then tapped a little, and waited a little longer; and
again, and again; and were about to retire, when
we heard his stride across the court. The door
opened, and a tall dark figure filled it, which,
standing on a step within, had to stoop to look out
at us. His countenance was dark and haggard;
and a vivid but subdued eye was the only feature
that then struck me. We paused for a few seconds;
his first inquiring demeanour passed gradually into
bashfulness : instead of demanding a reason for
the intrusion, he presently began to apologise for
detaining me so long at the door, as he was at
prayers, and thought the knocking was from his
brother, who, he said, with a smile, was his only
visitor. Expecting a different reception, I was

embarrassed by his meekness, and could not find a word to say, but followed him into his little chamber. He ran and placed a cushion from his oratory, on a raised stone-bench, that served for his bed; and this, with an earthen jug, was the sole furniture of his cell.

I sat down; he seated himself opposite, in a corner; the monk got into the window; and there we sat for some time, in irksome silence. At length, I said, that I was a stranger from Europe, who had been attracted by the fame of Mount Athos, and trusted he would excuse my boldness in my anxiety to see one of its brightest ornaments. He said, calmly, " You are welcome to Athos; as to the rest, you have been misinformed." He smiled, but with features that had lost the habit, and, abashed, dropped his eyes. I endeavoured to get into conversation about the history of the monastery, and at length succeeded. He told me, that he employed his very useless time in transcribing rare Georgian manuscripts. In speaking of the discipline of the monks, he said, that they were, on the one hand, cowards, who fled instead of fighting; and on the other, wise men, who knew and distrusted their own weakness; that the world had some temptations, and the desert others; and that their privations too often led to self-commendation and to spiritual pride.

After half-an-hour's conversation, which it had not been very easy to maintain, I retired, much

satisfied with having succeeded in seeing him; but
provoked at not being able to penetrate the veil of
mystery, behind which were concealed, I doubted
not, a powerful mind and strange history. My
conductor, as we descended, told me, that the
timid being we had just left, during the horrors
that succeeded the subjugation of Cassandria and
Athos, had bearded the ferocious Abul-Abut, in his
palace, at Salonique; and, amidst the thousand
victims of his cruelty, had sought in vain for the
crown of martyrdom.

This visit awoke in my mind a strong desire
to visit the romantic country of this singular man.
High mountains seem to have a relationship to
each other. It was on the summit of Olympus
that the desire of visiting Athos arose in my mind;
and as I looked on Athos, in returning from the
cell of the Caspian Hermit, my thoughts wandered
to the Caucasus; and the hope arose, that, some
day, my footsteps should tread its base and my
eyes rest on its summit.

CHAPTER XIII.

THE HOLY MOUNTAIN AND ITS INHABITANTS.

THE monks of Sinai, Lebanon, of the shores of the Red Sea, of Antioch, Alexandria, Jerusalem, and Damascus, of Greece proper, Georgia, Russia, and of all the monasteries scattered over Asia, and belonging to the Greek creed, look to the Holy Mountain as their model, and acquire reputation and consideration from visiting it, and from dwelling amid its consecrated groves. The monks of Athos itself, are held in the highest veneration; their rule considered the most perfect; their ceremonies the most holy.* Secluded, as it were, from the rest of mankind, by their position, their reputation of sanctity, their character for austerity, are not worn away by familiar intercourse. Their ranks are not recruited from family or local connexions: human frailty has no temptation; scandal no hold. If there is little piety, and less learning, to be found in these castled crags, still, unlike the cloisters of the western

* In the Eastern Church, there is but a single order of monks, that of St. Basil.

church, neither slothful penury nor luxurious in-
dulgence startle the novice, or scandalise the
pilgrim. Hither, from the wastes of Russia, from
the sands of Africa, resort the many-tongued vota-
ries, to worship and admire, amidst the most
sublime and elevating scenery; to repose on
luxuriant verdure; to drink from cool and crystal
streams; and to carry back to their unbroken
plains, and their arid deserts, the fame of the ter-
restrial beauties and delights of this region, tenanted
by holy men; and on which the eyes of angels and
of saints look down with favour and with love.

Amidst such scenes arose the palaces of the
monks, splendid and imposing, and adorned by the
former lords of Constantinople. The taste and
industry of thousands of monks, inhabiting detached abodes, had converted their cells into
romantic grottoes, led vines and creepers over
the impending rocks, contrived fountains and
bowers, and spread fruit-trees and flowers around:
or, ascending the bare sides of the mountain itself,
the stranger pilgrim might watch, at respectful
distance, for a glimpse, among the rocks, of the
cowl of some more aspiring ascetic—some prouder
spirit, which had mistaken its way, and now sought
consolation among such wild abodes, in carnal ab-
negation and in spiritual pride. There have dwelt,
and still dwell, hundreds of solitary beings; some in
insulated but comfortable dwellings; some in huts;
some in caverns; choosing their habitations, ac-

cording to their moods, and separating themselves from all communion with the more wordly
tenants of the Mountain. At certain stated periods,
they appear at the monasteries on which they
depend, to receive a supply of food, and to prove
that they are still in life. Some of these have been
known to pass years without speaking, and some
have reduced themselves to eating once a-week.
Besides these privations, they subject themselves
to discipline of various kinds, performing daily
some hundred genuflections: in the cell to which
I was admitted, the floor before the Panagia had
been worn into two holes by the knees of the
Solitary.

Belon, three centuries ago, writes thus:—" Of
the six thousand monks who live on this mountain,
I do not think there is one idle; for they leave the
monasteries early in the morning, each with his
tools in his hand and a sack on his shoulder, with
biscuit and onions. They all work for the community of the monastery, and every one must practice
some mechanical art. If there is any common
work, they all undertake it together; but they
have each one his particular occupation—some are
shoemakers; some are cobblers; some spin the
wool, others weave the cloth, and others make it
up into dresses; some are masons, some carpen-
ters, some build boats, some are fishermen, and
some millers; and this is a great difference with
the morals and manners of the Latin monasteries.

Yet all are equally industrious, and no one receives more than the rest for his industry or his sloth :"—that is, the frugal meal twice a-day, the cell to inhabit, two woollen shirts and one habit in the year, and two pair of stockings. This still is the rule of the κοινόβοι, or Cenobites—that is, those who have every thing in common.* I asked the Goumenos of Simeon, which is a Cenobite monastery, how he maintained such order without rewards or punishments : he replied, " Men who come to such a place as this, have been broken by care; they are of a religious turn, and are advanced in life; if indulgences are sought by them, they go to the other monasteries, where their means can procure such ; the poorer, the more devout, the more abstemious, come to us ; but if one man is very industrious, and seeks to profit more than the rest, he can obtain a κοίλον, and go and live by himself; if he is very devout he can become a φιλέρεμος, and go to the Mountain. Thus, those that remain in the κοινόβοι, are temperately devout and abstemious without excess, and perfect images of each other. The labour of our several avocations fills up days that no worldly passions distract, solaces or excludes regrets, and becomes the bond of our common friendship ; the silent approbation of our fellows is our chief end, and this harmony we never suffer to be disturbed by the admission of a brother unlike the rest."

* From κοινὸς βίος.

There are twenty-four monasteries; the principal are, Chelendari, Simeon, Vathopedi, Pantocrator, Iviron,—these are inland; Lavro, Agio Paulo, Dionysio Gregorio, Archangelos, and Castamoniti, are placed on the face of the mountain itself, towards the Ægean, and, standing forth in bold relief from the rock, are hailed by the passing fisher, mariner, or pirate ;* or hid, nestled amidst cliffs and foliage, the boatman quits his oar to watch for the spire, and having caught a glimpse of it, devoutedly crosses himself and resumes his labour.

Belon was enraptured with the botany of the promontory, he compares its Platani to the cedars of Lebanon; the creepers, he says, are so gigantic, that they would grow to heaven if they found a tree tall enough to twine round : but what surprised and delighted him most was, "qu'il n'y a plante insigne qui ne soit connûe aujourd'hui, par le même nom que Theophraste, Discoride, et Galen, laisserent par escrit."—"Les haults lauriers et oliviers sauvages répriment en tout temps l'ardeur excessive du soleil, et les arbousiers qui

---

* "The Turkish, as well as the Christian pirates, respect the monasteries; thus, those who would spare neither father nor mother, relative nor friend, but would sell them ' à purs déniers comptans,' have, I know not what, instinct which makes them spare the Καχοριον—nor is this by reason of their poverty; for these pirates take men for their body as well as for their wealth, and can get 50 ducats for a slave."—BELON,

communement sont ailleurs arbrisseaux, arbres."
The *Smilax lœvis* ascends the crests of the loftiest
platani, then spreads down over its branches,
forming a defence of perpetual verdure against
the impetuosity of the winds, or the ardour of
the sun's rays.

In the days of Hippocrates, this country was
celebrated, as now, for ague: he adduces several
cases, from Abdera and Thasus, of the malignant
fever and of intermittent fevers; he mentions the
Etesian winds that temper the dog-days—the daily
breezes during the hottest hours—from the south
in winter, from the north in summer. In no other
country could he have attributed such wonderful
efficacy to air, and water, and situation, which are
at this day examined, enjoyed, and venerated, as
in his: the first merit of a spot is its "cold and
clear water;" next, its "pure air;" and you hear
a mountaineer regretting—not, as with us, his hills
or his hearth—but his stream or fountain,* the
peculiar breezes, carefully distinguishing these, and
then the distant prospect: in hearing some of them
learnedly and curiously descanting on these topics,
attributing to peculiar situations and exposures
particular effects on the water, and then the effect
of temperature and water on the complexion,
voice, temperament, and health of man, I had
the same gratification of discovering resemblances
with antiquity, that Belon had in finding the

* Every fountain in a village has a name.

botanical terms of Hippocrates and Galen in common use.

At the extremity of the Peninsula, Athos rises into a lofty mountain, visible from 30 leagues at sea. Looking from the mountains of Macedonia, where you embrace at once the whole Peninsula, fore-shortened, it may have the appearance of a man lying on his back; for as the nose and chin would so be raised in the air, and an interval would appear between the chin and the breast, so the elevated portion of the extremity of the mountain seems detached from the rocks that lie below, and which spread on either side as it were the shoulders; then they seem to narrow and to rise in the centre and mark the navel; then spread towards the hip; then the abrupt escarpment of a mountain across the isthmus, seems to give the outline of the knees, bent and drawn up; after which the land, suddenly sinking, narrows where the joined feet might be supposed to touch the earth. From no other point is it possible to give to Athos the remotest resemblance to the human form. This, I therefore think, must have been the view of Stesicrates when he endeavoured to persuade Alexander to complete the resemblance, and place a tower in the right hand and a cup in the left; the more so as the town of Acanthus stands on the right side* just

* Strabo, it is true, places Acanthus in the west instead of the east, but he alone does so, and, by the context of the passage, he is evidently in error.

beyond the ridge that would represent the knees, and where, by the perspective, the hand in that attitude would come : corresponding to this point, on the left, is a knoll which might have been fashioned into the cup. This idea, it is true, has occurred to me since my visit to Athos, so that I do not feel that conviction which an inspection of the localities, with this view, would have given. When I looked on this scene, it was evening ; the sea reflected the rosy hues of the heaven so truly, that you could scarcely tell where the sea and sky met : not a cloud obscured the one, not a breath ruffled the other; so that, losing, by the height at which I stood and the uniformity of colour which effaced the horizon, all idea of level, the mass assumed the form of a vast image ; and an effect, still deeply impressed on my mind, recalls the resemblance of the promontory to the human frame, which, at the time, I attributed to the giddiness produced by the illusion of the prospect— the promontory seemed to rise into the sky, at first like a tree, and then like a colossus endowed with motion.

CHAPTER XIV.

KLEPHTS, PIRATES, AND SMUGGLERS.

THE robbery here placed in a most awkward position;—the Binbashi breathed nothing but vengeance; and how could that vengeance be satisfied? By fining the monasteries!

I may here remark, that the principle of all ancient government, by which the body is responsible for its members, is preserved in the East, and is the ground-work of laws, habits, and opinions. The district is in the first instance responsible, then the government. Here was an exceptional case, as the monks formed a distinct community. As military governor, the Binbashi became in the first instance responsible; and, indeed, he offered to pay me at once 5000 piastres as compensation.

I dreaded, however, being made use of as a pretence for extortion; and the monks, in secret, implored me to save them. I took occasion to represent to the Binbashi, that I was not at all incensed against the Klephti; that they had taken nothing from me; and that I should be more anxious to

favour their escape than their apprehension.   That
such being my feelings towards the Klephti, he had
no right to interfere in the matter.   He laughed
at my scruples; and, gradually working himself
into a rage, he vowed such vengeance, and vomited
such execrations, as are usual in similar cases.   I,
in turn, incensed, told him that he had better display his choler against the armed Klephts than
against the peaceable monks.   He swelled with indignation at this reproach; and pretending to apply
my allusion to the Greek guards of the Isthmus,
and perhaps, too, to shew me with what scorn he
could treat Christians and armed ones, he ordered
a Greek captain up to the room, abused him for
his culpable negligence, and told him that if he did
not find the Klephts in three days that he should
be hanged in their stead.   Then, suddenly changing
his ground, he accused him or his men of the robbery,—ordered them to be immediately mustered;
and those that were present to be immediately
brought to me, that I might identify them.   The
Captain turned on him a look of fury; and left the
room without uttering a word.   I protested against
this outrageous proceeding, but in vain; fifteen
men were presently paraded up stairs; I got up,
and, expressing to the Captain my regret at being
the cause of the unworthy insult offered to him
and to his men—left the apartment.

    After rambling about for a couple of hours, I
returned to my Konak; and there, to my surprise,

found the Captain and all his Palicars squatted round the room. As I entered, they got up, and, bidding them welcome, I seated myself; when they all squatted down again, and we remained for a couple of minutes or so in silence—I wondering the while at the cause of this strange visitation. The Captain's emotion would scarcely allow him to speak; and it was some time before I discovered that the object of their visit was to thank me for my good opinion, and for the manner in which I had treated the proposition of the Binbashi.*

" I have been a Klepht," exclaimed the Captain, " on land and sea; and then every bush in Athos trembled at my name! When I was Klepht, I owned it, and he (the Binbashi) dared not have reproached me with it; now I hold the Sultan's firman, and to me the mountain owes its security, and he dares call me robber!"

The Captain of Agion Oros holds his tenure as the Captain of Cassandra. He was chosen by the monks from among the robbers, and received a firman from the Porte, and a Buyourdi from the Pasha, constituting him Armatole; exempting him and his men from taxes, and intrusting to him the district of Agion Oros. He had twenty-five

---

* During several days of rough weather, the Binbashi was detained at Caries, not venturing to return by land; having become friends again, I offered him a note of hand, as a *sauf conduit* through the mountains!

men; with these he had to maintain the police, and to save his district from devastation by his " Chatir."

I have been often struck by the analogy between the Klepht of Turkey and the Contrabandista of Spain. The lives of both are spent in daring adventure on land and sea; their native inertness is roused by violent excitement;—their career is ennobled by exertion and danger;—they are alike branded with the name of felon by legitimate authority, and endeared to the popular sympathies, less, perhaps, by their adventurous lives, than by the practical good of which they are the unconscious agents.

If Spain has not succeeded in establishing a commercial inquisition as detestable in principle, and far more destructive in practice than her religious inquisition; if she has not entirely extinguished the resources of her territory, and the energies of her people, it is that her geographical position permitted her misrule to raise up the body of Contrabandistas. France, Gibraltar, Oporto, supplied dépôts of foreign merchandise; the thousand passes of the Pyrennees, an immense extent of sea-coast, lofty and difficult chains of mountains, intersecting the whole kingdom, afforded the smugglers ample field for the exercise of their calling.

From time immemorial, immense bodies of organised smugglers have carried on a great portion of the commerce of Spain; and the remainder of that commerce would perhaps not exist but for the indirect effect of smuggling, which rendered the customs wholly unproductive when restriction was carried to an excessive degree. " Except bulky articles, or those of trifling value or difficult transport, *even prohibition* has scarcely any effect on the markets of Spain."

But if the smugglers have so much contributed to the preservation of the commercial prosperity Spain still retains, they have contributed in a no less marked degree to her national independence. This alone, under such a government, could have preserved breasts not callous to generous purposes, and prodigal of ease and life in their country's cause. When the hundreds of thousands arrayed by the government against the French were scattered like chaff, when the central administration, and all that belonged to government,—all that bore the stamp of legitimate authority,—was wiped clean away, then it was that the Contrabandista stood forth the patriot; and bound on the brow of his ungrateful country the better half of the wreath which was struck from the victor's head.

The legitimate principles of the internal administration of Turkey are such, that no set of men could ever be the objects of public sympathy by the infraction of them. Such an opinion may appear strange; but I cannot resist a conclusion to which so many separate inquiries severally lead me : take this one for instance :—Not in Spain alone, but in every country of Europe, are the moral effects of smuggling most lamentable; our coasts are covered with preventive-service men; our prisons filled with culprits in the eyes of the law, who are victims in the eyes of the public: respect for government and for law is enfeebled,— the common retribution of dissimilar crimes diminishes the infamy of punishment; the standard of morality is lowered;—the effect of opinion is weakened. Yet it is only by such re-action, however deplorable, that the still more noxious effects of European commercial policy is to be corrected; and to it alone we will probably owe our emancipation from the wretched system. Most strange, most unaccountable is it, that Turkey should offer us such a contrast on a question of such vast practical importance. That contrast I cannot more strongly mark, than by stating this simple fact. In Turkey there are no smugglers. It will be inquired, Whether the exactions of government are lighter than in Europe? Clearly not. Whether their custom-house officers, their preventive-service men, are more efficient, their punishments more severe? Quite the reverse: there are custom-receivers and appraisers, but no custom-house guards, no preventive-service, and *no punishment* for smuggling. The fact is, that the government exactions being laid on property minutely calculated (by themselves), according to the amount of each man's wealth, there is so sympathy for a defrauder of the revenue. The Turkish government has never sought to disguise the amount of revenue, and has therefore preferred imposts on property to imposts on commerce; which seems to combine the greatest amount of revenue with the greatest freedom of industry; and, consequently, *cæteris paribus*, the greatest submissiveness to government.

But if the population of Turkey is not inimical to the principles of the administration, they detest the abuses of the local governor, whether the Pasha of the province or the Aga of the village. This, as far as I have been able to judge, is *the* evil of Turkey; and if the violence of these despots has been restrained, if the Porte has been encouraged and strengthened in having recourse to measures of severity against its inferior agents, it has been by the co-operation of the Klephti. The peasant, chained down by family attachments,— bonds of straw with us, but of flesh and blood with them,—by the responsibility of relatives and fellow-villagers for his conduct, endures labours, pays; but ventures neither to remonstrate nor complain, until some crowning indignity bursts all these bonds at once: he flies to the mountains, enlists with some of the Capitani as an Armatole, or joins some more ignoble party of marauders; and with Albanian kirtle, pistol in his belt, and musket over his shoulder, he presents the veriest contrast of what he has been. The tame, submissive, beast of burden, becomes the wolf of the plain and the vulture of the mountain.

Thus, then, the Klepht limits the arbitrariness of Turkish rule, as the Contrabandista limits the despotism of Spanish law. But the most remarkable parallel is between the seven years' war of independence in both countries; when, under foreign direction, with apparently the most contemptible military resources, the greatest military names of the Eastern and Western worlds have been tarnished, and overwhelming armies cut off in detail by Guerillas they despised. Each country, paralleled only by the other, has succeeded by a struggle of equal duration in a contest which appeared hopeless in the case of Spain,—madness in that of Greece. Here, I trust, the comparison will cease to hold; and that Greece, in escaping from the accidental evils of the Turkish rule, will not engraft on her national tree the systematic evils of Europe; the excess of which is so glaring in Spain. She will rue the day that she exchanges the Klepht for the Smuggler.

The Klephts on land have also been pirates at sea; but there are various kinds of pirates, and the distinctions between them may be worth pointing out.

The geographical position of Syra is nearly that of Delos, the most ancient free port; and during the late struggle, and in the wars of the

Persians and Greeks, the characters of the two
ports have been identical; depending on a similarity of local circumstances that still exist, and
political causes that have re-appeared. At Delos
was interchanged the commerce of the East and
the West, and the commodities of nations ignorant
of each others' language,—perhaps existence.
Here the commerce of remote shores found a central mart, and the vessels of warring nations a
neutral port. Here the pirates were received as
friends, and their plunder became legal objects of
traffic. So, at the present day, the little insignificant island of Syra has risen to an equality with
the first emporia of the Levant, from an interme-
diate position between the East and the West, and
the three quarters of the globe; from its being a
neutral port for the provisioning both of Turks and
Greeks, the importance of which was so sensibly
felt, that, without defences of any kind, it was respected by each, and paid tribute to both; and,
lastly, it was the rendezvous of the pirate,—the
receptacle of stolen goods; and to this source of
wealth has its importance to be chiefly attributed.

The number of vessels plundered by the pirates,
from 1823 to 1827, has been enormous. Piratical
enterprises were conducted by the three following
classes of pirates :—

The first class was composed of soldiers, who
secured boats on the shore, and made the fishermen pull them to be-calmed vessels, which they

boarded and rifled. Success, and impunity, and
necessity, gradually increased their numbers and
skill; so that the Macedonian followers of Cara-
tasso, who had established himself in the Devil's
Island (as the Protocols are pleased to call them),
had an exceedingly well-equipped flotilla, of sixty
beautiful mysticos:—such are the pirates which
generally infested the shores of Greece, from the
Echinades to Mount Athos. There is no organisation amongst them,—no means of disposing
of their plunder, and seldom any object beyond
immediate necessity; and they enter a vessel as
they would do a sheepfold, to obtain covering or
a bellyful.

The mystico is a long, low, and narrow boat,
with three or four masts, with latine sails, with a
gun in the bow; and impelled by from twenty to
ninety oars. These, lying close among rocks,
which no large vessel can approach, and whence
they can pick off the men in boats, coming
to attack them, would suddenly, in those calms
which so commonly prevail in the Levant, dart
on merchantmen, as they lay immovable logs,
or even board them in the midst of convoys;*
plunder them, and carry off their booty in open
day, and almost under the guns of the convoying
men-of-war. This is a species of pirate peculiar to

* They once even boarded and carried an Austrian man-of-
war brig; but that was at night, and by mistake.

Greece, and identical with the pirate of ancient days. The mysticos are probably not unlike the Homeric fleets and Athenian galleys:—the same calms, the same rocks, and the same political circumstance of the countries adjoining the sea, are causes which exist, and ever have existed.

The next class of pirates were the cruisers of the naval islands, who at a late period took to this species of industry. It may be advanced in extenuation of their offence, that they were often frustrated of legal prizes by false papers, by the interference of European men-of-war, and they were exasperated by the undisguised, though unavowed hostility of one European power: they were pressed by the hard hand of necessity, and encouraged by the impunity of the misdeeds of others. If for the greater crimes of the Ipsariots further palliation was wanting, it may be found in the blood and flames of Ipsara. These cruisers went out first to maintain the blockade of Turkish ports; they next searched for contraband of war. They soon adopted the English creed of maritime international law, and searched all neutrals for Turkish property. Scrupulous at first in their seizures, and strictly legal in their deportment, they found good prizes escaping from their hands; the judges, right or wrong, were suspected of collusion. These circumstances, but above all the decay of the consideration and hope which Europe had at first inspired, led to the frightful increase of the piracy

of these armed vessels, which was quite distinct
from the coasting piracy of the mysticos.

The piracy of the cruisers is such as other
nations have been guilty of when driven to the like
extremities; for instance, the Dutch.

The third species of piracy has resulted from
the other two; and resembles the Bucaniers of
the western hemisphere. These crews are composed of the most daring and depraved among the
Greeks, with desperadoes of all nations. They infested the central group of the Archipelago in
schooners' boats, or carried on in larger vessels
more extensive operations from their impregnable
fortress of Grabusa.

This new Algiers is a square rock, rising almost
perpendicularly from the sea, separated on two sides
by channel from the north-western extremity of
Candia; the opposite cliffs of which are equally steep
and regular. On the western side of the square,
looking to the sea, is superimposed another cliff,
narrow and abrupt, which can be reached by clam-
bering up one difficult path from the table-ground
of the inferior rock. This is the fortress; walled,
but needing no defence, and mounted with some
scores of guns. Its defence seaward is an impending cliff, of 700 feet, from which height it
looks down to the south and east on the bay, enclosed by a bar and reef, with rocky and dangerous
holding ground. To blockade or bombard such a
place by a naval force, which could not keep such

a sea without shelter or anchorage of any kind, is impossible; while the vessels blockaded could issue from, or retreat by, the two entrances, to the north and west. This place had above twenty beautiful schooners, well found and manned, belonging to the more piratically inclined of the naval islands, and connected with the commerce of Syra. The disturbed state of Candia gave it additional importance; and, at the period of its capture, 7000 men were assembled here. Some of the pirates had built houses, presenting a strange mixture of European commodities, that remind one of the establishment of Byron's Lambro; magazines, caverns, and the cisterns of the fortress and the church, were filled with French silks and wines, English cottons and hardware, Genoese velvets, Swiss watches, &c. Venetian mirrors, elegant time-pieces, and Marseillese commodes, adorned mud walls: their patron Saint was propitiated with the most incongruous offerings; and strange objects and unwonted luxuries were applied to the most homely and grotesque uses.

During the continuance of the piracies, I believed, and with justice, as the end has shewn, that piracy not only originated in political circumstances, but was entirely dependent on them. It was only by organising the islands that piracies of the coast were to be prevented, and, by giving legitimate employment alone, that unlawful enterprises were to be resisted. By attacking them they are exasperated, and their hopes extinguished; while the local circumstances favour their defence against our marine, which must attack under the most serious disadvantages, multiply itself on innumerable points, and risk both vessels and men for trifling advantages. To put down piracy by force, we must, like the Persians in Euboea, have joined hands to catch them on the rocks; or, like the Athenians at Pyla, have spread nets to take them in the sea. Yet the news of the recognition of the independence of Greece, and of the establishment of a government,—chilling and anti-national as it was,—had scarcely time to spread over the Levant, when every species of piracy had ceased.

The ancient history of the Levant has an episode peculiarly coinciding with this remarkable event. The pirates at that period, from their central position in Candia (as Lutro and Grabusa of the present day), and stations in many of the smaller islands on the coasts of Asia Minor, commanded the whole of the Mediterranean; and not only exasperated the Romans by depredations on their commerce, and by descents on the Latian coasts, but met in battle array their largest fleets with various fortune. It was no small necessity that induced the still jealous republic to place at the disposal of Pompey the enormous means voted to him for the prosecution of that war; which was the most extensive command that had ever yet been intrusted even to a Roman citizen. Yet in three short months,—in shorter time than it would have taken him to sail from one end of his province to the other,—was the war ended; the pirates had ceased to exist. The robbers became husbandmen; and the republic losing inveterate and powerful foes, found in them devoted subjects. Pompey gave them a country,—he gave them lands, habitations, independence, and connexion with Rome only by their own municipal institutions, to which they owed their distinguishing prosperity, and long attachment to the mistress of the world. " The successful management of this war," says a just observer, " which he finished in three months, is perhaps the most glorious event of the life of Pompey; and exceeds, in my opinion, the greatest actions ever performed by Cæsar."*

The amount of loss incurred by European commerce, during the Greek insurrection, is incalculable. I have heard the number of vessels captured, and formally confiscated,— captured by pirates,— or plundered in the open sea, stated to amount altogether to four hundred! Without admitting the accuracy of this estimate, the enormous extent of piracies is patent; and, besides the actual loss, a further loss was in reality occasioned by the interruption of communication, and the arrestation of commerce. And to this state of things is owing the more determined diplomatic interference of

* Arbuthnot's Tables of Ancient Coins, p. 250.

Europe in the affairs of the Levant.   The source
of that interference was no doubt the sympathy of
Europe for the name of Greece, and the antipathy
of Europe against the Mussulmans; systematically
excited by the long-foreseeing cabinet of St. Petersburg.   But it was the piracies of the Levant which
placed our government under the obligation of
acting; that action being directed of necessity by
Russia.

This is not the first occasion on which the
piracies of these seas have called into action the
diplomacy, and gravely complicated and compromised the relations of the great European powers.

A band of outlaws, under the name of Uscocks,
the refuse of all nations, occupied, under the protection of Austria, for nearly the whole of the 16th
century, a strong position on the coast of Dalmatia, committed depredations on land, and unheard-
of barbarities at sea: the commerce and the dependencies of Venice and the Porte were their
prey; and, after embroiling all Europe, and entailing on Venice a loss of twenty millions of ducats,
they were put down by a treaty, signed at Madrid,
under the mediation of France, between Austria
and Venice.

CHAPTER XV.

SUBSEQUENTLY to this period, my journey would be a sad and dreary tale, presenting but a succession of burning and shivering fits of the ague; against which I considered myself proof, and which, I doubt not, I should have escaped, had I adhered to the regimen I had followed for the previous year, and which I would recommend to travellers in this unhealthy climate when similarly exposed. The first point, is wearing the dress of the country and to have always an ample pelisse at hand, and constantly, on sitting down, to throw it over the shoulders. The open verandas, the crevices around, above, and below, even in the best constructed houses, and the excessive difference of temperature between shade and sunshine, produce constant draughts and currents—the tempting coolness of which beguiles one's best caution, unless provided with the facilities which the Turkish costume affords. The next point, is shaving the head—one of the greatest luxuries in a hot climate. The absence of hair and

uniformity of covering, prevent chills by cooled
perspiration; and, after exercise, the head can be
wiped dry, and a fresh skullcap put on. As to
diet, the principal object is to prevent perspiration
as much as possible; to take as little liquid as
possible; no wine or spirits; and I have found
that fruit supplied the place of liquids without producing perspiration. The Orientals generally have
a great prejudice against fruit; but what I have
seen of the fever, leaves me no room to doubt the
beneficial effects of fruit, both as preventive and cura-
tive. One meal a day is, in this climate, sufficient;
and that ought to be after the work of the day is
over; or, if made in the forenoon, a refreshing
and digesting sleep ought to intervene between it
and exertion. Turkish made-dishes are tempting,
but fat :* sheep roasted whole are dangerous
viands with a traveller's appetite; and a general
predominance of salt among the Albanians is intended to give the forbidden juice a stronger zest :
against this, the prudent traveller ought to be on his
guard; he would do well, if that were practicable,
to confine himself to pilaf, yaoort (a species of
sour milk), and eggs, which he can find every

---

* Turkish cookery is also a tempting subject. There are
several processes and principles new to us, and valuable. However, travellers, unfortunately, are not very liable to excess in
this way, for, generally speaking, they have such opportunities of
judging of Turkish cookery as a foreigner, from English taverns,
might have of judging of English comforts.

where : the first two form together a light, nu-
tritive, and not unpalatable dish.

Adhering to these maxims, though exposed to
all the malaria of Thessaly and Lower Macedonia
for the whole summer, I alone of our party, which
originally amounted to nine, escaped the ague.
While at Caries, I lived with the Binbashi; and to
this I can clearly trace the fever with which I was
attacked. I was delirious during the first night,
but was somewhat relieved next day by a copious
perspiration, and had the mortification to find my
servant nearly as ill as myself. There was not a
house without one or two invalids ; and no medical
assistance whatever to be procured, not even for
the letting of blood. The night after, during a fit,
I perceived a stranger most carefully attending on
me ; on recovering in the morning, I recognised in
my nurse the Abbot of St. Simeon, who, having
heard of my illness, had hastened to Caries to perform this service of charity.

It was important that I should be conveyed to
Salonica as quickly as possible; but the distance
was 80 miles; and nothing but the instances of
the Abbot would have induced me to have commenced the journey. I was placed on a mule, my
servant on another, and we were transported in
one day to Vathopedi, which is, if I recollect well,
a distance of ten miles. Next morning, I was
again placed on the mule, but was too weak to
proceed; a fishing-boat was procured, and I was

transported to Ozeros. My situation was most deplorable; I had but a pelisse for bed and covering; and a mat to lay on the ground I obtained as a great favour. The misery of the place was such, that I could not procure a spare capote, and it was already full of invalids. In the state in which I was, further progress was impossible; nor was there even a barber in the place to bleed me. After repeated inquiries, a man was found in a neighbouring village who professed to draw blood by a species of cupping with a horn, which they apply to the skin, slashed with a razor, and suck with the mouth, by a hole at the small end.

I ought not to omit the kindness of the Aga, a negro, who, during four days that I was detained here, came daily to inquire for me, and always drew something out which he had concealed in his sleeve: one day it was a water-melon; another day it was a fowl; "for," said he, "you are weak, and want something to strengthen you." I was at one time able to go and sit before the door, and he immediately bethought himself of amusing me by making the peasants dance. They had little will for dancing; but, before I was aware of it, a a score of them were brought from their vintage and ordered to dance: "What could they do?" said the Primate, "dancing is *Angaria* (corvée) like any thing else."

I here delivered myself into the hands of a celebrated Paramana, or nurse, who applied fre-

quent frictions of oil, which really did me a great
deal of good; and brought me a potion, which I
was deterred from taking by the strong smell of
prussic acid: it proved to be an infusion of indigo
and laurel water.

My servant was somewhat recovered; and,
after four days, we again resumed our painful
journey: still I was determined to pass through
Nisvoro, the principal of the Mademites, that I
might, at least, look on the locality of the mines'
which had been a principal object of my trip.   My
recollections of the remainder of the journey are
quite indistinct: the fever had become remittent,
and then continuous; the weather was wretched, for
the rains had set in; and considering that the
country was infested with robbers, that I had not
a farthing of money in my pocket, that myself and
my servant were in an utter state of helplessness,—
my passage from Athos to Salonica, fed, housed,
and watched over, whenever we halted on the
road, appears to me an indisputable proof of the
good-nature of calumniated mankind.   This was
not the first time that I have found myself penni-
less in a strange land; and my own experience
would lead me to say, that such a position is in-
valuable for instruction, and leaves not unpleasing
recollections.   I remember passing immense heaps
of slag and scoria, I think in the mountain above
Nisvoro; but in such a condition was I, for, besides

shivering with the fever, I was drenched with rain,
that I let myself slip several times from my mule,
and entreated the strangers who were conducting
me to allow me to lie there and die.   When I
reached Mr. Charnaud's door, at Salonica, I was
recognised only by my mule and clothes; and the
good folks there were startled at the apparition, for
general credit had been given to the report of my
assassination.

Shelter, repose, comforts, and medical attend-
ance, in a short time worked a great change in
me; and in a fortnight after my arrival, I was able,
though very feeble, to walk about.   My first
thoughts were naturally given to Cassandra, and
I determined on laying before the Pasha a formal
complaint against the Aga.   While I was considering how this could best be done, I learnt that
Hassan Aga, the former governor, and my kind
friend, had arrived at Salonica under escort; and
that he actually was in the castle, suspected, it was
said, of some traitorous correspondence, for which
his head was to answer.   I now delayed no longer,
and though I had not requested the intervention
or assistance of the consul, he, on learning the circumstances, entered warmly into the business, and
accompanied me to the Pasha's; and I do not
think that I lost any thing thereby: but the Pasha
had in his remembrance an incident, by no means
pleasant to him, which occurred during my pre-

vious visit, in consequence of his shutting me out at night, when landing from an English man-of-war.

I stated to the Pasha the conduct of the Aga of Cassandra—his violence, but especially, unmannerly conduct—and did not keep in the background the extortions of which he had been guilty, or the hatred of the people against him; and contrasted his conduct with that of Hassan Aga.

The Pasha merely said, " Very well;" and I quitted the Seraï with the conviction that the Pasha was going to act very decidedly ; for I felt that I had touched the Turkish chords of his heart. In two hours afterwards, while lying on a sofa, exhausted with the effort, I felt my hand seized and fervently kissed. I opened my eyes, and beheld Hassan Aga, who poured forth expressions of devotion and gratitude for his deliverance. He had been arrested some days after my departure by the Aga, charged with a plot for inviting the Greeks to Cassandra. The petition of the local Greeks in his favour had given colour to this accusation ; and their complaints against the Aga were thus interpreted as proving the guilt of Hassan Aga. Report on report, to this effect, had been sent to Salonica; and especially by my Cavashes, who were exasperated against me for treating them as a Turk in my position would treat them, and against Hassan Aga, for treating me as a Mussulman. They, therefore, on their return, loudly proclaimed the notoriety of Hassan Aga's treachery; declared him a Giour, in league with the Greeks and the English. The Pasha no longer doubted the criminality of Hassan Aga: public indignation was aroused against him; and, at this moment, he arrived a prisoner. His fate might have been immediately sealed, had it not been for the incident above referred to, respecting an English man-of-war; this induced the Pasha to pause till my return. Hassan Aga, meanwhile, had given himself over as lost, and was considered as such. After our interview, the Pasha, much excited, sent for and cross-questioned Hassan Aga: he, standing between a couple of soldiers at the bottom of the room, and expecting from the Pasha's manner an order for his execution. After musing for a while, the Pasha ordered the soldiers away, told Hassan Aga to be seated: Hassan Aga threw himself at his feet. The Pasha said, " I see how it is;" and gave orders for a couple of Cavashes to proceed immediately to Cassandra, seize the Aga, and bring him to Salonica without an hour's delay.

A few days after this incident, I was summoned by an officer of the Pasha's household to the Divan. The Pasha received me with extreme affability: we chatted for some time about indifferent matters; coffee and pipes were served; and then, on a sign, the numerous train withdrew, and the little ill-favored Aga of Cassandra, looking the image of terror, and the representation of squalid misery, made his appearance between two of the regular soldiers with muskets. I got up from my seat beside the Pasha, and, retiring to the lower end of the room, said, I demanded justice against that individual, who had used his delegated authority to insult a stranger (guest) and the bearer of the Sultan's firman, and on whose head was the curse of the orphan and widow. The Pasha said, " He is in your hands;" and on a sign, he was removed; his sentence was displacement from his governorship; confiscation of his property; was to be imprisoned, for a space of time which it was left to me to fix; and he was to come to ask my pardon: this last was (considering the position of Christians) the most remarkable part of the transaction; and anxious to profit by it, to improve the position of my countrymen, I would not admit him when brought for the purpose, but said that he should go to the Consul and obtain his pardon, and that he should fix the term of his imprisonment. I had the mortification to see the advantage that might have been derived from this incident entirely lost. Thus ended the only complaint I have ever had to make, during ten years' wandering amid pirates, bandits, rebels, and warring foes.

Before I left Salonica, a purse of enormous dimensions, and of delicate workmanship, found its way into my hands, and for years I cherished this reminiscence of Cassandra and of Aglaë.

From Salonica I embarked for Negropont, and

after three months spent in the midst of interests and events, very distinct from those I have been describing, I returned to England. I omit my journal during the subsequent excursion, as it would be of no interest without entering into details, and I prefer carrying the reader back to Albania to view the conclusion of the drama which he there saw commenced; and I am anxious myself to return to that Eastern mind and character which is no longer to be found on the soil of Greece.

I have disposed of most of the *dramatis personæ* connected with my expedition to Mount Athos. I have still to mention that Capt. Anastasi became, for a time, sole regent. His father was named Captain of Polygiro : Hassan Aga went to Greece. I received the Pasha's promise that my captors should be pardoned, and my faithful Hadji become a respectable maccaroni manufacturer at Salonica—having learnt that art when he accompanied me to more civilized regions. Eighteen months afterwards, on visiting Salonica again, Hadji escorted me with several servants of his own ; and, without any infraction of forms, I could ask him to sit down to the same board. As illustrative of the social ties that connect you in the East with your servants, I may mention that, on returning to Greece, I found commandant of the first post, a man who had formerly been a groom in my service ; and the secretary and deputy of the

Governor before whom I had to appear at Egina, I had picked up a destitute orphan, and taught to read and write while officiating as my pipe-bearer. Little do we suspect the amount of enjoyment we lose by the harsh lines drawn between the various grades of life amongst ourselves, while we pride ourselves on social equality; or how much we injure ourselves in mind and character by the degradation of those who are constantly about our persons.

CHAPTER XVI.

SECOND VISIT TO ALBANIA—CHANGE OF CIRCUMSTANCES—
CHARACTER AND EFFECTS OF LOCAL GOVERNMENT—AR-
GYRO CASTRO—MUNICIPAL DEBTS—DRAGOMANS—GREEK
MANNERS.

A few months spent in the sober clime of the
West; a few months of comfortable beds; rain-
tight roofs; smooth, level roads; gas-lit streets;
cloudy weather and monotonous faces; had gradually
recalled—first in my slumbers, and then in my
waking dreams—the bright skies and stirring scenes
of the East.   Presently arrived the news of a fresh
gathering in Albania ; of a general movement at
length, headed by the tardy Pasha of Scodra, and
of Reschid Pasha's mustering his Spahis and Nizam
from far and near.   The embers of the fire that
seemed almost extinct had burst forth afresh, and
again were the destinies of the Ottoman Empire to
be staked upon a cast.

After a few days' combat between inclination
and prudence, the former obtained the victory.   In
November 1831, I made a sudden start across the
channel : a rapid flight of twelve days landed me
at Otranto.   In crossing from Otranto to Corfu, it
was with heartfelt delight that I looked again on

the mountains of Albania; but words cannot express the thrilling effect of the unexpected peals of artillery that welcomed me on the Adriatic wave. At Corfu they had some general notions of insurrection and war connected with Albania, but I could gain no information as to the relative state and position of parties. I heard, indeed, of a disastrous defeat of Mustapha Pasha, and of a beleaguering of Scodra; but the artillery I had listened to in crossing, proved to me that the sphere of hostilities was still very extensive. Nothing shaken in my resolution, convinced I should fall in with friends in one party or the other, with little to encumber me, and less to make me an object of plunder, trusting, as heretofore, to the ready hospitality and the human sympathies of the many-tongued tribes of the land of the Skipetar, I determined on throwing myself on the opposite coast, and on plunging into the midst of the convulsion.

It was necessary, however, to disguise my project, from the same dread which had attended my last entrance into Albania, that I might not be placed under arrest from kindly regard for my safety, and that my servant might not abandon me. Therefore, after receiving my friends' commissions for Cephalonia and Greece, instead of stepping on board the steamer, I slipped down to the Lazaretto, and resolutely passed that irrevocable barrier between civilization and barbarism.

Next morning found us on the beach at Agia
Saranta; and no sooner landed, than engaged in a
quarrel with an Albanian Buluc Bashi, who housed
his dignity in a ruined barn, and uniting in his
person the various functions and attributes of
harbour-master, custom-house collector, quarantine
director, commander of the place, and guardian of
the passes, conceived he was fully entitled to the
gratification of inspecting my baggage, of scru-
tinizing my person, of fingering my passport, and
of making me pay for the quarantine I did not
perform. To the whole of these pretensions I gave
a decided negative. " Do you presume," he indig-
nantly exclaimed, " to examine our passports, make
our boats pay, rummage our goods, and then clap
us in a prison (Lazaretto), without expecting that
we shall do the same to you ?"—" No," said he,
" vallah, villah, tillah—you must pay for your quarantine, and I must see every article in your saddle-
bags." " Do you know the length," I retorted,
" of the Sadrazem's beard? Do you know the
length of your own body without the head?" and
passing by, without waiting for the reply which
seemed faltering on his tongue at this unexpected
conjuration, I ordered my unopened saddle-bags
to be taken up to the Aga's own apartment, and
seating myself on his own rug, I ordered his attendants to bring coffee and pipes, and to get
something quickly ready for breakfast, as I had
been all night on the water. The Aga, thus unex-

pectedly stormed, resigned himself, scarcely be-
lieving that I could be a Frank, slowly entered the
apartment as I was concluding my directions to his
household, and quietly sat down.   I then informed
him that no further notice would be taken of what
had passed, but that he must immediately send and
get horses, and let me have half-a-dozen men to
escort me to Delvino, as soon as I had breakfasted;
and at Delvino did I arrive the same evening,
mounted on the cattle, and attended by the guards,
of the Aga of Agia Saranta.

I had landed opposite to Corfu : the people,
and particularly the men in authority in that
quarter, were contaminated, and rendered both
insolent and rapacious by the neighbourhood of
what we call *civilization*.   I had made my calculations on their own natural and hospitable character.   I had neither firman nor authority from
the Porte, nor the means of resisting violence, nor
even of buying services at the rate which would
have been exacted from me, had I suffered myself
to be imposed on.   There was but one course
open—that which I adopted, and which, though it
did succeed, might have failed.

It was a real pleasure to me to find myself
again domesticated in the East—that contrast of
the mild, quiet, docile existence of the household,
with the stormy agitation of the court and camp—
that easy and elegant costume—those tasteful
rooms and comfortable divans—that heavenly

climate, and that existence passed in constant
communion with nature : what a relief, too, from
European tedium, politics, theories, systems, argu-
mentation, and learning !   The East owes much of
its attraction to contrasts, which fade when the
novelty is past ; but it possesses positive merits,
which certainly increase upon you with experience
and habit, and which never seemed so prepos-
sessing in my eyes as at the present moment.   But,
beyond these, to me it presented one peculiar
source of gratification.   Arriving straight from
Europe, having passed through a scene of unparalleled misery in the South of Italy, having
quitted England immediately after the brutal riots
at Bristol, having in my rapid course been the first
to enter Lyons after the more systematic but more
bloody tumult of that city, it was not without a
feeling of self-satisfaction and of pride, that, considering the opinion I had ventured to form of
Turkey, its institutions and its populations, in
despite of the universal reprobation of the wise
as well as the simple, that I contemplated, in
the midst of the convulsions of Albania, the
scene presented to my view under the hospitable
roof where I was lodged, and in the aspect of the
lovely burgh where my first Eastern evening was
spent.

When I was last in the country, it displayed a
general picture of anarchy and convulsion.   The
success of the Albanians led evidently to the utter

destruction of the very sources of population and production: the success of the Sultan appeared to me to promise little, or, at all events, distant amelioration. I now found the Sultan triumphant, and the Grand Vizir besieging, and on the point of taking, Scodra itself. The inquiry, therefore, immediately arose in my mind—an inquiry which scarcely presented itself before—What will be the effect of this triumph? My attention was therefore anxiously turned to every trivial circumstance that could enlighten me as to the actual state or expectations of the population: the first glance at Delvino revealed a condition of things for which I was utterly unprepared. I shall endeavour to describe it.

On arriving, I had dismounted at the door of the Governor Youssouf Aga: Italian and French books were lying on his sofa; and in his hand, when I entered, there was a work on Greek coins. He received me with extreme urbanity, spoke to me with enthusiasm of the happy change that had been effected, told me that I had arrived at a memorable epoch for Delvino, (which, indeed, I had seen crowded with people as on a festal day); for that next morning they were to commence levelling the castles of the various Albanian Beys, that overlooked and commanded the town. He shewed me a schedule of the population of the district, with a scale of taxes that they were in future to pay, and which was to be published, to prevent illegal extortion; and which was fixed in lieu of all former exactions, as follows :—

The Charatch (poll-tax), according to the classes, as formerly.

The tenth, or Spahilik, was to be paid to the Governor, and not to the Spahis.

A compromise for all other taxes, 60 piastres per fire, equivalent to about 15s.; and beyond this not a single asper.

He conceived this arrangement to be a reduction of two-thirds on the amount previously exacted; while it would return to the public treasury a larger sum than was formerly received. " The Sultan," he observed, " deserves to profit by his victory; but the Christian and labouring population, through whose co-operation that victory has been gained, must also share in it." This leading us directly to the question of Greek independence, I observed that the independence of Greece might in one way be instrumental to the re-organization of Turkey, if properly used. He turned his eyes on a Turk sitting by him, and said, " Now, do you see the truth of what I was saying to you?" and, looking again at me, he said, with a sigh, " People are always the last to comprehend themselves."*

What was most surprising, was the perfect resignation of the Beys, whose castles were to be

---

* It is to be observed, that this was the first time this idea was put forward by a European.

destroyed. " Our day is gone," they said, " and God is great. If we had triumphed we should have done worse, and quarrelled amongst ourselves and our Tchifliks; if tranquillity is general, it will be better than our swords."*

Every person I addressed, with the exception of some few of the very old Albanians, seemed to set no limits to their expressions of devotion to the Sultan, and admiration for the Grand Vizir. Their amiable governor came in, too, for a share of praise and affection. They had even determined on building a Seraï for him at their own expense. In allusion to the towers about to be condemned, that frowned from the steeps that overlooked the town, they said their Aga's Seraï should rise in the *heart* of the town (εἰς τὴν καρδίαν τῆς χώρας); and, subsequently, a deputation of the elders of the place begged me to be the channel of this request to the Grand Vizir.

Such was the aspect of my first halting-place in the distracted land of Albania, after arriving from the civilized regions of the West, where Turkey was considered by one half the world as a living exhibition of barbarous anarchy and crime, and by the other as a vast and inert mass, from whose nostrils the last breath of existence had already fled.

* One of them, rather advanced in years, told me that a new era was beginning; and that he himself was " tearing his eyes out" with learning French.

I was guest in a modest establishment, deficient in no comfort—not wanting in many luxuries; my host's attentions were unremitting, but never obtrusive; his deportment respectful, as it was intended to be, derived not less of its merit from the style and manners of the country, than from the kindliness of the man. His conversation was that which would have been considered in Europe as refined and instructive in any class; and as infinitely superior to that class to which he appeared to belong. I was sedulously attended by several lads, his children, who, down to those of the tenderest age, performed their parts with a dexterity, and conducted themselves with a decorum, which spoke habitual practice; and which, to a western, appeared perfectly incompatible with the waywardness of their age or the habits of their rank. Comfort, neatness, and extreme cleanliness, characterised the whole establishment; and the general calmness of deportment, and elegance of manner, might have led a stranger to believe that it was the retreat of one whose dignity could command, but whose taste rejected, the external signs of splendour and of power. My host was but a tanner, a Greek Rayah, whose means of existence did not exceed 60*l.* a-year! He was also an elected elder of the place, a judge and arbitrator, a collector and assessor of the government taxes; an office held for six months, to which the community nominates, and is gratuitously performed.

It was on that day that these various points struck me in connexion one with the other, and upset all my previous notions of government and history; and make me look back at this present moment to the thoughts then awakened in my mind, as to an epoch in my existence.

But, to give some indication of the circumstances which produced on me such an effect, I must mention a scene which I had witnessed a few days before in Apulia; and but for which the social and domestic features presented to me by the family of the primate of Delvino, and the political state of its population, would have passed by without producing any more decided effect, or awakening any deeper reflections, than thousands of similar instances had awakened in my previous rambles.

Some twenty or thirty miles before reaching Otranto, the road became almost impracticable, so I left my carriage, and proceeded on horseback; and being accustomed to travel alone, on account of the greater chance thus afforded of coming in contact with the simple and real characters of the country, I left my attendants behind—and lost my way. Perceiving a village at a little distance, I made for it, and inquired as to my road; to my surprise I found that none of the inhabitants could speak Italian, but some sounds struck my ear as not unlike Greek. Great was my delight when I learnt that the name of the village was Kallimera— no doubt now remained: here was a Greek colony—here was, on the soil of civilized and Christian Europe, a portion of that highly gifted and attaching people, whose lot I had bewailed, and whose misguided energies I had so long lamented over, perverted and repressed under the doubly chilling atmosphere of political despotism and religious imposture. All this rushed upon me in a moment; I leapt from my horse, and entered the first open door,—all attention and all suspense,—expecting to look upon a brighter metamorphosis of the Greek race; and prepared to lose no fraction of the meaning that might be drawn from the new incidents I was about to behold. But to represent a tithe of the surprise and disappointment which a momentary glance around me sufficed to convey, is impossible; no hearty welcome from the host; no clustering round of " classical profiles," and picturesque costumes; no curious and anxious, but not obtrusive looks; no busy preparations among the family; no corner swept; no carpet spread; no pillows carefully adjusted; no children, striving which should first fill the pipe, or bring the coffee; no bashful maiden, approaching to pour water over the stranger's hands! And can these be Greeks? And Greeks, too, transported into the bosom of Christianity and civilization! Have they left in the land of barbarism that liveliness of air and manner, that smile of kindness and pride of hospitality, which for years I had witnessed and enjoyed, and conceived to be qualities and attractions inseparable from their name and race? After some essays, I found conversation with them in Greek practicable. They were but a recent emigration, yet they had become such as I saw them!

While I sat quite bewildered with the contrast this population presented with their cognate tribes across the Adriatic, my eye wandered across the street, and settled on a small building on the opposite side, of massive structure, and without windows; the door was strengthened by numerous iron bolts, and was secured by five enormous padlocks; above it was an escutcheon, like the sign of a pothouse, bearing the royal arms, and under it the words " SALE E TABACCO."

When conversing on the distribution of taxes with the primate of Delvino, this sign and motto recurred to me; *here* (in Turkey) were no Apalti— *here* were no police officers—*here* were no government tax-gatherers—*here* was no bachelor clergy, connected with a political system; but here *was* a village administration—*here was* the mind of the villager directed to his village affairs—here *was* the opinion of the village omnipotent as regarded its elders, stewards, priests; and though they might suffer from the irregular excesses of ephemeral governors, they had not to wither under the undying errors of legislators. The excesses of the first tended to strengthen their natural intelligence, the errors of the second did not pervert the idea of justice, and confound the sources of right and wrong. These differences in their political existence,—were they sufficient to account for the contrast between the visible and material circumstances of the two people ? Was the annihilation of local administration sufficient to account for the dereliction of the faith of their fathers, for the corruption of their language, and the degradation of their intellect ? Was the difference of the scene I witnessed at Kallimera, and that presented to me by the family of my host at Delvino, to be referred to modes and principles of taxation ? Are, then, morality and politics, religion, language, and administration, so intimately connected ? These were some of the inquiries which tumultuously arose in my mind, and directed my attention from that moment with intense interest to all the details of eastern existence, and to all the contrasts between their state and ideas and ours. How far I have been able to reply to the questions then raised, I will not venture to say; but I do look back to the circumstance that suggested the inquiry as to a fortunate event—as to one which has been the source of much enjoyment to myself; which has agreeably occupied many a solitary ride and bivouac; which has relieved the tedium, or has multiplied the attractions of the circumstances and scenes which have been spread over the years that have rolled on from that hour to this.

At Delvino I ascertained that Selectar Poda, the wary old fox who had refused to go to the

Grand Vizir because he had seen no returning footsteps—that he, too, had been caught like the rest; his fortress, so long proclaimed impregnable, had been taken even without a blow; that the independent chiefs of Middle Albania had entirely submitted; and that the insurrection had been wholly put down, after a great battle between Mustapha Pasha and the Grand Vizir, near Perlipe, in which the former had been routed, and his army completely dispersed. But still Mustapha Pasha held out in the fortress of Scodra, where, although it was the middle of winter, the Grand Vizir was besieging him with all the force he could collect. It was even reported that the castle of Scodra had surrendered; but as the same rumour had been spread before, implicit faith was not then given to the intelligence.

I therefore determined to make all expedition to Scodra; hoping that I yet might be in time to witness the final catastrophe of the tragedy, in the earlier scenes of which I had been so deeply interested. In every case, Scodra was the point of attraction. There was the Grand Vizir, the chief men of all Roumeli, the survivors amongst my own Albanian friends; and, scarcely less interesting than these, the city and castle of Scodra itself. This point being settled, how to get there was the question. The horses and cattle throughout the whole country had been greatly diminished in numbers, and those that remained exhibited evident

proofs of the (to them) inglorious hardships of the
campaign, which had, in opposition to all previous
experience, been carried on during winter; the
first, and perhaps the most important, effect of the
employment of regular troops. I could not pos-
sibly perform the journey in less than ten days;
and the mud, clay, mire, marshes, and sloughs, the
cut-up roads, and overflowed rivers, which stretched
between Delvino and Scodra, were displayed in
strong, if not vivid colours, by my new friends.
Those who became acquainted with my project
called it madness. The idea of a European crossing the country at such a moment, where, indeed,
a European had not been seen for twenty years;
and where, though the Grand Vizir had been victorious, no order had been established, while the
country was filled with reckless bands of the discom-
fited chiefs, appeared indeed an enterprise in some
degree deserving such a character. I merely told
my friendly counsellors, that at Corfu I should
have been considered a madman if they had known
I intended coming to Delvino; and that I trusted
for the rest to *Kismet*, and the name of the Grand
Vizir. And thus, after a single day's delay, I started
for Argyro Castro, with an escort of a few men,
which the governor could ill spare me.

Between Delvino and Argyro Castro rises a
ridge, of about 3000 feet in height; looking, with
its bluff and rugged face, towards Corfu, and shelving down rapidly, but evenly, towards the north

and east. At the bottom lies, parallel to it, the long narrow valley of Argyro Castro. Standing on the summit of this ridge, I turned back to look on the Ionian Sea and the Adriatic Gulf, stretched north and south; and divided from the sky, along a considerable portion of the horizon, by the hills of Italy. Before me lay the verdant vale of Argyro Castro, thirty miles in length, and four or five in width; and up rose, immediately behind it, and parallel to that on which I stood, a ridge of equal height and extent, presenting towards me its bold and beetling face. An opening in the wall of rock shewed a third escarpment again behind; so that the mountains appeared like gigantic waves, rolling after each other, and turned to rock just as their threatening crests were about to break.

These ridges are of mountain limestone, passing in the loftiest range into beautiful lithographic stone, interstratified with layers of silex, which sometimes becomes red jasper. In some place the silex lies in layers of nodules, some of them perfectly spherical. The tendency to fracture rectangularly of this formation gives to these strata their peculiar character; the loftier part having on their face the appearance of a perpendicular wall. Above the limestone is a succession of layers of sandstone and aluminous shale, soft and friable, covering the lower part of the mountains on both sides, and rendering most toilsome the mountain paths; which the passage of beasts of burden

during the winter had converted into a succession
of deep holes. The plains below are of clay; and,
flooded as they almost universally are, the pas-
senger on descending exchanges the chances of
sliding over the rocks for the certainty of sticking
in the mire. The castle of Argyro Castro, or the
Silver Castle, is perched on a mass of conglomer-
ate, lying inclined on the back of the ridge which
I had traversed. Around it is scattered a town of
2000 Albanians, and 200 Greek fires. The governor, an Albanian, Ibish Aga, who speaks neither
Turkish nor Greek, occupied an old and ruinous
Seraï; and was surrounded with a train of armed
retainers, who had any air except that of keepers
of the peace. Notwithstanding the unpromising
aspect of his person and establishment, I found
that the same beneficial changes had here also
taken place.

The rate of money is now one all over the
country; previously the governors of districts were
in the habit of altering the value of the currency,
so as to enhance the Turkish piastre at the period
of the payment of their troops, and to depress it at
that of receiving the tribute. Indian corn, their
chief means of subsistence, has fallen (taking into
account the difference made by the establishment
of the common standard of Constantinople) 48 per
cent in two years, and other things nearly in proportion. The debt of the Greek community here
is 130,000 piastres.

Throughout the whole of Roumeli the municipalities are oppressed with enormous debts; which have been contracted during the last years of unceasing wars. Had it not been for the depreciation of the currency, a general bankruptcy must have taken place. One of the first objects to which the Grand Vizir gave his attention, was the relieving of the communities from these burdens, in as far as that was practicable, consistently with the preservation of the rights of property. The creditors, it is true, deserve little sympathy; as the money that has been so lent has principally been the fruit of malversation on the part of governors or bankers; and the rate of interest exacted usurious. The Turkish law, it is true, does not recognise interest; but the deeds were so framed as to avoid the direct violation of the law. The Grand Vizir, however, dealt with the whole question in a summary manner; invited the communities who felt themselves aggrieved, either in the form or spirit of their contracts, to make their complaints to him directly, and these he adjusted as he thought fit; reduced the rate of interest, fixed a time for their liquidation, and even sometimes disallowed claims, or diminished the capital, when the communities had suffered from the exactions of their creditors.

It was very singular, to see the tranquillity and expedition with which an affair of such vast importance as this was disposed of,—where so many

powerful and contending interests were at issue,—
where the obstacles in the way of arriving at the
truth so great, and the difficulties of judging rightly
so numerous. Yet the Grand Vizir, in his camp
of Scodra, while besieging the castle, managed to
conclude the greater part of this intricate affair;
and while that settlement was considered by the
Greeks a benefit, only second to their deliverance
from the Albanians, it scarcely occasioned a murmur of complaint among those who had suffered
by his decisions.

There was an inherent difficulty in this decision,
which, however, must not be omitted. The major
part of the suitors were Greeks, while the defend-
ants were Turks or Albanians. It will, therefore,
at once be perceived how completely at the mercy
of the interpreters were both the Greeks and the
Grand Vizir. The discovery of some flagrant cases
of deception led the Grand Vizir to inflict capital
punishment on two of his principal interpreters
and scribes, the one a Greek, the other a Turk;
and this anomalous display of judicial vengeance
was repeated from mouth to mouth with unbounded
delight and satisfaction. Since that period, all
memorials presented to the Grand Vizir in Greek
are sent back by him, that the memorialists themselves may get them put into Turkish.

While the Governments of Europe, which rule
populations derived from different sources, have
used every effort to extinguish the national feel-

ings, and the mother-tongue of their subject-people, Turkey has uniformly adhered to a policy of non-interference, or, rather, to express myself more according to their ideas, of honesty. Turks, as other Orientals, never start by laying down an abstract principle which is to rule their practical conduct. They do not adopt, for instance, as an axiom, that the language of the state is to be one, that the laws of the provinces are to be uniform; and then build or destroy to enforce the application of this abstraction : they, on the contrary, never interfere in any way unless forced, by some necessity, to do so. They have not laid down non-interference as a principle of government ; for that idea could only come as a result of interference — a result, by the by, that no legislating people has ever yet arrived at. Each population, accordingly, preserves its own language and habits; and, for the most part, is regardless and ignorant of that which pertains to its neighbours. The Turks, in like manner, seldom know the language of their subjects, or of foreign countries; and thence arises a great and crying evil: the governors, the administrators, the judges, the merchants, are at the mercy of interpreters in all the details of government, law, finance, and commerce. These interpreters form a class linked together in interest and intelligence, which, extending from the centre of power to the lowest gradations of official existence, and spreading from the capital to

the remotest frontier, form a vast net, from which
nothing can escape; and which controls, by slight
and invisible, and, therefore, effective bonds, the
circumstances and the minds of men.   The means
by which you get entangled in the insidious web
are so gradual and minute, that they baffle detection; and the power subsequently exercised by
the Dragoman over his victim so absolute, that all
thought of resistance or of vengeance passes away.
Men become attached to their Dragoman in that
sort of way that men become infatuated with a
mistress; from the moment they adopt his opinions, or identify themselves with his acts, they
are entirely in his power.

These reflections were forcibly brought before
me by the conversation during the day I spent
with the Archbishop and Primates of Argyro
Castro. There was a Turk present, who exemplified
the ruin brought upon Turkey by the Dragomans
(he alluded only to the internal administration),
by the following anecdote:—

A few miles from Triccala, to the west, appears
on the naked plain, the ruined minaret of a mosque,
which, ten years ago, stood in the centre of a
flourishing village. I have mentioned it as the site
of a village which had been ruined by the plague
of 1812; so I was told as I passed it: I now
learnt the real cause of its desolation. This village, called Capidji, was a tchilik of Veli Pasha,
son of Ali Pasha: on his fall, this property de-

volved to the Sultan. (I may remark, *en passant*, that when property is held over the cultivator of the soil, the cultivator does not lose his right of occupation; and the landlord's interest is reduced to a *pro rata* interest in the produce.) By the arrangement with the farmer, the Sultan's agent was bound to furnish the seed. A Pasha, Essad Pasha, had been sent from Constantinople; at that time, the farms were under the superintendence of the Pasha. The country, owing to the insurrection in Albania and in Greece, was in the most distracted state, and the sowing time was come; the elders of the village had made several fruitless attempts to obtain the seed necessary for sowing, as well as for their own necessities; and, finally, the whole population of the village — men, women, and children—assembled round the Pasha's palace, calling aloud for seed — in Greek, *sporos*. The Pasha, from the genial clime of Southern Anatoli, had taken refuge from the January blasts of Pindus in the recesses of his harem; and, hearing this tumult without, sent for his Dragoman, Ata Effendi, a Turk; but a Turk, if a Dragoman, is quite a match for a Greek, a Copt, or a Frank. Ata Effendi represented to his highness, that the people assembled were come, in a tumultuous manner, to demand money to buy wine for a festival of their idolatrous church, at which a great many of their sons and daughters were to be married. " But," said the

Pasha, " what means that *Sporos! sporos?* "
" Oh," said the Dragoman, " that is dance!
(*choros*) dance! — they want to be merry." The
Pasha, indignant, immediately gave orders to
drive the peasants from the court-yard. My in-
formant was master of the Pasha's hounds, and,
a few days afterwards, proposed to his master to
course; the day being fine, the hares abundant,
and the dogs in excellent condition; and managed
so as to bring him through the village of Capidji.
On entering it, not a soul was to be seen; the
doors stood open, the furniture and effects had
been cleared away, and no living creature was
discoverable; until, apparently by chance, they
found an old man, purposely placed there to tell
the tale of the village. When he related how
they had come to the Pasha's gate to suppli-
cate for corn, and had been driven away with
blows and imprecations,—the Pasha got up, rode
home, and stopping but to make some indispensable arrangements, continued his journey to Constantinople; leaving his brother, until the arrival
of a successor, to administer the pashalic which
he renounced. He has, however, been made Pasha
of Erzeroum, where he has no need of Dragomans. I inquired what was done to Ata Effendi—
nothing!

I supped with the governor. The supper was
an exhibition in the most uproarious Albanian
style; but through the cloud shone a ray of light

as pleasing as unexpected, and contrasted singularly with the reckless air of himself and his attendants, and the general views of his companions in adventure. "We have done more," he said to me, in parting, "than you see or believe; because we have rooted out the evil that prevented the growth of good. Hitherto it has been but 'destroy,' 'kill,' 'burn;' come back in five years, and you will see the fruits of last year's manure."

It is a remark of some great man, that "men are always superior to their circumstances." What a paradise might not be made of Albania or of Turkey, were the men in the higher places capable of bearing onwards, to less imperfect fructification, the germs of excellence which men and nature there alike present! But, might not any and every portion of the globe equally become so?

At Argyro Castro, I have said the debt of the community amounted to 130,000 piastres; no alteration had taken place with respect to it, nor had any application been made on the subject to the Grand Vizir. On inquiring the reason for this, the primates told me that their creditors were all Turkish proprietors in the neighbourhood; that the money was lent readily and kindly, to assist them in their necessities; that the interest had never been rigorously exacted,

and that the rate was only 8 per cent. Ali
Pasha had, as it was well known, appropriated to
himself an immense amount of private property
throughout his numerous satrapies.

This property has fallen to the crown; and
the amount that has been restored, where flagrant
abuse could be proved in the mode of acquisition,
has still left it a considerable, if not the principal,
portion of the revenue which the government receives from Albania. A system of administration
for it has been formed, according to the routine
pursued in collecting those branches of the revenue
which are farmed. These lands are very numerous in the neighbourhood of Argyro Castro. The
general director sub-lets them separately to middle-
men, who are like middle-men all over the world.
The peasants upon these properties have recently
sent a deputation to the Grand Vizir, with a request to be permitted to pay directly into the treasury the sum which the middle-men at present pay
to the superintendant. The value of this fact, as
regards the facility of effecting an important change
— I may say, the all-important change for the Ottoman Empire, which is here indicated—is what I
cannot pass over without pointing out, although I
cannot now stop to discuss it.

At Argyro Castro, I was more struck with the
family of my Greek host than even I had been at
Delvino. I have never seen three handsomer

young men than his sons : two of them were
married ; and if I were to attempt to describe
the mode and style of their intercourse, I might
be supposed to be describing the court of a By-
zantine prince, rather than the family of a Greek
shoemaker. Yet how much happiness may be
traced in this domestic etiquette of the East,
where authority is the gift of affection, and where
love knows no office, menial or degrading. To
each man his village is his country, because his
home is his world. In the present unsettled times,
it is more than country or world—it is sanctuary;
and the respect paid to woman by the most reckless, there casts a shield over the weakness and
pusillanimity of father, husband, and brother. But
when, in quieter times, such protection is unsought,
still does the home of the East not sink into the indifferent appendage or burden it so often is amongst
us. It is with unfeigned gratification that I can
bear testimony to the harmony that reigns, there
—to the courtesy that characterises its internal intercourse—to the privation which absence causes
—to the delight of return. During several years
of continual intercourse with these people, I have
never seen a family quarrel : I have never observed,
or at least my memory does not serve to recall,
one of those incidents which so constantly strike
and annoy the visitor and the guest in our own
country. It is this difference of domestic manners that makes them prefer their own country to

Europe.   How many temptations are not held out
to endangered governors, to wealthy delinquents, to
the needy adventurer, to the curious, to the disappointed, to visit Europe and to reside in it? and
yet, until very recently, I may almost say until
after the period of my visit to Argyro Castro,
scarcely had a dozen living Easterns visited Europe.   Nor are they by any means deficient in
curiosity, or in love of travel: Europe presents to
them great and solemn subjects of inquiry; but
the specimens of Europe and of civilisation that
haunt the capital and the seaports, and the
general impressions which they have received of
our individual character, have hitherto averted
from Europe every feeling of respect, and have not
suffered individual bonds of regard and affection
to be formed.

It must not be supposed that these domestic
manners, and, consequently, this national character, is to be found amongst the Greeks either
of the Morea or of Constantinople.   Wherever
the influence of the revolution has extended, old
ideas, habits, or feelings, have been obliterated or
upset.   In some individuals, their place has been
occupied by a high degree of Western accomplishments; but the mass of the Greek race, wherever
it has abandoned its old customs, has given away,
without compensation, the elements of its past
prosperity and of future progress.   In political
institutions, compare the present state and hopes

of the Morea with its progress of ten years under
the Turkish government, before the revolution.
In mind and manners, compare the disgusting exhibition of a Greek festal evening in the Princes'
Islands, decked out in tawdry finery, which they
call European, with such scenes of domestic happiness and comfort as I have attempted to describe
at Argyro Castro, and which may still be seen in
every village of European and Asiatic Turkey inhabited by Greeks. M. de Lamartine has pointed
out what he considered to be a strong contrast
between the Asiatic and the European Greeks,
highly commending the first and reprobating the
last. He has met, in his flight through Asia, some
instances of the Greek character, deteriorated,
but still original; he has met in Greece some
of the Europeanised Greeks. Struck with the remarkable contrast, M. de Lamartine at once gene-
ralises, as any man must do who makes a volume
out of the observations of a month, and builds up
a political theory, or overthrows an empire, in
consequence of a single observation or a single
mistake.

In speaking of the disastrous influence exercised by the revolution over the Greek mind and
character, I do not mean to say that the *war* of
the revolution exercised a deleterious influence
over the Greeks—quite the reverse: that war
aroused the energies, and tempered the mind, of

the Hellenic race ; and their success, while it freed
them from those causes of complaint which existed,
either in their former habits or in their previous
government, emancipated Turkey also from the
chilling thraldom of the janissary rule ; and, while
it placed within the Sultan's reach the means of
their destruction, it awoke the mind of Turkey
from that lethargic slumber which was gradually
creeping over its senses, and closing its eyes to the
complications of foreign wrong and policy which it
could not fathom, and under which it must otherwise have inevitably sunk. Such were the elements, as regarded the East, presented by the
triumph of the Greek revolution ; namely, the
pacification of the Levant, and the consolidation
of Turkey ; and immense might have been the
results, had an enlightened spirit and a master-
mind directed the councils of Great Britain.
That position which she did not occupy, and
did not comprehend, has been otherwise filled ;
and millions of treasure, and oceans of blood,
which she may yet have to expend in defence
of her own interests, never can undo the evil
that has already been done. A single intelligent
agent may prevent what twenty line-of-battle-ships
may be required to redress ; but you cannot have
agents intelligent unless they are profoundly versed
in the knowledge of the country with which they
have to deal. Total absence of information can

alone account for the policy of England, or for the events of the East for the last twenty years; and the commonest foresight must suffice to shew, that a very short period of similar progress must lead to a general convulsion of Europe; where England must enter the arena, not to acquire, but to preserve; and where she must appear in arms, to destroy what her own unconscious influence has been used in peace to bring about,

CHAPTER XVII.

HABITS AND EDUCATION OF EASTERN CHILDREN.

THE demeanour of the youngest child towards his parents, as towards strangers, its habitual sedateness and docility, would lead a European to believe that children in the East are ruled with a rod of iron; that their spirit is broken, and the buoyancy of childhood crushed by the continual exercise of despotic paternal authority. It is just the reverse. If a man were to beat his child, there would be a general uproar in the street, and all the neighbours would run to its assistance.* The source of Eastern despotism has, by some writers, been discovered in the domestic tyranny exercised

---

* A little romping boy, of five years old, began to pull his father's beard and whiskers, till the old man roared with pain. He looked in a fearful rage, threatened unutterable things, but never thought of using his hands. I asked him why he had not beaten the child; "Ah!" he said, "what clever people you Franks are!"

throughout the East. Volney, who has been called the philosophic, and Heeren, justly styled the learned, have particularly dwelt on the great analogy that existed between, as they term it, the two species of slavery — paternal and regal. Whatever sentiments the scene presented by, I may almost say, every family in the East, might inspire for the learning and the philosophy of the one or the other, still does the analogy pointed out hold true; the structure of Eastern government is but the enlargement of the paternal roof; and the authority upon which Eastern despotism exists, as that which the paternal despot exercises, is granted alike by the affections of those who obey, and whose obedience would be inexplicable in a European school-room, or in a European parliament.

I had written thus far, and was about to quit the subject, in despair of rendering the mode of existence of Eastern children intelligible, when I was interrupted by a visit from a Turkish friend, accompanied by his little son. He mentioned an anecdote of one of the Sultan's children, at the time a boy of nine years old, and of his own son, then four, which appeared to me a curious exemplification of the respective observances of these little personages. The Sultan, in an excursion, had slept at my friend's house. The young Prince had laid himself down, complaining of a severe headach, which my friend said he thought he could cure by reading from the Koran;* and, kneeling down beside him, commenced his practice. In the middle of it, however, the Muezzim's call to prayers was heard, and " the Shah Zadeh (the Prince) turned," said he, " to me, and asked my permission, as if I had been his own father, to go and perform his namaz." His carpet was laid for him, and when his namaz was over he returned, and we concluded our reading; and whether it was the effect of the prayers, or God's blessing on my good intentions, or his natural recovery, the Shah Zadeh's headach was cured. But little did I think of the misfortune that was going to befall me, for the Shah Zadeh said to me, he was sure I had children of my own. Now, I had only this good-for-nothing youth whom you see, so I began trembling all over, knowing what my child was. I have now found my misfortune, thought I to myself; I am lost—my child is lost—we are all lost. This is the Shah Zadeh; he has asked me, and I must tell him the truth; when I tell him, the boy will be brought. So I answered, " Your slave has a child—a young child, but a very graceless one, that has been born and brought up in the mountains, and does not know what respect and

* In performing this operation, they lay the hand on the afflicted part, in a way that resembles animal magnetism. I certainly have seen pains thus suddenly relieved. The magic of Egypt, and that of India and Asia, is clearly a branch of magnetism.

duty mean." "Vai," said the Shah Zadeh, "I want so much to see him; Kuzum (my lamb), send for him immediately." I wanted to go for him myself, that I might give my Ali Bey (his child's name) a lesson how he was to conduct himself; but the Prince, guessing my intention, would not let me stir, and there I was, trembling all over, expecting to see Ali Bey rush into the room, get upon the sofa beside the Shah Zadeh, lay hold of him, or, perhaps, ask him what his business was there, and tell him to get out of the house. But Ali Bey, on entering the room, came running up straight to me. I had only time to whisper in his ear " *Shah Zadeh!*" and the little lamb went straight up, and, falling on the floor before him, kissed the ground, and then the hem of his dress; and after that, retiring backwards, crossed his hands on his breast, and did his divan. Whenever the Prince spoke to him, he gave the exact answer, and did his temenas. My face was white again, and the Shah Zadeh, turning to me, and laughing, said, " Mashallah Effendim, is this your little mountaineer ?"

When the Sultan's eldest son was scarcely eleven years of age, I was paying a visit to the favourite of the day, who was in the room adjoining that in which the Sultan was with his children. Without any previous intimation, we were surprised by the curtain over the door being suddenly raised, and the Shah Zadeh walking in, accom-

panied by a black eunuch, half a tutor and half a
dry nurse, and followed by about thirty little boys
of his own age, young slaves, or sons of the grandees who are brought up with him.   My host
prostrated himself before him, and the Prince, to
disembarrass us from ceremonial, nimbly stepped
to the divan, and, jumping up upon it, sat himself
down in the place of honour, the corner, but in
the attitude of respect; that is, half kneeling, half
sitting, with his hands placed before him on his
thighs.   The host then went and kissed the hem
of the sofa, to which the Prince replied by a temenas, and desired him to be seated.   He immediately seated himself on the floor before him, but
no sooner having done so than he rose, and stood
with his arms crossed on his breast.   The black
Hodga then approached the Prince, and, bending
down, whispered something in his ear; his quick
brilliant eyes were immediately turned on me, and
he desired me to be seated, motioning to a place
near himself on the sofa.   After a moment's pause,
observing the pipe I had been smoking lying near
me, he ordered it to be filled.   The only thing
I recollect of the little conversation that passed
was, that he was very anxious to learn French,
but had nobody to teach him.   A present had
been prepared for him of a very beautiful model
of a ship, which he accepted with great delight;
it was delivered over to the special charge of four
of his little attendants, who carried it off, each

holding a corner, with a degree of anxiety for its welfare painted on their childish faces, which provoked my Western risibility.

Then came a very handsome toy, which was presented for his approbation — a kaleidoscope. After looking at it and admiring it for some time, he laid it down, and shook his head, and being asked why he would not take it, he said, " I have taken the ship, because women have nothing to do with ships; but a gay thing like this I can't accept, unless there is one also for my sister." I wore, suspended by a riband, a small folding-up opera-glass, which attracted his attention; so I took it off and hung it round his neck, when the old black Mentor again approached, and whispered in his ear. He took it off in a great hurry, and would have brought it back to me, had he not been anticipated by his attentive little troop, saying, " If you wear it you must have use for it; you can't get another like it here, and therefore I ought not to keep it." What struck me in this was his sudden deference to the simplest suggestion of his black preceptor, who, on his part, seemed to approach him with every mark of reverence.

The young Prince, as soon as he felt there was nothing more to say, got up in that sudden way which Turks adopt to cut short the ceremonial of leave-taking, made a little hop, jump, and race to the door, while the youthful troop, who had stood ranged at the bottom of the room in motionless silence, and who probably for some time had been watching the signal for departure, were dispersed in the twinkling of an eye, poured out of the room, and were seen ranged in two lines on the outside, some of them straining to hold up the curtain. As the young Prince retired, my host's servants fell down and kissed his footsteps.

There is something inexpressibly interesting and attaching in the children of the East; and what can be more attaching than children neither backward nor fatiguing, who receive as a favour any notice that is taken of them, and conceive it to be their place and their duty, to watch and to serve their parents and their elders? Their old-fashioned manners are rendered more remarkable by the forms and complications of Eastern salutation, ablution, services, and modes of being and acting; and by the, to us, singular effect of seeing those little bodies equipped exactly in the same costume that is worn by grown people. In many places they even wear diminutive arms (in Circassia they wear them and use them too). I once saw the petted child of the old age of a silly man, with a complete establishment of his own; and though scarcely more than nine years of age, he was seated on the sofa opposite to his father, and presented with a pipe by his own Tchiboukji. I could not help thinking, at the time, that if a book-making traveller had seen the scene, we should have been treated to a new series of philosophical inductions respecting the system of paternal and political government of the East.

At Monastir, where I arrived after leaving Scodra, the second son of the Grand Vizir, Ibrahim Bey, a boy of thirteen years of age, resided. The news had there spread of the favour which I was supposed to enjoy, and of the reception which the Grand Vizir had given me at Scodra. The tutor and chief of the household of Ibrahim Bey came to welcome me on the part of his pupil and master:— my first visit was therefore to the Sadrazam-Zade. A family divan was held as to the ceremonial of my reception—the question being discussed first in the harem, which is the upper house here as in all the rest of the world, and subsequently in the selamlik, where the whole establishment was of course assembled, down perhaps to the sacca (water carrier). A difference of opinion arose between the two houses, and my servant was called and cross-examined as to my mode of reception by the great man, and by those of his suite whose opinions might carry weight, and whose acts were valid as precedent.

The female portion of the establishment, combining in their persons the double infallibility of rank and sex, took the truer and most statesman-like view of the question. They unanimously decided that Ibrahim Bey should not merely get up, but even that he should go to the door, to receive the Ingliz Bey-Zadeh. This decision on the part of

the ladies might bear, and, indeed, requires a word
of explanation. Strange tales had been whispered
in the harem's inmost recesses of the external sovereignty of the sex in Frangistan, of the obsequious-
ness that there attends their steps, the humility that
waits on their frown, the happiness that is dispensed
by their presence and their smile. The lords of
the creation there bend their necks to the willing
yoke; and the proudest of the earth, the first in
power, in glory, and in arms, yield submissive obedience to womankind. Startling, head and heart
perplexing thoughts! What men must those
Franks be! All this rushed to their lips, though it
came not forth in this warm debate; and thence the
unanimous decision, " Ibrahim Bey *shall* go to
meet the Bey-Zadeh." A few messages exchanged
between the harem and the selamlik led to a compromise—viz., that Ibrahim Bey should be walking
in the ·corridor before the room-door—that our
meeting should appear accidental, and as if he had
been quitting one room to go to the other at the
moment of my arrival. But the arch boy gave the
victory to the women; for on the signal of my
approach (in the houses of Turkish grandees, the
arrival of a guest is indicated by telegraphic signs),
quickening his movements, he gained five seconds
upon me, performed his walk to the opposite door,
then returned and met me. My visit over, and
it was a curious one, and one to which I may
afterwards have occasion to refer, I went to pay a

visit to the governor of the place, and found with him the Mollah and the chief of the troops. I had scarcely been seated when Ibrahim Bey, to shew me what a great man he really was, notwithstanding the reception with which I had been honoured, suddenly and unannounced made his appearance; wrapped now in a flowing harvan, and with an assumption of stately grandeur marched up the room, and, seating himself in the governor's place, signified his pleasure that we might also be seated. He returned the salutations paid him with a most patronising air; and not one of the greybeards present, by the slightest look or motion of any kind, evinced a consciousness of the circumstance being liable to be considered extraordinary by a stranger. Ibrahim Bey accounted for his visit by his anxiety to see as much of me as possible during my stay. But he only waited long enough to display his position by ordering up pipes and coffee, and to receive, as master of the house, the salutation after it had been drunk, and then vanished as abruptly as he had made his appearance; and we presently heard in the court-yard the clatter of horses bounding away at full speed.

I might fill a volume with instances of social demeanour of ability in the transaction of business, of daring and bravery in war, on the part of Eastern children, quite beyond what we should expect at such an age; the instances which I have given will, however, suffice to shew the self-control which they are taught by social habits, and by the consideration and respect with which they are treated by their elders and parents.

The subject of Eastern education is one which certainly ought not to be entered on lightly, and I by no means feel myself equal to deal with it; but when a few philosophical inquirers have turned their attention to the study of the East, education will become the subject of a most interesting and valuable work. Important as education has latterly become amongst ourselves, and that importance, regarded as it is at once as the sign and the means of the most advanced state of civilisation, cannot fail to strike a European with astonishment, when he finds that education is considered by Eastern populations as of far greater importance than it is with us; and that Eastern legislators have provided for it a place among the fundamental institutions of the state. Education is there invested with a solemn and religious character, pervading every class of the community, and extending back, by the proof of public records, for thousands of years. Public documents of Hindoo villages, of above 3000 years, place the charge for the school and the schoolmaster as the first obligation incurred by the community: no fee was paid; yet education had not the stigma of charity. By the institutes of Menu, and the code of Mahomet, the parent was obliged to place his child at school in his fourth year. Reading, writing, and a certain knowledge of religion and of laws, were considered an amount of instruction which the state was bound to see conferred on its members; and Mahomet further imposed on the chief of every community the obligation of seeing orphans instructed in some handicraft, so as to enable them to gain their daily bread. Placing the child under the authority of the schoolmaster, was an act to which was attached the character of a religious sacrament; and the schoolmaster was rendered responsible for his conduct and behaviour. From the Hindoos, and from other portions of the East, have we ourselves borrowed the system of mutual instruction; and many of the forms of that system are now to be found in every Turkish schoolroom. In Persia, the proportionate number of children instructed in reading and writing is supposed to exceed that of any country of Europe. In Turkey, there is not a Sultan that has not left behind him his endowed college; what Sultan is there that has left behind him a palace?

The day upon which the child is delivered over to the schoolmaster is a family festival — the relatives, friends, and neighbours, are invited; the ladies in the harem, the male folks in the sclaamlik. The little hero of the day, though generally there are several, is paraded backwards and forwards from one assembly to the other, bedizened with finery; and kissings, blessings, and presents, are showered upon him. The Kourban lamb has been selected before, with the greatest regard to colour, form, beauty, and sprightliness; it has been fed on the choicest dainties, tended and watched with the greatest care; it is now brought forth with pomp, the splendour of its whiteness exalted by festoons of gaudy ribands and brilliant flowers. The sacrifice, performed by the father, and the child blessed by the Imaum, is delivered over to the schoolmaster.

Whilst the child remains at school, the authority which may be exercised by the father is, as it were, in the name of the schoolmaster. The child lives at home, and goes, for a certain number of hours in the day, to the school; if guilty of misconduct, the father sends to the schoolmaster, to say, " Ali, or Achmet, Effendi* has done so and so — it is for you to act as you judge fit; but I have not failed to tell him my opinion on the subject." The schoolmaster is, by no means, so ceremonious in the exercise of his authority — has the little delinquent down on his back, with his feet cocked up in the air; while the falatea, or long rod by which they are supported, is sometimes held by the whole school together, and the bastinado is calmly administered by the schoolmaster, sitting on his haunches, the indus-

---

* The title of Effendi is given to the child the moment he takes the pen, or reed, in his hand.

trious courbash in his right hand, the decorous tchibouque in the left.

I would particularly request the reader's attention to this separation of the castigation from the parent, while the child is not separated for the purpose of instruction in grammar from the only valuable education for man—that of the parental hearth.

However, even at school, chastisement is of very rare occurrence; and a Turkish child invariably, till he is six or seven years of age, is allowed to do just as he pleases; no restraint is placed on his free will or on his caprices, and no idea of punishment, corporeal punishment at least, exists, as far as I have been able to perceive. I do not recollect ever seeing even a pat of the hand given in anger, or in the way of correction; and such an act would be felt to be what might be rendered indecent. How, then, are produced, it may be asked, that sobriety and tranquillity of temper and disposition so remarkable in Eastern children? Might we not as well inquire why European children are boisterous, and rendered so wayward as to call for correction? Is there not that in our domestic habits, which, by withdrawing the natural control of respect and diminishing the domestic sympathies and affections, renders children unmanageable, and leads us to form an erroneous estimate of human nature? I feel I could easily explain to an Eastern why European children

are so little like theirs. It would suffice to tell
him that our children were not taught to kiss their
parents' hands—to stand before them—to serve
them,—that our servants were mercenaries, hired
by the month,—he would immediately comprehend how young minds, left without occupation,
become wayward; how family affections and sympathies are chilled; and it would hardly be necessary to enter with him into the graver causes of
our intellectual and political habits on the separation of children from their parents, and their
congregation in schools.

The external portion of this difference resides
in the forms and ceremonial which habit and imitation impress upon Eastern existence from its very
dawn; so that, in fact, no greater punishment can
exist than to be debarred from the fulfilment of
these observances; the fulfilment of which, according to our mode, would be enforced by punishment. A Turkish child is punished at school, by
being denied water for washing himself, by being
forbidden to go to the mosque, or to say his
prayers. Compare that with our thrashing for a
dirty face in infantine years, or the confinement
to chapel in our universities, as punishment for
maturer offences. The first duty which the
infant is taught is to kiss the hand of its parent;
the first use to which its tender muscles are
applied, is to carry that hand to its lips; the
faculties of mind, as they are successively deve-

loped, are applied to the expressions of affection and respect; while, from its tenderest years, it is itself the object of unceasing and undeviating kindness, and even respect, from those around it. The little boy, three or four years old, standing with crossed hands and humble mien before its parent, is addressed by that parent with the titles of his house; and the girl of the same age, so standing before its mother, is addressed by the same word that the subject applies to the sovereign. Manners are the code of the East; indeed they are so all over the world; but we can only become sensible of their value, I may say, we can only perceive their existence by coming in contact with new varieties and unaccustomed applications.

The character thus allowed to grow up, if I may use the word, naturally, while, at an earlier age, it acquires the reflectiveness of manhood, preserves, in the after years of life, much of that warmth and simplicity which, amongst us, flowing to excess and running to waste in our early years, is lost in the character of manhood; and while you see a Turk, in the vigour of manhood, delighted with the trifles, and giving way to the frolicsomeness which a child alone will enjoy or exhibit amongst us, you may see the young Turk, of ten or twelve years old, conducting affairs of intricacy and importance, demeaning himself, and treated by others, as the equal of those of triple his years. And if, amongst them, the public intercourse of the two sexes, which has been so powerful and exciting a cause in the progress of Europe, is forbidden, still does the constant, though never coarse or familiar, intercourse of all ages wonderfully tend to the increase of domestic enjoyments and affection, and to the maintenance of that dignity of demeanour, and that equanimity of character, which extend almost from the cradle to the tomb, giving to the child the experience of the sire, and to the grandfather the light-heartedness of infancy.

A man of respectable or elevated station may often be seen walking about fondling a child in his arms, obedient to its caprices, and rendering it the services that a nurse or a menial servant would alone be called upon amongst us to perform. As the tradespeople or artisans return in the evening from their daily avocations, scarcely one will you see without some little token of family affection in his hand—a flower—an apple—a bunch of grapes —a quince. The following circumstance may serve to illustrate this intensity of parental affection.

An inhabitant of Broussa, a man of some substance, labouring under a chronic disease, consulted a European physician who was passing through that place. This physician informed him that his life could only be saved by an operation; and that it would be necessary for him to send for an able surgeon then resident at Constantinople, and that this surgeon must be retained at Broussa two or three weeks. The Turk wrote to ascertain the expense of this visit : the surgeon mentioned a certain sum as the remuneration he should expect—I believe about 100*l.*; and the Turk declined sending for him. The physician originally consulted now expressed his amazement at his throwing away his only chance of life. The Turk made this answer:—" I have lived long enough ; I am blessed with kind, excellent children, and why should I diminish that which I have to divide amongst them, from a silly wish to live a few years longer ?"

The calmness and resignation of the Turks, under privation and misfortune, has been often dwelt on with enthusiasm; in nothing is it more remarkable than in the loss of children and parents. Devoted to each other during life, they deem excess of grief for their loss as a species of rebellion against the dispensations of Providence, and consider an external display of mourning as unworthy of their character, and as revolting to the feelings of sincere affection.*

In every Eastern family, the great object of respect and devotion is the mother. The children, whatever their affection for their father, never admit of a comparison between the duty they owe to the two parents ; witness the familiar expres-

* The Turks, therefore, do not wear mourning ; this is, however, a national, not a religious habit, for the Mussulman Arabs delight in ostentatious ceremonies and loud wailings.

sion,—" Pull my father's beard, but do not speak
ill of my mother." The mothers of the Sultans,
and of the great men in Turkey, have exercised
greater influence over its destinies than the Ninons
de l'Enclos, the Maintenons, or the Nell Gwynnes
of Europe; and may that influence never be less!
Even in the house of Othman, that house wholly
exceptionable in its position, and where the fratri-
cidal horrors of that of Athens has been for centuries renewed—in that house, where the sacred
tie of matrimony has been forbidden by the jealous
policy of its nominal slaves, but real masters, still
there has the Turkish tie of son and mother retained its power, and benignly displayed on many
an occasion its signal influence.

There is no loss which a Turk can suffer equal
to that of his mother. If his wife dies, he says,
" I can get another;" if his child is cut off,
" Others," he says, " may be born to me; but I can
be born but once, and can have but one mother."
I once witnessed a remarkable instance of mental
fortitude under the sudden announcement of a
mother's loss.

Husein Pasha, of Belgrade, subsequently Roumeli Valessi, was to receive a visit of state and
ceremony from the Archduke Ferdinand, then
making a tour of inspection on the Danube, on
the opening of the steam navigation of that river.
Various circumstances contributed to render this
interview important, and every means were em-

ployed to give it effect. An hour before the arrival of the Archduke, Husein Pasha received the news of the sudden death of his mother. He prevented the communication of the intelligence to any one, and went through the duties imposed upon him by the circumstances of the day, as if they had been his only care, and as if all his thoughts had been devoted to his guest. When, next day, I learned the circumstance, I, in common with some other Europeans, was struck by it in a way which it is impossible to describe. Here is a trait which would be designated Roman; but should the real Turkish character ever be appreciated, and its excellent parts brought into evidence and consideration by the elevation of their political state, then may traits of the history of Rome be designated Turkish. The great similarity of the two people I feel in this; that it seems to me that I had no idea of the Roman character or of the Roman system of administration, until I had made some progress in the study of the character and the institutions of Turkey; and I shrink not from avowing, that my opinion of my fellow creatures has been raised by my intercourse with the Turks.

This family affection, coupled as it is with dignity, forms the character of the people, and *is* the education of the youth. Education can never be any thing save thei mpressing on the young generation the stamp of the old.

Having expressed myself thus favourably respecting their moral and domestic education, I must not leave unsketched the dark side of the picture, namely their intellectual education. For this I am sorry to say little has been done. The Turkish language, which, at this present moment, is the only means of instruction for the numerous tribes of the East extending from the Caucasus to the Persian Gulf, is unfortunately amongst the Turks themselves despised and neglected. Children are set to study Arabic and Persian, and the Turkish is so mixed up with these two languages, that it has become unwieldy in use, and so difficult of acquisition, that the zeal and ardour for instruction which prevail throughout the whole empire, and even amongst its most wild and ignorant tribes, are fruitless in great and material results. The backwardness in matters of science amongst the Turks has invariably been set down as a consequence of their rejection of every thing foreign, and their want of imitativeness. The case is exactly the reverse; it is their imitation of others to a degree, without a parallel, that has encumbered the language with foreign idioms; and thus has rendered the acquisition of two foreign and difficult languages a preliminary step to the use of their own. That imitation has not been directed hitherto to Europe, but to Persia and Arabia; and while they adopted, with fatal facility, the manners, customs, ceremonial forms of administration and diplomacy of the tottering Empire of the East, they adopted in the same spirit ·the prosody of Persia and the senile prolixity of the once vigorous and splendid rhetoric and philosophy of Arabia.

Recently we have seen that imitativeness turning round to Europe. Let the philosopher or the statesman now put together those various elements,—a moral groundwork of education, which I venture to assert to be infinitely beyond the level of any thing presented in Europe,—a universal desire for instruction, a respect for science and for letters,* a desire of imitating Europe. What may not be made of that people, if the proper direction is given at this present conjuncture, and the dangerous chances· to which every change must give rise, are set aside?

---

* I once found a little Turkish boy rummaging amongst my things, and pulling out all the books he could lay his hands on; whenever he got hold of one, he carried it reverentially to his lips and forehead. I asked him what he was about; he said he was kissing the books. "Why?" "Because they would not be printed unless there were good things in them." Fortunately there were no travels in Turkey amongst them. A Turk never passes a scrap of paper or a crumb of bread, without lifting it from the ground, shewing his equal respect for the food of the mind, of which paper is the vehicle, and the food of the body. I once had to complain to a country governor of a drunken Tartar: the only attempt made by the delinquent to justify himself was, by narrating that I wrapped things up in printed paper, so as to prove that I was unworthy of any credence.

I have been much struck to find in another European precisely the same ideas as to the effect of the domestic education of Turkey on its national manners. The following extracts are from a pamphlet on " La Question d'Orient," by Mr. Fourcade, formerly French consul at various scales of the Levant. The writer of them will, I trust, give us something more than a political pamphlet.

" Domestic education, and the well-understood and respected principle of social equality, have formed these national manners. It is the patriarchal life from which we are so removed.

" Also we are greatly deceived, when we take that respect of the subaltern towards the man of dignity for servility—a grave error. There exists in the whole empire a hierarchy recognised and indispensable ; *et avec des traits moins irritans mais plus prononcés qu'en Europe.* In every grade, in every class, and in every family, each shews to his superiors in rank or age that respect and submission which he in his turn obtains from his inferiors. It is the same in public as in private life. A woman never speaks of her husband without employing the words Agha Effendi, corresponding to Monsieur Seigneur ; in which she is imitated by the children, who listen to her.

" These present themselves before their father with downcast eyes, the hands joined upon the breast, and with a countenance most respectful. Upon the grand fêtes, as in frequent events of their life, they never fail in kissing the hand of their father, and of their mother, and of their aged relatives, to demand their blessing;—all attach thereto the highest idea of happiness.

" Even between brothers, age is the object of marked deference. It is to the force of this domestic education, common to all classes of society, that is to be attributed *cette égalité de bonne tenue*, and of dignity that strikes one in all the men in office, even those drawn from the most indigent class of the people; which happens frequently in a country where hereditary nobility is not known."

" Deprived of our accomplishments of dancing, music, and painting, and games of chance, being wisely forbidden by their religion and their manners, eating only to live, and not living to eat, the society of the Ottomans is not very attractive for a European; but it is sure and instructive. Would that we might copy from them that which is good; and that they might gain from us the useful knowledge, in which they are deficient!"*

* Question d'Orient, par M. Fourcade, p. 97.

CHAPTER XVIII.

TURKISH LITERATURE.

To those who, anxious for the progress of Turkey and of mankind, are studious to examine the elements of improvement which that country possesses, the observation with which the foregoing chapter concludes must be one of deep importance, and they may be anxious to obtain evidence, first of its truth, and secondly, of the recognition by the Turks of its truth; which recognition is necessarily a preliminary step to that direction of their national literature, which can only result from a conviction of the advantages of a change. Shortly after the preceding observations were written, respecting the injurious effect upon the Turkish mind of the imitation of the literatures of Arabia and Persia, and the benefit that might be derived from cultivating their own mother-tongue, I found myself in the society of several learned Mussulmans; and the conversation falling on the comparative merits and advantages of the West and the East of Europe, and of Turkey, one of them attributed the degradation of the power of

Turkey to the absence, on the one hand of scientific instruction, and on the other of religious fervour. " A nation," said he, " must be bound together by one of those two cements; Christ did not create an empire, but he revealed to man the wisdom and the science that now flourish in Europe. Mahomet told us that all science was contained in the Koran; that he who was strong in the faith would vanquish all his foes; we have lost the strength of our religion—we have not gained the wisdom of Europe." I thought this a good opportunity of putting to the test my doctrine respecting the causes of the mental backwardness of Turkey. I commenced by asserting that the opinions he had expressed respecting the relative state of Turkey, and of Europe, were not his own, that they were not Turkish, that they were not true; that he merely retailed them from some European traveller; in which assertion I was immediately supported by some of those present, and it was admitted by my antagonist himself. I then requested him to listen to another explanation of the state of things, of which the following is the substance:—" Christ preached a religion, neither political nor worldly; it was one of faith and dogma,—not of forms and watchwords. He did not raise a standard to rally under it the great of the earth, but preached submission to the powers that were;—self-denial, self-mortification, and contempt, both for worldly science and worldly greatness. It was not, there-

fore, true that Christ had revealed those sciences
to Europe that had made her great and powerful;
and it was quite the reverse of the truth that
Mahomet had impressed upon his followers, and
upon the political edifice which he had raised, a
character hostile to science. It was only when
the Christians came into the East, in a spirit
hostile to the views and character of their religion, that, by their contact with the followers
of Mahomet, the first seeds of science and literature were communicated to them; and, at the
present day, the great proportion of the scientific words employed in Europe are words of
Arabic origin.   Whence, then, the present difference between Europe and Turkey?   It is that the
branch of Turks who migrated into Europe (not
Islamism) were unscientific; and, having a language splendid in its construction, but meagre in
words, they have imitated, and continued imitating,
without ever mastering the Arabic and the Persian.
The use of language has, therefore, for them been
in a great measure annihilated; and when some
degree of proficiency is acquired, they are set adrift
on a sea of words and phrases, and literature thus
becomes no exercise of the judgment, but sterile
labour for the memory; so that the language of
their people ceased to be a vehicle of useful instruction, and language itself became a barrier to
knowledge."   This was the first occasion on which
I had given utterance to these opinions, and great

was my gratification on observing the effect they produced; an effect which soon became visible in the tone of the society where it took place; and, lest it might be suspected that complacency for a foreigner might have led to a readier adoption, or to a waving of the opposition which freer discussion would have called forth, I may state that the principal interlocutor in this conversation (Osman Bey of Ismid) was not at the time aware that I was a European.*

" The greater part of the Turks of Siberia are entirely without literature: many of them are even ignorant of the use of alphabetical characters; and very few possess any interest to arrest the attention of the curious: it is therefore with no feeling of regret that I turn from these barren and uninteresting regions, and approach towards the contemplation of the literature of the Osmanlis;— a people of the same race, indeed, as those of the northern wastes, but one whose love of learning, and whose efforts towards its attainment, have raised it high above the level of its kindred. The prejudices which have so long led us to consider the Turks as ignorant and unlettered barbarians are now, for the most part, happily removed. The age is past in which the praise a Christian people

* Many Turks are authors of Persian and Arabic works; but two centuries ago the literature of Turkey surpassed that of Europe. It was from the works of Chelebi Effendi that D'Alembert took the idea of the Encyclopedia.

would have elicited would be denied to Moham-
medans; but we have still to contend with our
imperfect knowledge of the Osmanlis, added to a
certain degree of prejudice, arising from our education. The difference between the genius of the
East and West is almost a barrier to our arriving
at an impartial judgment on the subject of Oriental
literature. Formed on the model of Greece and
Rome—tempered by the nature of our climate—
the literature of Europe possesses little in common
with the offspring of Asia. The climate of the
North differs not more from that of the Oriental
regions than the literary taste of their inhabitants:
the beauties of the one are the blemishes of the
other; and what the one admires, the other despises. Of all the Eastern nations, the Osmanlis
have made the nearest approaches towards uniting
the genius of both hemispheres. Situated both in
Europe and in Asia, drawing their origin from the
one, but having constant and continued relations
with the other, they have, in some measure, learned
to unite the beauties of each, and will gradually
succeed in effecting a more complete union. But,
although the difference of genius and style is thus
rendered less perceptible in the Osmanli than in
any other of the languages of Asia, it is not the
less an Oriental idiom; and, if we judge it by the
test of the European model, we still find it, in
many respects, not consonant to our ideas. In
thus trying the literature of the East, however, we

are subjecting it to a somewhat prejudiced judgment; for whatever differs from the standard we employ, must be condemned; and but little, consequently, will escape the censure of the critic. In the physical world we judge of things relatively: the various species of animals we judge by themselves: we do not compare the ant with the elephant, or the eagle with the fly; each may be excellent, nevertheless, in its degree: let us not, then, follow the opposite course in examining the literature of nations essentially differing from each other in taste and opinions: let us endeavour, if possible, to eradicate this prejudice of education from our minds; and let us not hastily condemn all differing from that to which it has rendered us accustomed.

" There is no nation more passionately attached to literature than the Osmanlis. Instead of the religion they profess restraining their pursuit of knowledge, as the ignorant have asserted, we find their prophet himself commanding it :—' Seek knowledge,' says he, ' were it even to China. It is permitted to the Moslems to possess all the sciences.' The mandate of the Prophet was re-echoed by the Sultan. The library founded by the conqueror of Constantinople bears its paraphrase, as an inscription:—' The study of the sciences is a divine precept for true believers.' Neither the Prophet nor the Sultan has been disobeyed. The Osmanlis have eagerly sought science, have zealously cultivated literature; and it will be the object of this part of my Essay to endeavour to shew that their efforts have not been entirely unsuccessful.

" The dialect of the Osmanlis is the most polished of all the Turkish idioms—rich, dignified, and melodious: in delicacy and nicety of expression, it is not perhaps surpassed by any language; and in grandeur, beauty, and elegance, it is almost unequalled. The perfection and regularity of its derivation, and the facility with which it may be performed, render it extremely adapted for colloquial purposes. The addition of a letter or syllable makes the Verb Passive, negative, impossible, causal, reciprocal, or personal; and combinations of these are produced in the same manner, and by the same kind of mechanism.

" The conjugation is rich and regular, and is principally executed by the aid of the verb substantive. But the most singular feature in the Osmanli, as in all the other Turkish dialects, is the inversion of phraseology which pervades the language: the sense of a passage, suspended throughout by the employment of the numerous participles, is determined by the verb which concludes the sentence: the prepositions are subjoined instead of prefixed: and, in construction, the governed precedes the governing. These peculiarities give a gravity and picturesque effect to the periods of a Turkish composition, which adds greatly to the dignity and expression of the language."*

The Osmanlis have enriched their language by the adoption of numbers of words : and all scientific terms from the Persian, Arabian, and Greek, and traces of the Chinese are visible in their titles, and in many of their roots.

" From the earliest periods of their history, the Osmanlis have devoted themselves to the cultivation of literature. The last words of Othman to his son Orkhan—' Be the support of the faith, and the protector of the sciences'—were religiously observed : and no sooner had his triumphant arms planted the crescent on the walls of Prusa, than it was adorned with a college of royal foundation, which the learning of its professors soon rendered celebrated throughout the East; and students even from Persia and Arabia did not disdain to become the disciples of the Osmanlis.† The example of Orkhan was imitated, and surpassed

---

* " Sir William Jones thus sums up the relative qualities of Persian, Arabian, and Turkish languages :—'Suavitatem Persica, ubertatem ac vim Arabica, mirificam habet Turcica dignitatem : prima allicit atque oblectat; altera sublimiùs vehitur, et fertur quodammodo incitatiùs; tertia elata est sanè, sed non sine aliquâ elegantiâ et pulchritudine. Ad lusus igitur et amores sermo Persicus, ad poëmata et eloquentiam Arabicus, ad moralia scripta Turcicus videtur idoneus.'—Vol. II. p. 363:"

† " Cantemir Hist. Ottom. tom. I. lib. 1. p. 71."

by his successors. Bajazet, each year of his reign, endowed an academy of science. Amurat, his successor, did not omit to decorate his conquests by the munificence of his foundations;* and, long before Constantinople became the seat of their empire, the schools of the Osmanlis were both numerous and celebrated. The conqueror of Constantinople, Mohammed II., was perhaps one of the greatest patrons of literature that perhaps any age or country has produced. Learned in the languages of Asia and Europe, he did not confine his patronage to the productions of his own nation or country. The poets of Persia and Arabia, the scholars and artists of Italy, were alike the objects of his distinction; and Noureddin Jami, the author of the beautiful poem of Yussuf and Zuleikha, and Philelphus, who addressed him in a Latin ode, were equally indebted to his munificence.† Two universities owe their existence to Mohammed II.— Aya Sofiya, and the Mohammedieh. The first consisting of six colleges, amply endowed, was furnished with the most skilful professors of science; but the second, raised by Mohammed himself, was on a more magnificent scale. Sixteen colleges,

* "Cantemir Hist. Ottom. tom. 1. lib. 2, p. 266."

† " Gentil Bellin, a painter, of Venice, was sent for to Constantinople, to display his art; and was handsomely rewarded. He drew the portrait of the Sultan."

adapted for the reception of six hundred students, were comprised within its compass: the most celebrated of the Osmanlis were numbered among its teachers, and Constantinople still considers the Mohammedieh one of its greatest ornaments. It has been the constant practice of the Ottoman Princes to attach *Mudirisehs* (مدرسه) or colleges to the buildings they dedicated to the purposes of religion. More than five hundred such institutions, each bearing the name of its founder, are still existing in Constantinople. In addition to these are a multitude of inferior schools, termed *Mektebs* (مكتب), in which the lower branches of education are taught; and above thirty public libraries, exclusive of the mysterious collection of the Seraglio, complete the literary resources of the capital, and attest the zeal and regard which the Osmanlis have displayed for the cultivation of literature.

" Before proceeding to survey the literature of the Osmanlis themselves, it may not be improper to examine to what degree they have cultivated foreign learning, and how far they are indebted to other nations. Notwithstanding the pride of ignorance, and contempt for foreign learning, usually attributed to the Ottomans, we find them at all periods anxiously seeking the enrichment of their literature from the stores of other countries. In the reigns of the early Sultans, when the whole range of classic literature was in their hands, many

of the authors of Greece and Rome assumed a
Turkish dress. A Turkish version of Plutarch's
Lives, made by command of Mohammed II., is
known to have existed: the Commentaries of
Cæsar became accessible to the Osmanlis in the
reign of Soliman I.; and Aristotle and Euclid are
also found in their language. These works are
known to have been translated into Turkish; but
it cannot be supposed that they were the only
monuments of classical antiquity that attracted the
attention of these enlightened princes; and it is
not even now impossible that some of the long-lost
fragments of classic literature may yet be recovered
from the versions of the Osmanlis. Even in modern times they have not failed to procure translations from the works of various European nations.
The Sultan, Mustapha III., introduced the ' Prince'
of Machiavel to the Osmanlis; not, however,
omitting, at the same time, to annex its refutation—
the ' Anti-Machiavel' of the King of Prussia.
Krusinski's Journal, the Works of Boerhaave, our
English Sydenham, Bonnycastle, Vauban, Lafitte,
Truquet, Lalande, and a translation of some un-
published manuscripts of Cassini, the astronomer,
presented by his son to the Turkish ambassador,
are found on the shelves of the public libraries of
Constantinople, and many of them have been
thought worthy of being submitted to the Imperial
Press. To the Persians and Arabians the Osmanlis

are certainly under many obligations; and they possess numerous translations and imitations from the authors of those countries."*

These extracts are from the Introduction to Mr. David's Turkish Grammar. It was with a feeling of astonishment, not less than satisfaction, that I came upon idea after idea, in turning over the pages of that little essay. Death has, however, put an end to his labours and his usefulness: he lived long enough to witness the commencement of the mutual renunciation of antipathy, which must precede that fusion of the genius of the East and the West, which he so confidently predicted. But rapid, without parallel, as the progress has been, how much has it not been retarded, how much even is it not endangered by the ruthless destroyer which, in so short a space of time, has mowed down every useful and gifted labourer in this field; and has cut off those who, by the powers of their mind, and their equal acquaintance with those two worlds, were calculated to become links between them—Mr. David himself; then—within an interval of a few months, and even before

* "'Turcæ, ut suprà dictum, Persas sequuntur, imò, sæpe, ita fidè, ut verbum de verbo reddant. Sed Alcæum, Archilochum, Bacchylidem, Anacreontem, alios, permultis in locis imitatus est Horatius: Latina tamen non minori voluptate quam Græca legimus. *Multi sunt prætereà versûs Turcici, qui, è Persicis non redditi, videntur esse valde belli.*'—*Sir* WILLIAM JONES, *Poës. Asiat. Comment. Lond.* 1799."

his powers became known, or his reputation established, at least in Europe—Osman Noureddin
Pasha. In August, 1836, Mr. Blacque, so long
the sole champion of Turkey in the *Courrier de
Smyrne*, was suddenly cut off at Malta, on his way
to Europe; there to have employed, in defence of
that cause to which his life had been devoted, the
power of his eloquence, his energy, and conviction.
His place at Constantinople had been supplied by
Hassuna d'Ghies; who, after long and instructive,
though not unclouded, acquaintance with Europe,
had just arrived on the natural field of his usefulness, and was mowed down only four months after
the death of his predecessor. An Englishman, a
Turk, a Frenchman, and an Arab, had each, in
different positions, arrived at almost identical views.
They had all, by patient study, and long acquaintance with the East and the West, fitted themselves
to become the instruments of counteracting the
destructive march of events. They are gone; but
they have left behind them a regret, which proves
that their labours have not been all in vain; and
that the cause they espoused is one which has
already established a claim to regard from the
sympathies of mankind, and to interest and ex-
amination from the cabinets of Europe.

At the time that Mr. David's essay was written
and published (1832), no communication had taken
place between those or other individuals in whose
minds the germs had been separately formed of

those ideas respecting the East. One unqualified voice of reprobation pervaded the whole of the Western nations; and not a doubt, even at that period, remained of the practical extinction of the Ottoman empire, which, indeed, alone could have justified the opinions of the public, or the policy of the cabinets. At that moment, the publication of the essay of Mr. David derives no less merit from the boldness of the act, than from the intrinsic merits of the work; and though he alludes neither to politics, administration, commerce, military, or diplomatic relations, the portraiture he has given of the literature and the mental dispositions of a people devoted to destruction under the pretext of humanity and civilization, is one of the bitterest satires ever penned against dogmatic fanaticism, or national madness.

Appearing, as it has done, as an introduction to a bad and faulty grammar of a language which nobody in England thinks worth studying, though spoken along sixty degrees of longitude, and some-times ten of latitude, of the most important regions on the face of the earth, and some of them in our own possession, it has excited but little attention, and been but little read. I am therefore tempted to extract from it a passage or two more, more particularly as they contain the admission, by the Philo-Turkish author, of the extreme ignorance of the Turks in matters of practical science, which I have already so strongly dwelt upon, and an alteration in which I conceive to be pregnant with results wholly incalculable, not only as regards Turkey itself, but as regards the whole of the East, even to the shores of the Yellow Sea.

" Though it must be admitted that the Osmanlis are inferior to the European nations in the sciences, they have been far from neglecting the study, and they possess numerous treatises on astronomy, mathematics, algebra, and physics. In philosophy, they have all the speculative knowledge that the Greeks and Arabians were masters of; but in experimental science they have made but little progress. In moral philosophy, however, and in treatises on the art of government and political economy, the Osmanlis particularly excel; which is the more surprising, as our ideas of the Turks and their polity would lead us to imagine quite the contrary.

" From their earliest periods, the Osmanlis possessed the best masters of astronomical science. Salaheddin, or Kadi Zadeh Roumi, was an excellent astronomer and mathematician. He was born at Prusa, in the reign of Murad I.; and became the preceptor of the celebrated Ulugh Beg, under whose patronage he commenced the Zidg, or astronomical tables, which bear the name of that prince. He died before their completion; and the work was finished by his son, Ali Kushdgi. Mustafa ben Ali, who lived in the reign of Soliman, was the author of several much esteemed astronomical productions. Mohammed Darandeli composed the excellent Ephemerides, entitled *Ruz Nameh*, روز نامه which contains perpetual tables of the day, the hour, and the minute of each lunation, and a variety of information essential to astronomical accuracy. There are a multitude of astronomical works in Turkish, many of which display great science. In most of the mosques of Constantinople, solar quadrants are found, fitted for taking observations; and astrolabes, telescopes, and other astronomical instruments of their own manufacture, are in frequent use, some of which are extremely well constructed. They have even the honour of invention; and Hadgi Khalifeh records, in his chronological tables, that in the year A.H. 987, a Turk, named Tashieddin, invented a beautiful instrument for observing the stars. Mathematics, geometry, algebra, and arithmetic, are considered by the Osmanlis among the necessary acquirements of a man of education; and a course of *Hindeseh v'al Hisab* هندسه والحساب, which comprises these sciences, forms a portion of the studies to which their schools are devoted. Bajazet II. was much attached to geometrical and astronomical studies, which he cultivated under the instruction of the celebrated Salaheddin. In the science of numbers their proficiency is very great; and the facility with which their calculations are performed has been frequently noticed.*   On these subjects they possess many excellent works.   The philosophical productions of the Osmanlis are very numerous.   Their speculative and metaphysical writings, *Hikmet ve Kelam* حكمت وكلام are similar to those which issued from our schools during the reign of the Aristotelian philosophy; and, like them, have usually a theological cast.   The light of Newton, and the philosophy of modern times, has not yet shed its full lustre over the empire of the Ottoman; though, to their honour, it should be mentioned, that Raghib Pasha—the talented vizir of Osman III., and his successor, Mustafa—the contemporary of that illustrious philosopher, sought to procure a translation of his philosophical system.†   Their moral philosophy, which is termed *Adeb* ادب, is, however, a science on which the Osmanlis seem to have bestowed some of their best energies: it is the subject of many excellent and valuable treatises.   Their mode of conveying the

---

* " 'Ils calculent très rapidement par une méthode simple et fort courte.   En quelques minutes de temps, ils font, sur un quarré de papier, un compte que nous ne ferions pas sur quatres feuilles en deux heures . . . . . Notre Arithmétique gagneroit à la traduction de quelques livres Arabes et Turcs, qui traitent savamment et sommairement de cette matière.'—*Toderini de la Lit. des Turcs. Cournand.* Vol. I. p. 90.   *Par.* 1789."

* " 'Réflexions sur l'état critique actuel de la puissance Ottomane,' without place or date. — *Toderini*, ib. p. 118, ascribes it to ' le savant et érudit Eugenius, archevêque de la Nouvelle Russie et de l'Esclavonie.' "

principles of morals, by means of imaginative dis-
courses and apologues, adds great force and beauty
to the sentiments ; and, strewing the path of knowledge with flowers, it renders its acquisition at once
agreeable and impressive.　An elegant work of this
nature is the *Humaiun Nameh* نامه همايون.　It is
written in mingled prose and verse, and is one of
the most beautiful specimens of the Turkish language that its literature can produce.　It was composed by Ali Tchelebi, for Sultan Soliman I., to
whom it is dedicated : there is also a poetical version by Gelali, by command of Bajazet II. : the
former is, however, the most esteemed.　The
Humaiun Nameh is formed upon the model of a
work whose excellence is evidenced by its existence in almost every language, ancient and modern
— the fables of Pilpay.　Upon this, Ali Tchelebi
has raised a system of ethics, couched in a series
of amusing tales and fables, inculcating various
principles of moral philosophy, and teeming with
beauties of thought and language," &c.

" If the Osmanlis are our inferiors in the depth
of scientific research, in the *belles-lettres* they do
not yield to us the palm of superiority.　In poetry
they display great genius and taste ; and all classes
are its ardent admirers.　To so great a degree has
the love of poetic composition been carried, that
there is no grade of society in the Ottoman Empire
but has contributed towards it : the ladies, the

Sultan, his ministers, doctors, soldiers—all have devoted themselves to the cultivation of poetry; and the divans, or poetical collections of above six hundred authors, are existing evidences of the taste of the Osmanlis for the productions of the muse," &c.

I take this opportunity of filling up a *lacune* in Mr. David's Essay. Isaak Effendi, late chief professor of the Sultan's own college, was some time ago required by his Highness to draw up a course of mathematical instruction, to be used generally in the higher colleges. It has issued from the Constantinople press in three thick octavo volumes, and comprises the elementary parts of algebra, dynamics, hydraulics, optics, &c.; and conducts the student in the region of abstract calculation as far as the third section of Newton's " Principia," comprehending that portion of each of these sciences which a man, reading for a class at Oxford, would have to study. I have been led to mention this fact by observing inserted, as a " *pièce justificative*," in a publication,* the object of which is to justify the occupation, by an ally of England, of the capital of another ally (on the plea of civilisation), an extract from the work of the chaplain to the British Embassy at Constantinople, and a writer of several books on that country, as follows :—

* Russia, by a Manchester Manufacturer.

" Extracts from various writers illustrative of the condition of Turkey.

" GEOGRAPHY AND THE USE OF THE GLOBES.

" Lord Strangford sent the Porte a valuable present. He had brought with him a pair of very large globes from England; and, as the Turks had latterly shewn some disposition to learn languages, he thought it would be a good opportunity to teach them something else; and he determined to send them over to the Porte, and asked me to go with them and explain their object. . . . . . This important present was brought over with becoming respect. A Choreash (Cavash), went first, with his baton of office; then followed two janissaries, like Atlases, bearing worlds upon their shoulders; then myself, attended by our principal Dragoman in full costume; and, finally, a train of janissaries and attendants. When arrived at the Porte, we were introduced to the Reis Effendi, or Minister for Foreign Affairs, who, with other ministers, were waiting for us. When I had the globes put together on their frames, they came round us with great interest; and the Reis Effendi, who thought, *ex officio,* he ought to know something of geography, put on his spectacles and began to examine them. The first thing that struck them was the compass in the stand. When they observed the needle always kept the same position, they expressed great surprise, and thought it was done by some interior mechanism. It was mid-day, and the shadow of the frame of the window was on the floor. I endeavoured to explain to them that the needle was always found nearly in that direction, pointing to the north : I could only make them understand that it always turned towards the sun ! The Reis Effendi then asked me to shew him England. When I pointed out the small comparative spot on the great globe, he turned to the rest, and said " Keetchuk," little ; and they repeated all round " Keetchuk," in various tones of contempt. But when I shewed them the dependencies of the empire, and particularly the respectable size of India, they said " Beeyuk," with some marks of respect. I also took occasion to shew them the only mode of coming from thence to Constantinople by sea, and that a ship could not sail with a cargo of coffee from Mocha across the Isthmus of Suez. The newly appointed Dragoman of the Porte (Isaak Effendi), who had been a Jew, and was imbued with a slighter tincture of information, was present; so, after explaining to him as much as I could make him comprehend, I left to him the task of further instructing the ministers in this new science. Indeed, it appeared to me as if none of them had ever seen an artificial globe before, or even a mariner's compass."*

* Walsh's " Constantinople," as quoted by Mr. Cobden.

This Turkish Dragoman, instructed by Dr. Walsh in the use of the common compass, and in the relative areas of England and India, is no other than the translator of Wood, Hutton, and Newton. If this fact should bring home, to any dispassionate inquirer, the humiliating conviction of the nullity of the oracles who have so long been suffered to direct the opinions of an enlightened nation on so great and vital a question, it will have been worth recording; but there is connected with it a consideration scarcely less humiliating, which the reader will draw, if he will but picture to himself the scene here described, and imagine the effect produced on the minds of those present, by the pitiable exhibition here recorded by the actor himself.

The value of the information of modern travellers may be estimated by the boldness of assertion, and the hardihood with which the faith, character, and destinies of these countries are disposed of. Useful inquiry requires, while it instils, temperance of mind and frugality of imagination. Theories and speculation are called in to conceal the scantiness of observation, not to methodise the abundance of facts. How truly applicable to the present times are the observations of the learned Ockley, on the writers on Turkey and the East of his day: " If fortune did not envy merit, our Eastern travellers would all have been Plenipotentiaries and Secretaries of State."

In this age, when literature is so extensively circulated, and possesses such great facilities; at a period, when so many subjects of interest, when interests of such paramount importance, coincide in calling attention to the state of the East, it is most incomprehensible that nothing should have been done—I say, not worthy of our powers, the subjects, merits, or the urgency of the times—but nothing which can bear a comparison with the labours of individuals of former periods, who had to contend with innumerable difficulties, when little attention had been wakened in the public mind, and when their labours, not as at present, leading to great political literary and commercial results, could only aim at transplanting, into the literature of Europe, some of the historical and philological lore of the Orientals. The character of modern writers on Turkey, is too frivolous and childish to merit even censure ; they have nothing in common with the inquiries which that country presents ; and, with the exception of the above quoted work of Mr. David, and the geographical and ethnographical labours of Colonel Leake, I know of no contribution made to our stock of information, in latter years, by any Englishman, on the religion, manners, literature, administration, politics, or statistics, of Turkey. Since the time of old Knowles, there has not even been an English history of Turkey.* There is scarcely an

---

* A couple of volumes, entitled a " History of the Ottoman Empire," has been published in Constable's Miscellany. It is needless to say more of it, than that Dr. Walsh is taken as an authority.

Englishman acquainted with the Turkish language. A late ambassador, desirous of having a private secretary who understood Turkish, discovered that the qualified persons from whom he could make a selection, amounted to one — Mr. Mitchell, the assistant secretary to the Asiatic Society. There are three, or two, old residents in the Levant, who speak the Turkish language, and there is one young Englishman now educating, to fill the situation of Dragoman. Such is the amount of the means possessed by England, for maintaining its communications with the Ottoman Empire ; such is the amount of chances which it has prepared for itself, for gaining some insight into the character of its people, or the nature of its government ; such is the amount of the means by which her intelligence is to be represented to the eyes of the East, and through which her character is to be sustained, and her influence established.

Before blaming, therefore, the Turks too severely for their ignorance of Europe, we must consider our claims to applause for acquaintance with Turkey. What Englishman has gone to make a study of Turkey ? Yet, how many Turkish disciples are now in England and in France !

Those portions of the East, which approach the confines of Europe, appear certainly inferior, in intellectual developement, to the regions that extend further eastward. The metaphysics and mythology of the Persians, Arabs, and Hindoos,

have given an original character to the literature
of these people—have developed their reasoning
faculties, stored their minds with literary wealth,
and filled their imagination with pleasing images:
these various causes have rendered the study of
their language and literature attractive to the inhabitants of the West, and have afforded to those
who have made themselves proficients in such
studies, the door to intercourse and respect, among
the learned and influential. It is to the seeds of
respect thus scattered by a few gifted Englishmen,
that our Asiatic power and influence may perhaps be remotely traced. Metaphysics are the
most powerful of all political instruments, as applied to the East; without metaphysics, and the
facility of their application, to every trivial incident, a man can never obtain amongst them that
character which, flying from mouth to mouth, is
the source of power; without a competent knowledge of their ideas and learning, he cannot come
off with credit from those trials of wit and strength;
which contests, whoever seeks to acquire character
or consideration, must not only not shrink from,
but seek, and where he must triumph. In Turkey
this state of mind exists, but by no means to the
same degree as further eastward; while the character of the traveller, who visits Turkey, is infinitely lower than that of those Europeans who,
educated in England for Eastern service, have
acquired the native languages, mastered their sci-

ences, and become acquainted with their authors,
and thus possess that knowledge, without which
no useful intercourse can exist, but have also improved their own minds, and extended their views
as men. The traveller in Turkey is invariably
ignorant of the Turkish,—a knowledge of Turkish
literature is of course out of the question,—but the
commoner advantages of intimacy or friendship
with natives of the country are also wanting ; consequently it is not surprising that no Englishman,
or no European, has produced an impression on
their minds, or, I may say, is known to them at all.
Yet what powerful influence might be exerted by
any individual possessing but a few of the conditions requisite, and what a ground to work upon
in the strong attachment of the whole population
for England, and in the general conviction pressed
home upon them by the dangers and the difficulties of the times, that their political reorganisation,
and their national existence, now solely depend on
Great Britain.

CHAPTER XIX.

TEPEDELENE—RECEPTION AT BERAT—THE GUEGUES.

AFTER this long digression, I must remind the reader that we have left Argyro Castro, on our way to Scodra. I arrived next at a place, the name of which calls up a thousand interesting associations, and which I entered with a feeling of respect which an Albanian would have been proud to observe in a stranger;—that place was Tepedelene, the Croya of the modern Skander Beg. Arriving at it from the south, the beauty of the position, and the effect of the castle, are lost. I came at once upon a heap of ruins, and wandered about amongst them for some time, and under a shower of rain, before I found the house of the Aga. On approaching it, I had been met by companies of peasants, dragging towards Janina the guns that once had frowned over its battlements. The once proud Tepedelene, now sheltered but one hundred and fifty Albanian, and eight Greek families, and, as if this amount of ruin and desolation were not sufficient, the troops there assembled

were busied in levelling the fortifications to the
ground. That work, however, had not yet commenced on the lines of white walls and towers that
crowned the steep that looks to the north, and the
base of which is encircled by a rapid, and not
inconsiderable stream; so that, as I left the place
after being ferried across the water, I turned back
to cast on Tepedelene, the last stranger glance
which ever would fall on its doomed battlements
and towers. This scene of surpassing beauty led
me, forgetful of the coming night, to linger there
ere I turned away: the evening sun gilded the
snow-white walls, while the recent shower had
brightened the deep winter-green of the surrounding landscape, over which rose the brown steep
sides of the hills, their crests powdered with snow.
Tepedelene, on its rock, stood boldly forward in
the midst of the picture, and the swollen torrent
dashed foaming round its base.

But I must not leave this place, without some
record of my visit to the Governor. He told
me that twenty-four guns were to be dragged to
Janina, but that the weather was so bad, and the
country so difficult, that the labour was immense;
that one heavy gun had fallen over the side and
lodged in the river, and that it had been necessary
to collect two or three thousand men to get it out.
This, while it might appear on one side an Eastern
metaphor, was, on the other, a real representation
of Albanian mechanics. I took occasion, upon

this, to extract a calculation of the labour requisite to drag these twenty-four guns to Janina, which amounted to one day's labour of ten thousand men. This being by his own admission, I suggested the advantage of constructing a road, which perhaps four times that amount of labour would suffice to do, which would not only enable them afterwards to drag these guns with oxen instead of men, but which would facilitate the transport of all they ate, wore, consumed, produced, bought, and sold. My logic was, however, superfluous, for the chief, and all the by-standers, had already arrived at the same conclusion, and the answer was, "Tell that to the Grand Vizir." The destruction of the Castle was, however, a sore subject, even to the victors; they asked me if I did not think it was dreadful to destroy what it had cost their fathers so much labour to build? I could only answer by some commonplace remarks about the blessings of tranquillity and universal peace; and was asked, if we had not got a great many castles in England. Being tired of recurrence to those wooden fortresses, our superiority in which is so often quoted, only that our inferiority in all other material force should be inferred :—I answered that we had " a great many castles — our breasts!" and immediately arose an exclamation, in Turkish, Greek, and Albanian, one in sense, but diversified in sound, " Doghru der," " Kala lei," " Mir thoet," or, " He says well!"

Here, as elsewhere, there was a great interest evinced in Poland, and anxiety for news or information respecting its condition; they inquired why the Poles, who had taken refuge in other countries, had not come to them; that Turkey would not only have received and protected them, but would have given them lands and wives. But the refugees mistook their way, as the revolutionists miscalculated their hour. I had seen the Albanians in their wildest mood, and their worst days; I now saw them in a state of subjugation, but which, I hope, is also one of transition. If ever I should again visit their beautiful country, I may be rolling over terraces and roads in the midst of tranquillity and peace, the landscape formalised with fields and hedges, and the romance of war, and the interest of alarms, replaced by homely industry and ignoble wealth. Tranquillity, it is true, did now exist, but it was the tranquillity of fear; security I enjoyed, but it was a security bought by an apparent partisanship with the victors.

As I advanced, the country became less wild and rude, and the river, swelled in volume, was still in sound, and straitened in its bed. Night soon overtook me, and, after two hours' toiling in the dark, through the deep mud of the roads, and under torrents of rain, which, thanks to Mackintosh, fell upon me but touched me not; I was received under the miserly covering of a wretched

Khan, toasted in the smoke of a green-wood fire, and treated to a not unwelcome supper of Indian corn and resinous wine. In order to reach Berat next night, I had to start three hours before daylight. The rain continued, mixed with snow; peals of thunder rolled over our heads, and flashes of lightning, now and then, happily directed our uncertain steps. The blasts from the Albanian mountains became more piercing, as we ascended the passes of the Glava; and, though the sun rose not to our eyes, day broke over one of the most bleak and dreary prospects I ever beheld; the heavens were black, and the earth white. This rugged and inhospitable pass was crowded, however, with Albanian coulias, or little castles; one by itself, or two together, or ten at most, in the same vicinity, forming a *soï*, or race, which are bound together for the purposes of injury and defence; and if not always linked by consanguineous ties, are united by the undistinguishing vengeance of stranger blood, which may have been shed in their ceaseless feuds.

A numerous guard had attended me as far as Tepedelene. I had there got a fresh troop; but difficulties respecting horses having arisen, even though I had paid for them, and not wishing to be detained, I proceeded, attended only by a couple of Skipetars; and I afterwards ascertained that this, the only portion of my journey where I was unguarded, was precisely the most dangerous portion

of the whole route. I confess that I would much
rather have found myself at Corfu than where I
was, when, towards the summit of this pass, notorious for the handiwork of its savage inhabitants,
I perceived several of these mountaineers armed
to the teeth, hastening to intercept my passage.
The traditional mode of commencing business in
that quarter is to demand, not your purse or your
life, but — snuff! My new acquaintances asked,
indeed, for my snuff-box — a very modest sort of
inquiry to make. I answered, that the days of
" snuff" were gone by, but still, that they were welcome to my tobacco-bag. They answered, sullenly,
that they had not yet learned to smoke, and allowed me to pass without molestation. A little
after I reached a Khan, where there were several
Albanians. A Greek boy, the Khanji, served me as
interpreter. They told me that their country produced corn sufficient only for four months con-
sumption in the year; that the Sadrazem had
taken the bread from Albania, and they never
would enter the Turkish service. I asked them
what they intended now to do? The Greek lad
burst into a fit of laughter, and said, they are
" sitting," waiting for the Grand Vizir to die; and
treated them in other respects in a way which I
was astonished not to see bring down ready
vengeance on his head; but the spirit of the
Albanians is broken; each individual of the nation is a changed being; and, as they said

themselves, " their hearts are cold and their lips parched."

It was nearly sunset when I reached Berat, the Arnaout Belgrade, romantically situated between the lofty rock on which stood the castle, and the mountain from which that rock has been severed by the river Beratino. Along either bank of the winding stream is spread the town, and the two banks are united by a high and handsome bridge. Here the Greek women wear yashmacks and fe-ridgees like those of the Mussulmans. I forgot to mention, that at Delvino the Mussulman women wear the most ludicrous dress that woman's fancy ever invented; which consists of a white wrapper, covering them from the top of the head to the feet, with two half sleeves, into which their elbows are thrust, their hands being crossed upon their breasts, and their elbows stuck out at right angles. In this way they stalk about like rough-hewn marble crosses. This white wrapper opens at the face, however, to display a black mask, with two holes for the eyes. To all my inquiries as to the origin of this singular costume, I got one invariable answer, ἔτσι εὑρέθικε—" so it has been found."

At Berat my reception was of an extraordinary and instructive nature. I have before dwelt on the social distinctions made between Mussulmans and Christians; and the reader has seen some of the difficulties in which I have been involved, in consequence of attempts to emancipate myself from the common treatment reserved for Europeans. But I have . re-written, when better acquainted with the subject, the account of circumstances which occurred in the process of gaining that information. Notwithstanding all the means of intercourse I had previously had, I feel myself indebted to an incident at Berat for ideas on the subject, which rendered it more clear to me than it had been before.

The news of my return to Albania had reached some of my old friends, who were delighted at a mark of so much interest taken in them by a European; and among whom the curiosity respecting Europe, which, during the last few years, has been so rapidly growing throughout the Turkish dominions, had been quickened by the incidents of my last journey, and by those personal associations which are the necessary basis of international regard. Not only, therefore, did I find at Berat every disposition to receive me in the most friendly manner, but letters had also arrived, enjoining the exhibition of those dispositions which were already so favourable. The Governor, it was true, was absent; but his son, a youth of twenty, who filled his place, seized, with the warmth of his age, the opportunity of gratifying his predilection for the new order of things.

The Bishop being absent, the young Bey had the Episcopal residence prepared for me, and sent thither his own train of Mussulman attendants. I was visited by the most distinguished people of the place; and, thus surrounded by all the necessary appliances, caught the practice of Eastern ceremonial with that ready scholarship which ever attends the assumption of greatness. For the exact mode of salutation to guests of all degrees—for the particular point of the room or stairs where they were to be met—for the mode and degree of rising— the exact measure of the salutation — the spot where they were to sit — for the inquiries that were to be made, or the answers that were to be returned — I must refer the reader to the details I have given, in a previous sketch, of Turkish manners.

Next morning, I took leave of my youthful host, not without a promise of returning to Berat. He could now, he said, only dream that there had been a European at Berat; and that my short visit had left him with wishes excited, but not gratified. A few months afterwards I learned, with sincere regret, that this fine young man had met with an untimely grave.

I now entered on the beautiful champaign country that stretches to the north, and travelled twenty miles across a dead level, which appeared like the unruffled surface of a lake, and was cropped close by sheep. I had a letter from Berat to a Turkish Bey, at whose house I was to sleep; and here, for the first time, I was served in a Turkish house before the master. " Nothing is so striking as the change of manner now so rapidly taking place; every day, the attentions I receive seem to exceed those of the preceding one." The foregoing phrase was written at the time : I did not then understand that the change was in me, not in them.

The next day, in the afternoon, I arrived at Cavalha; and on entering the place, which contains between two and three hundred Guegue families, I met Ibrahim Bey, the proprietor of this place and the surrounding country, accompanied by a troop of savage and picturesque looking horsemen; but they all fell short of the ferocious air of their leader — a man guilty of every crime, and stained with every vice, and detested alike by Turks and Christians. The blood of his nearest relatives was on his head.

He possesses — in the way that an Albanian Odjack possesses — an extent of country thirty miles in every direction. I had now fairly entered into the country of the Guegues : they are the northernmost of the three general divisions of Albania ;—the first, to the south, called Châmi, of which Janini is the capital; the second, composed of the Toxides, the Liapes, and others, extends to Berat; the third, from Berat to the mountains of Monte Negro and Bosnia, are the Guegues. These last, though speaking a dialect of the Skipt, or Albanian, are strongly tinctured with Sclavonian blood ; whereas, to the south, the

influence of Greece has more prevailed. The
Guegues have a distinct costume : they wear the
fustanel, or large white kilt ; but the short jacket
of the southern Albanians is with them prolonged
into a skirt—descends as low as the extremity of
the fustanel, and is bound under their belt, so as
entirely to cover the fustanel behind. The colours they affect are crimson and purple ; and
these, with their red caps, white fustanels, red
leggings, and gold-embroidered vests, gives a
richness and splendour to their appearance, especially when assembled in numbers, which exceeds,
even in effect, that most elegant of costumes, the
southern Albanian. I never saw any thing more
beautiful than the groups of children. The pale-
ness of complexion which, even in infancy, casts
its invariable shade, here yields to the joint influence of the mountains and the north. The
little creatures wear, in miniature, the formal
dresses of their sires ; and the delicate crimson of their cheeks is matched with that colour
which supersedes every other in their costume.

CHAPTER XX.

MIDNIGHT ADVENTURES — DURAZZO—TURKISH NOTIONS ON
COMMERCE—EUROPEAN CONSULS AND RESIDENTS — THE
FRENCH IN EGYPT—MEHEMET ALI PASHA — NORTHERN
ALBANIA.

LEARNING that an old friend of mine was Governor
of Durazzo, I resolved to hasten on to that place
the same evening. The distance was three hours;
so, leaving the inhospitable Cavalha at an hour
before sunset, I hastened on alone, to reach Durazzo as early as possible. My haste, however,
brought me no speed; instead of following the
coast, to reach Durazzo, situated on a narrow
neck of land, I struck to the right, and got on the
road leading from Durazzo northward. I spent a
miserable night, having two or three times got
entangled in quagmires; and at length reached a
village, where I was assailed by troops of dogs. I
succeeded, however, in arousing the inmates of a
house. My appearance, or at least the noise I
made, soon created an alarm, but there was no
possibility of understanding a word on either side;
and a light presently appearing within, I had the
satisfaction of seeing half-a-dozen men shadowed
forth at the different windows, each with his

musket. I thought it now high time to retreat, even if to the quagmires; and, making the best of my way out of the enclosures that surrounded this inhospitable abode, I did conceive my troubles were all over, when I came to a well-beaten road. This, of course, could only lead to Durazzo, and I proceeded confidently, if not heartily, along; but a few hundred paces brought me to the edge of a small river. Seeing the path directed to the ford, I pushed in without hesitation : the water came up to the middle of my saddle; but I thought my horse was just about to step up the opposite bank, when he suddenly lost his footing, and we were both carried down by the stream. My accoutrements put every attempt at swimming out of the question; but though carried under, I still held by the bridle, and relinquished it only for the tail of my steed; which, turning, struck out for the bank we had left, and which we soon regained. But my horse no sooner reached the firm ground, than, shaking me off, he scampered away, leaving me in as pretty a plight as any lover of adventure could desire. But, what was now to be done? It was no consolation whatever for me to think, that it might have been at the very spot that the same accident befell the Emperor Commène, on the night that followed the memorable battle of Durazzo; when the imperial army, composed of Greeks and Turks, Circassians and English, was routed and scattered to the winds by the victorious lances of Robert de Guichard and his Normans.

I had escaped from the bogs, I had been snatched from the river, I had run from the dogs and the muskets, which way was I now to turn? Without a horse, unable to walk, without a word of any intelligible language at my disposal, hungry, shivering, and exhausted; drenched from top to toe, my boots filled with water, my ample shalvars and cloak weighing what might have been worth something in gold, and this on the 18th of December! The only thing to be done was to sit down on the bank of the river, and to wait for the 19th. It dawned at length; and, not long afterwards, one of the wandering Vlachs (shepherds) came down to water some cattle, at the spot where I had entered the river, and to which I had returned. I then discovered, that what I had taken for a path and a ford, was merely a place for watering and washing the cattle of the village. In the plight in which I was, I would have carefully concealed myself from a Guegue, who might have fancied my shalvars, though neither the shape nor the favourite colour of the country; from a Vlach I had nothing to fear, and, giving him to understand, by dumb show, and by the state of my vestments, the misfortune which had befallen me during the night, he gave evidence of his comprehension, by thrice devoutly crossing himself on the forehead and breast, and uttering a long whistling

ejaculation. But, from his calling, it was natural
that his first thought should be respecting the welfare of my horse; so, putting out the forefinger of
his left hand, and crossing it with two fingers of
his right, he began a trotting motion, casting his
eye the while from me to the river, and then all
along its banks, as if to ask in what part the trotting animal was to be found. I answered, by a
galloping motion of the hand and arm, and pointed
to the road to Cavalha. He suddenly set to work,
like a man who had got a new idea, took my wet
cloak, folded it, and threw it on the back of one of
his animals, which he led to the side of a bank,
and, repeating the foregoing diagram with his
fingers, intimated to me an invitation to ride,
which he had not twice to give. He also mounted,
and, driving his other cattle before him, commenced screeching what they call a song, and left
me to follow as I might. I thought, of course, we
were going to the village, but we turned off to the
left, and in about half an hour reached a small
encampment of Vlachs, where, stopping at a door,
he shovelled me in, and went on about his business. It was just sunrise, and I found myself in a
solitary *tête-à-tête* with an old woman. She stared
at me, and waited to be spoken to. I thought it
necessary to utter some sounds in the way of
speech: she immediately cried, " Whisht," putting
her finger to her lips, and placing a stool near
where the fire had been, motioned me to sit down.

She then pointed to a bed entirely covered up with a coverlid, which had an air of finery ill suited to the place, and, inclining her head upon her open hand, gave me to understand that some great personage there reposed, whose existence and slumbers I soon became convinced of, by that involuntary music so modestly disavowed by its most successful performers. A blazing and comforting fire was lit in silence, and, while the steam rose all around me, I was left for a full hour, to ruminate on the character of the invisible personage in whose presence I was, when suddenly the bed-clothes were thrown off with a jerk, and a figure bolted up to half its height, displaying, under a white wadded night-cap, a dark lank countenance and long black beard, and I perceived that I was the guest of the priest of the Vlach encampment. After the necessary yawns and stretchings, the obsequious handmaiden succeeded in directing his attention to me, when, taking me for a Cavash, he jumped up, came to kiss my hand, and to inquire, in sounds unknown, the purport of my visit. I soon discovered that he spoke Greek. His apprehensions quickly subsided; and after crossing himself, and wondering at my adventure, began to make himself more merry at my expense than I was inclined to be satisfied with. However, a comforter was soon produced, in the shape of a bottle of rakki, which was followed by a breakfast, by no means to be despised, of a hot Indian-corn cake,

and fresh drawn milk. My clothes were hung up
to dry; and after that, two good horses were at
the door, one for myself, and one for the Papas,
who declared he would accompany me back to
Durazzo, which I found I had passed six miles.
On the way I met some soldiers, who had been
sent in quest of me, my disappearance having excited some alarm; and although my friend, the
Governor, was absent, his Vekil had sent parties
out in various directions to look for me.

Durazzo is a place, the importance of which is
illustrated by the historical events with which its
name is connected. Barlettius, the contemporary
historian of Scanderbeg, and who had seen Dyracchium at the closing scene of the drama of Rome,
thus describes it :—

" Dyracchium is the most ancient and powerful of the maritime towns of Illyria, fortified by
nature, and rendered impregnable by art. He who
sails by is struck, on looking on the height of the
walls, not only with admiration but with terror, for
it is surrounded by rocks and the sea, except
where it joins the land. Here is a most safe and
commodious port—here are ample and beautiful
plains, most fertile soil, and abundance of all
things—here are consecrated buildings, august and
sumptuous temples — here are to be seen the
images of kings and emperors, and the monuments
of their ancient princes. The Colossus (Colossus
ingens) of Hadrian, of cast metal, stands in a

lofty position at the Cavalha Gate. To the west there was, besides, an arena or amphitheatre, constructed with wonderful art and beauty, and walls strengthened and adorned with towers and splendid works: but it is particularly remarkable for its saltpans and convenience for commerce. This is that Dyracchium which saw the Roman senate, and was no less renowned than unhappy by civil blood and intestine war; and finally, what the greatness of this city has been—*ipsa ruina docet.*" But the ruins themselves have now ceased to teach.

The present Governor of Durazzo, although he knew not of the past splendour and prosperity of Dyracchium, although ignorant of the traffic here carried on by the Venetians, yet expressed himself respecting it in the following terms:—

" Along our western shore, which looks on Europe, we have not a single safe or convenient harbour; so that the peasantry, through all these districts, have to supply themselves from Monastir with goods, brought sometimes sixty days' mule carriage, ·from Leipsic, Constantinople, and Salonica. Durazzo only requires a mole to be run out from the horn of the at present exposed bay, to give shelter to large vessels within, and afford them, at the same time, the immense advantage of a mole for lading, which no port in Turkey, save Constantinople, possesses. This place is, besides, the centre of all communication by land; and from twenty to thirty hours, in all directions, the

roads are level, and might be easily rendered pass-
able for wagons. I would undertake to drain the
marshes, make three roads for that distance, and
construct the mole, if I were allowed for five years
to retain the customs of the now unfrequented
port, and the produce of the scarcely productive
salt-pans."

  'But,' I observed, ' if your government pursues the course it has commenced to adopt respect-
specting commerce, the mole, if built, would not
be much frequented. By your treaties with us,
three per cent is all you have a right to exact for
the entry of foreign merchandise ; and in this very
port you exact at present five per cent.' " I say,"
replied the Governor, " the three per cent is robbery ; because our harbours are filled up, our moles
ruined, for the support of which alone that per
centage is claimed. It is commerce alone that
gives *value to our possessions,* and turns our harvests into treasure. If a government affords it not
a shelter, a landing-place, nor a road, it certainly
has no right to fees or tolls." What would he
have said of a government whose *science* resides
in impeding commerce, either under the plea of
raising revenue, of improving prosperity, or of
protecting agriculture ?

  There was a shipment at the time proceeding
of most wretched tobacco, for the supply of the
Austrian monopoly of Italy, at the rate of rather
more than one halfpenny per pound. It is delivered

damp, ill made up, and in the worst possible state;
it heats on the passage very often, and has then to
be thrown overboard. I was expressing my surprise, that when the peasants were at the trouble
of sowing, reaping, and transporting tobacco for so
small a sum, they did not expend upon it the
additional labour necessary for drying and packing
it, which would more than double the value of the
article. The Bey answered (and to this answer I
beg particular attention), ' The care and labour
required to cultivate and prepare tobacco well are
very great; and how can these peasants expend
that labour upon it, when they have to grind their
corn, and to *manufacture their clothing, with the
rudest machinery ?*' He was of opinion, that if
England manufactured for the tastes of the people,
and if Turkey could venture to abolish the pro-
hibitions on exportation of her own produce,
which have been silently and one by one introduced,* England would have the entire supply-
ing of Turkey, and *Turkey would be benefited as
much as if one-fourth were added to her population.*

* The exportation from Turkey of all the articles which are
staple products of Russia is forbidden by the Turkish Government. They now feel the bearing of this suicidal measure, and
did hope, at one time, to obtain the concert and support of
England, so as to venture to abrogate it.

While correcting this sheet (July 18th), I observe, in the
correspondence from Constantinople, that, in spite, as I must
say, of the concert of England with Russia, Turkey has abolished
the prohibition of the exportation of grain.

On entering the town, I was stopped upon a narrow causeway by a string of mules laden with bales of Manchester goods and Birmingham wares: goods which figure in our exports to Austria, and which had been brought from Trieste in three vessels, then anchored in the bay, and which were to take back the tobacco to supply the Austrian Appalto of Italy. Such are the links that now bind Italy and Dyracchium. The bales of goods, however, and the ships in the bay, cast into the picture of the place some Western touches, which were multiplied in passing through the streets by the mean figures of European sailors and petti- fogging merchants. I felt quite ashamed of the quarter of the world to which I belonged, when I was told by the captain of the Albanian Guard that I would now find myself at home, as there were *compatriots* of mine in the place, and that the Consul was already prepared to receive me. *The* Consul! an Italian Consul at Dyracchium! the descendant, the representative, too, I suppose, of the first Cæsar, who here had intrusted his fortunes to a fishing-boat. Scarcely had this im- portant fact been communicated to me, when the Consul himself was announced; and hardly should I have been more surprised at the apparition of the ghost of the great Consul himself, than I was at the appearance of the representative of the house of Lorraine, vulgarly called Hapsburgh, who now stood before me! A red coat and a pair of

epaulettes were not enough to shadow forth the
dignity of this personage.   A cap of purple velvet,
embroidered with gold, was displayed in one hand,
held carefully by the lining, so as to exhibit without damaging its splendour; while in the other
dangled, with the apparent carelessness of an
every day companion, an elegant pouch of crimson and green velvet similarly embroidered on
the seams: containing, no doubt, a specimen of
the tobacco of which he was superintending the
shipment to the warehouses of his imperial master.
These Austrian consular costumes might furnish
an appendix to Sibthorpe's " Flora Græca;" no
doubt they astonish the natives very much, and
give them a high notion of the dignity of the
empire; certain it is, the wearers are enchanted
with them: and I have known one Austrian Consul, who, after investing himself with the prized
insignia, could not, for three successive days and
nights, be induced to relinquish one item of his
new wardrobe; surpassing the hardihood of the
knight of old, who did unbuckle a single spur
when inclined to unbend his knighthood.

   The dignified person in question soon communicated to me a vast mass of information.   He informed me that the Albanians deserved to be all
hanged; that the Greeks merited no better fate;
that the " poveri Turchi" were much to be pitied
between them; that the Grand Vizir had gained no
victories, obtained no success; but he gave me to

understand that, if *he* had only a few regiments of the Hungarians that were doing no good in Lombardy, he would put all things soon in order.

The Austrian agents, somehow or other, manage always to disgust the people amongst whom they reside,* as the government itself, with all its calmness and judiciousness, is always a decade in arrear of events. While the Austrian government counselled the Porte to that resistance, justifiable no doubt, but untimely with respect to the affair of Greece, which led to the war of 1828 and 1829, an Austrian Consul to render the Greeks as dissatisfied with Austrian views as the Turks had been with Austrian advice, declared that he "could no longer believe in a Divine Providence after the battle of Navarin !"

However, Austria had another sort of representative at Durazzo in the person of a young man, the agent of a commercial house at Trieste, who spoke fluently Greek, Albanian, Turkish,

* At the time this was written, I had only come in contact with Austrian Consuls of Gothic, and more especially of Italian origin; since then I have had the good fortune to know two or three Austrian Consuls of Sclavonian origin, whom I highly respect, and to whom I feel much indebted. A Sclavonian holds in the East a most commanding station, and possesses, without labour, the key of the Russian, the European, and, in some degree, of the Eastern mind; he is, also, invariably acquainted with the French, German, and some Sclavonic dialect, and with the literature of these people.

Bulgarian, and Wallachian; who frequentèd freely all the fairs of Roumeli, laughed at the alarms of Europeans, and assured me that he had never suffered molestation of any kind, and found in his European character (combined with a knowledge of the country), not only protection against the accidents of the times, but immunity from many of the inconveniences which native merchants had to endure. There were one or two other young men who travelled in the same way, and to the connexion thus established between Albania and Trieste, was owing the importation into the former from the latter of the English goods, the caravan of which I had met as I entered the town. English colonial produce, re-exported from the free port of Trieste to the coast of Albania, is smuggled into Hungary through Roumeli and Servia. This occurred during those times of trouble which would appear to put an end to all peaceable intercourse; two years later, I found at Widdin, coffee that had been transported across the country from Durazzo, in consequence of the tendency at Constantinople to imitate European customs, and to embarrass the operations of commerce.

The facilities, and the freedom enjoyed by the agents of these commercial houses, in the midst of war and revolution, is a valuable illustration of the habits of thought of Eastern countries; because the position of those persons here was not the consequence of any exceptional circumstances, it was merely the consequence of the rare fact of familiarity with the language, without which no useful intercourse of any kind can be practicable ;* and if there is one portion of the Ottoman dominions more than another where such an intercourse would offer little promise of reciprocal benefit, that portion certainly is Albania.

This circumstance recalled to me the conduct of the French merchants in Egypt. Previously to the expedition of Bonaparte, the Directory left no means untried to pick a quarrel with the Beys, and on withdrawing their Consul, ordered all the French merchants to retire. Some of them did so, but the major part refused to quit the country, and laughed at the representation of the government agent respecting the dangers to which they would be exposed when the regular protection of the nation should be withdrawn. This not suiting the views of the French Commissioners, and the merchants having expressed their determination of not quitting the country, these latter were denounced to the Egyptian authorities as disobedient subjects, in whom the Republic took no further interest; thus exciting the lawlessness or the avarice which they pretended to dread,

---

* Heeren, in speaking of Phœnician trade, remarks, that the advantage the Phœnicians enjoyed of transacting business " without the intervention of roguish interpreters, sufficed alone to give them the monopoly of the commerce of the Levant."

and which would have afforded to the French government some pretext for the greatest outrage on public justice which has occurred for centuries : namely, the invasion of Egpyt without declaration of war — an outrage unfelt in Europe, because its victims were the Turks.* The French merchants, to avoid the persecution of their countrymen, retired up the country to Cairo ; and there, unmolested, carried on the traffic up to the period of the invasion.†

When such is the conduct of warring Mamelukes, of rebel Arnaouts, towards unprotected European merchants, it may cease to be a matter of wonder that the Porte respected the rights of the British on the flight of Mr. Arbuthnot from Constantinople in 1807 ; or when, at a later period, the inconceivable policy in which we were plunged, forced the English Ambassador to abandon to their fate those of his compatriots whom he left behind him.

At Durazzo, for the first time, I heard of Mehemet Ali, as connected with the affairs of Albania. I got into conversation with a man whom I understood to be a Turkish merchant, but

* At the time of writing this, the events of Constantine, of the Texas, the affair of the Vixen, the blockade of the coasts of Mexico, and other occurrences indicating the extinction in this age of every sentiment of international right, had not occurred.

† See " Olivier's Travels."

our acquaintance having rapidly ripened into confidence, I learnt that he was one of those agents
whom the Porte employs, or rather whom influential members of the Divan employ to collect
information. In this capacity he had travelled
into Egypt, Arabia, and Bagdad, and was returning to his patron, the Grand Vizir, with an account
of these countries. I gathered from him what I
had subsequent opportunities of becoming well
acquainted with, the views of Reschid Pasha upon
Egypt. I had hitherto looked upon the war of
Albania as a finite object. Now the connexion
between the state of that country, and the destinies
of the whole empire, became practically evident,
I perceived that Reschid Pasha looked to drawing
large resources both in means and men from
subdued Albania, which should be directed to the
subjugation of Egypt. He had been defeated in
the object next to his heart — the reduction of
Greece—by the insubordination of the Albanians,
and by their settled resolution not to put an end
to a war which, to them, was an unceasing source
of pay, plunder, employment, and power; he
had now subdued Albania, and therefore could
have directed an overwhelming force against
Greece, but European diplomacy had stepped
in and closed against him, by an insuperable barrier, this career of greatness and renown. What
enterprise then presented itself worthy of the
position he had acquired? What field offered

itself to occupy that military spirit of the Albanians, which, if not directed now by the Porte, could scarcely be mastered by it, and would probably soon again be directed against it? Egypt was that field, and Mehemet Ali the rival, and the enemy of the Grand Vizir of old was an antagonist worthy of him. These ideas suggested themselves in consequence of the following answer, which I received from the secret emissary to the inquiries I made respecting the state of Egypt: " Mehemet Ali," he said, " has done well in every thing that he has created, ships, sailors, arsenal, and soldiers; but the poor are oppressed, and he neither has the hearts of his people, nor the name of the Sultan. His troops and his ships would beat ours, but if our Sadrazem were to appear in Egypt only with 10,000 men, Mehemet Ali's troops and ships would be his, and he would not find a mountain to fly to, and has not a tribe to defend him."

My horizon was thus suddenly extended, not that a great deal of uncertainty did not overhang these lucubrations, but that uncertainty was to be dispelled by a trifling incident which occurred in paying for the horses which were to take me to Scodra — I *received the change in Egyptian coin.* Whence did this money come? The troops mustered against the Grand Vizir by Mustapha Pasha had been partly paid with this money, incurring, of course, a considerable loss in the exchange. Me-

hemet Ali had then a strong presentiment of the
views of the Grand Vizir and of his own danger,
and had made this sacrifice, precipitate and lavish
as the mode shewed it to be, to prevent the subjugation of Albania, and to occupy there the Grand
Vizir. I was now, of course, ready to prophesy the
affairs of Syria, and the news of the attack of Acre
was scarcely a novelty. But, good God! what was
English diplomacy about?

Full of these ideas, I wended my way from
Durazzo northward along the coast. From Berat,
northward, the country may be called champaign.
The plains form basins, bounded by low argil-
laceous hills. The limit of this formation, to the
north, is the chains of Leche, Croia, and Gova,
bearing N. and W., S. and E., dipping to the
E. N. E., and exactly corresponding with the chains
of Argyro Castro and Longaria. This limestone
formation, described at Argyro Castro, has been
broken in fragments, and is scattered over the face
of the country, from Scodra down to the Gulf of
Lepanto. It is distinct from the central range of
the Pindus, against which it sometimes rests: it
dips, in Middle Albania, to the north and east, and
in Acarnania, to the east. To the north of Argyro
Castro, on the back and on the face of these eleva-
tions, rests a formation of mixed aluminous shale
and slate; some layers are very soft, and decom-
pose readily into clay. Thus, all the valleys and
plains, and even the sides of the hills, are covered

with clay. To the north of Leche, where the Drin bursts through the hills, this formation does not accompany the limestone, which here wears the aspect of the uninteresting limestone of the Morea, not being of the fine lithographic grain parallelly stratified, and alternating with silex, consequently not forming bold and picturesque escarpments; which appearance (being, in that case, accompanied by the aluminous formation) is indicative of fertility, wood and water. Over this whole tract of country are scattered some other strata; but of no mineralogical or agricultural interest: they are a sandstone (near Delvino), sand and shale (Glava), breccia and amigdaloid. On an insulated mass of the latter is seated the Castle of Argyro Castro; but nowhere are any traces of organic remains to be found. The appearance of the country, from the loftiest ridges, is that of an ocean, with the waves of the limestone rolling after one another. Towards the west the plains exhibit from below a perfectly levelled surface, from which the hills and mountains, as it were, detach themselves, as islands or coasts, springing from the sea. Between the larger ranges, the aluminous formations are cast about in all directions, forming dunes and monticules of most exquisite beauty, insulated in groups, or stretching in straight lines, or forming the first steps to the mountains.

These three days I have been riding or walking along, enjoying the most pleasing and agreeable

sensations;—the mildness and softness of the
climate—the scenery of extended plains or bold
mountains, " wild, but not rude"— the richest
possible soil; forests no longer in their pride and
stateliness, but romantic in their mossy and de-
crepid age, over which the creepers of the cle-
matis, wild vine, eglantine, and bramble, hang
like roofing, weighing down their branches, or en-
circling their broken trunks; the huts of the
scanty peasants, made of wicker, as also the reservoirs for the Indian corn, of all sizes and shapes,
covered or thatched with the broad and husky leaves
of the maize, looked like grotesque baskets, deposited by some giant hand in the open spaces.
Here is to be found every element for a new settlement: vicinity to Europe —facility for the construction of roads —marshes, indeed, and ague,
there are, but those could easily be drained, and
these would disappear, while the discharges would
serve for harbours for the small coasting craft —
fertility that cannot be surpassed — a climate for
every richest produce, where a long torpid winter
consumes not the produce of the summer; now,
in December, every field was verdant.   Oak for
use—platani for shade—game for luxury—wild
vines for grafting, but withal large spaces cleared,
and now serving for pasturage — excellent breeds
of sheep and horses, and an immediate demand
on the spot — wicker and rushes for domestic
uses, and, if stones are distant, every where ex-

cellent clay for bricks, tiles, and vessels. This
district, unlike the relics of Ali Pasha's satrapy,
has not suffered from the ten years' anarchy that
followed his fall. Here Turks and Christians wear
arms, and are more equally balanced : it is at present a waste, from long innate barbarism and
Illyrian dulness. The servility of the Greek, the
lawlessness of the Albanian, differences owing to
their castes, are redeemed by an extraordinary intelligence and acuteness. But when you have
crossed the Beratino—Guegues, Merdites, Greeks,
Latins, and Turks, without the excesses, without the
anarchy or hate of the former, are pervaded by an
absorbing spirit of stupidity and barbarism, which
the traveller feels in every house he enters, every
shepherd he questions, every transaction, great or
small, that brings him unwillingly in contact with
them. The traveller, I say ; but when, heretofore,
has a traveller ventured his " plachica," or his neck,
amid these lawless tribes? They tell me of one
twenty-four years ago. However, send off Ibrahim
Bey of Cavalha and all his race, and a few other
chiefs; disarm them, and they will make good
beasts of burden: they are at present terror-
stricken, and this is the first step. The name of
the Grand Vizir is a talisman ; but he is sadly deficient in men capable of making that talisman
efficacious for good. If it is his fate to live for five
or six years, and if the good stars of this land
preserve him in the same mind till the youth are

somewhat formed, this country is regenerated. His life would be long, if the prayers of the Rayah avail. In one place they said to me, "May God take five years from each of our lives to add to his!" May he merit the holy aspiration, re-echoed as it is, whenever the local governor understands his views and effects his purposes, *but only then.*

Dec. 24th.—Here am I, at length, at Scodra. Now, like Sterne at Calais, I can assure myself that no future event whatever can prevent me from having been here. When I look at the map, and run over Argyro Castro, Delvino, Tepedelene, Berat, Scodra, I can scarcely congratulate myself enough on having visited these spots I have so often traced on the same map with so much longing, but so little hope to visit.

CHAPTER XXI.

SCODRA.

It is only one who has mingled in the events of the Greek and Albanian wars who can understand the feelings with which I found myself in Scodra. There, in a fortress supposed impregnable, guarded round by impassable mountains, resided, on the very limits of the Turkish world, a chief whose character was involved in mystery, but whose power was indisputable, and whose election seemed decisive of the various struggles which agitated the country to the south.

The Pasha of Scodra was claimed by all parties in turn as their ally, and by all parties was he dreaded. The Greeks never wearied in their relations of the devastation which had marked the track of his crimsoned Guegues and his black Mirdites; yet they admitted that, under his mild and paternal sway, the Christian was equal with the Turk; and, indeed, Christians had formed the bulk of the army which had followed his standard to Greece. The Albanians considered him as the chief and head of their race, as the most potent chieftain of Turkey, and whose family, for two hundred years, had maintained their sovereignty in defiance of the Sultan. Yet he had marched into Greece with a view of effecting this purpose of the Sultan, and would have done so but for the treachery of the Albanians, who sacrificed his army. These wrongs, and the willing, though very inefficient, support which he had given to the Grand Vizir in his first operations against Albania, justified the assertions of the Turk that he was their ally; that it was in his power to render triumphant the party he espoused, was evident from the strength he put forth, and which he used so ill, after the Grand Vizir had triumphed, first over Aslan Bey, and, secondly, over Selictar Poda. It was said, when Mustafa Pasha mustered his followers, every gun fired from the battlements of Scodra was a signal for a hundred men to gather under his standard; and the bards of Albania told how seven hundred signal guns of his grandfather, Geraldin Pasha, had collected seven hundred times a hundred followers, whose devotion had saved their chief from the Grand Vizir of the Sultan, and their country from the devastating incursions of the Bosniacs and Servians.

As I looked on the ruined towers of this rebel chief, little did I anticipate the feelings of esteem and regard which I should one day entertain for his amiable character and refined mind. It would be curious to contrast my impressions respecting him at that time with a recent period, when, after a long absence, he met me with fraternal greeting, and led me into his library to see an excellent assortment of French books, which he said he had placed there to overcome his natural indolence of disposition, and to spur him to the study of the French language, by the sight of the treasures he possessed, and could not use.*

But associated with the Fortress of Scodra were other remembrances scarcely less interesting, illustrated, as it had been, by the heroism of a Loridano, and by the frustration of the military genius, and the discomfiture of the martial pomp and power of the conquering Mahomet.

In approaching Scodra from the south, both the town and the lake are hidden by the ridge, the summit of which is crowned by the castle. There is a suburb, however, to the south, called " The Gardens," where a few of the most respectable houses are situated, scattered amongst gardens, and overshadowed by a grove of fruit-trees and stately chestnuts. In the skirts of this suburb

---

* Mustafa Pasha had opened at Scodra his valuable library to the public; any one could borrow books, leaving a receipt for them. Before abandoning his pashalic, he constituted this library Vacouf, that it might be consecrated to the same purpose. When, subsequently, the Sultan offered him a pashalic in Asia, he replied, that he would rather have the command of a printing press.

were the breaching-batteries, and, between them
and the base of the hill, a small plain of four or
five hundred yards, encircled by a bend of the river
Dreno. Reschid Pasha's quarters were unremoved
from this suburb, where they had been established
previous to the surrender of the castle. The town,
lying below the castle on the other side, between
it and the lake, was afflicted by the cholera, so that
the principal persons were lodged in the few houses
that still remained erect, and roofed, in the
suburb of "The Gardens." The Grand Vizir would
not suffer me to go into the town, but ordered me
to be received in the house of the Mollah or
Imaum, which had not been occupied by any of
the pashas or officers out of respect to the character of its possessor; and here I was served from
the Vizir's kitchen.

I was all anxiety, of course, to find some of my
old friends. While my baggage was depositing,
and a room preparing for me by the active hospitality of the Imaum, I wandered into the garden.
The indiscriminating shots of Mustafa Pasha
having opened free passage into the neighbouring
enclosure, I ventured through, and, coming upon
an old dilapidated hovel, on which several shots
had done their worst, I perceived, to my infinite
surprise and delight, looking through a small window, my old friend, Gench Aga, whose timely escort
had saved me from the hands of the bandits on
the Pindus, and who had been the higher agent in

the tragic plot which had concluded with the common destruction of Veli and Aslan Bey. The old man's surprise surpassed, as may well be supposed, my own. He came running down the ladder, which served him for stairs, took me in his arms, kissed me on the forehead, poured out a thousand inquiries, without giving me time to answer one, and during my stay at Scodra his time was almost entirely spent as my guest at the Imaum's abode, for which he was glad to exchange his own miserable quarters, and not more attractive fare; and yet he was no less a man than Tufenkj Bashi of the Grand Vizir, and Deputy Governor of Thessaly.

I staid but ten days at Scodra; but a couple of volumes would scarcely suffice to detail all the interest of that sojourn. Here were assembled the chief men of the party of the Grand Vizir, the relicts of the different factions subdued by him; men of distinction from every part of Roumeli, and also from Anatoli, and all these collected in thirty or forty houses, standing close to each other, where, from morning to night, we were constantly mingling; and where my position was so very different from that in which a traveller from the West is usually placed, mistrusted without the means of direct communication, without sufficient knowledge to interest them in discussion, and therefore unheeded and unknown. If now, for the first time, I had landed in the East, or if in travelling through it, I had not mingled in their wars and dangers,

I should have found myself in the midst of a
scene most interesting, indeed, to the eyes, but
where I should have been absolutely interdicted
from all intercourse of thought. As it was, how
different was my position! Wherever I went to
pay a visit, the house was immediately crowded;
when I returned home, I found visitors waiting
me; when I proposed an excursion, companions
presented themselves. The young Beys were full
of the adventures of the late wars, replete with
interest and diversity. The soberer minds looked
to the political changes to be effected in the policy
or the administration of the empire; and, as if
these subjects did not suffice, we had the position
and the character of the populations of the Pashalic
of Scodra, of the Bosnians, Montenegrins, and
Servians, supplied by people from those countries,
or governors who had resided there. But two
paramount feelings cast a tint over all their
opinions; and, whatever subject was commenced,
to one or other of these did the conversation
revert. The one — the political regeneration of
Turkey — which was dwelt on with an enthusiasm
really affecting in the midst of a camp, and in the
hour of victory. The other — England. How
often in a whisper, and under promise of secrecy,
have I been questioned with regard to the expense
of going to England! The interest thus excited
about England might certainly have had its immediately exciting cause in my previous visit to the

country, and the habit into which they had got of talking about Englishmen, and now by this second visit. But of this I am certain, that a native of any other European country, whatever the consideration in which he might have been held, would never have had the pride and satisfaction of seeing those feelings turn from himself to his country. Austria and France are the only two nations which, of course, could enter into competition with us in point of influence and consideration. Now Austria inspires no Eastern population with respect. France formerly enjoyed paramount influence* throughout the whole of the East. The invasion of Egypt as a fact, but far more the mode of that invasion—a buccaneer expedition, destitute of the forms consecrated by the invariable practice of mankind—has left a stain on the character and the honour of France, which centuries will not efface from the memory of the East. The common epithet, " Kandgik Fransiz," dates from this event.

These feelings were now revived by the connexion of France with Mehemet Ali, and by the occupation of Algiers, which they consider no less an outrage on the rights of nations than the former expedition to Egypt, while it possessed characters

---

* Before Napoleon, Louis XIV. was the only European sovereign that so far valued the opinion of the East as to seek to make himself respected among them. He had a history of his wars translated into Arabic.

of a baser description, in the robbery of the public treasury, the violation of private property, and the religious fanaticism which they conceived to be the motive for acts of another description, which brought no advantage to the victors. All the details of the expedition, and the subsequent conduct of the French, were repeated from mouth to mouth, and public indignation was excited throughout the empire by the emigrants from Algiers. They contrasted our conduct with that of France formerly in Egypt, and more recently in Algiers.* The first it was that gave to the East an idea of the power of England; the latter it is which has established her character for integrity and justice. " You had a right," they said, " to attack Algiers, because of the piracies which she committed; in four hours you levelled its battlements with the ground; and, having extirpated the evil, you sought neither to acquire that which was not your own, nor to injure those you had vanquished."

With respect to our immediate policy as regards Turkey, contemptible as it has been, it has never exhibited either duplicity or design.† Discussing the subject with Turks, it is easy to bring them to see that the fault lies at their door more than at ours. They were ready to admit that their haughty manners towards us personally had hitherto prevented our travellers and residents from receiving ac-

* Also the occupation of Dalmatia by Napoleon.

† This, it must be recollected, was only at the commencement of 1832.

curate ideas, and impressed them with feelings of ill-will, while they had taken no pains to open direct communications with us; and, consequently, in these European complications, where they were unrepresented both in the presence of public opinion and diplomacy, they appeared as an accused man before his judges, who condemn him, on the testimony of his adversary, because he holds his tongue.

Such were the subjects of daily discussion which presented themselves in a thousand new forms, and of which the record can be but faint and unsatisfactory. I will conclude this chapter with the opinions of a Turk on the press.

Talking with Negib Bey, whom I had formerly known at Larissa, on the different changes that had taken place since we had parted, we came to the Turkish newspaper, on the advantages of which he summed up thus:—

" It lets us know the price of corn and several other things, and this is an inestimable benefit; it lets us know the quantities furnished by the different commissariats. Young soldiers are excited, by seeing those that distinguish themselves having their names recorded in print, and read by every high functionary in the empire; and who would expose himself to be branded with infamy before such a company? In Turkey, we all know well enough what is right, though we very seldom do it; and we will be all improved by reading the

z 2

good deeds of others. It is very true, we might find examples among our forefathers, but present example is warmer.

" The learned Alwakidi tells us, that he who is acquainted with former events raises his mind, and prolongs his existence; but how many are there amongst us, that know perfectly the history of Omer and Osman, that know not that of Mach-moud: while we extend existence backward, it would be more useful to extend it to the present time, and to understand something of the age in which we live, as well as of the age of our great-great-grandfathers. Here (in the newspaper) we have information about Frangistan, about the Jeni Dunia (America), which is very useful. If my neighbour gets more corn from his land than I do, I would be a fool not to go and sit at his chiftlik and learn something. When we see your ships, your guns, the cloth you wear (passing his hand over my coat), and hear and feel the effects of your power, should we not wish to know how all this is come to you; for are we not all men alike, and have all one friend in Allah, and one foe in Shaitan? Now, this paper will instruct us about these things, and those that can read it will ex-plain it to others, and will be justly proud of their instruction; while the man that cannot read, and thinks his pistol better than his pen, will be con-sidered, as he is, no better than a brute. When this happily takes place, other books besides this will be as cheap by the *basma*,* so that they may be as common."

" We will know what men ought to know, and by becoming a wiser, we will be a happier people. How many men, that sit idle all the day, either cannot read, or cannot afford books, or if they can afford them, cannot get any to buy, or not such as please them ! It is with books as with friends; a man who has seen the world will choose a good friend, and no man, who can have the company of wise and pleasant men, will sit by himself. Books are the friendly parts of the souls of all the wise men that have ever lived ; their tongues are cold, but their thoughts live and are multiplied ; and when we have these within every man's reach, the whole people will have gained wise counsellors and pleasant companions, and what it is now an honour to know, it will then be a disgrace not to know."

---

* This is both a metaphor and a Turkish pun, *basma* (print) being applied equally to printed paper and cotton ; the cheapness and fineness of our prints has superseded their cottons, stamped or painted by the hand.

CHAPTER XXII.

MILITARY MOVEMENTS—DEFEAT OF THE PASHA OF SCODRA.

I MUST now narrate the circumstance of the struggle which ended by the fall of Scodra.

During the last Russian campaign, the Pasha of Scodra was led by Diebitch to believe that the Russians marching to Constantinople, he would remain independent Prince of his own province, with accessions of territory and influence, if not authority, over the Beys of Albania; and the Russians were suffered to pass the Balcan unmolested. Finding, at the treaty of Adrianople, that they had been deceived, Mustafa Pasha saw, when too late, the error he durst not avow; and it required the intervention of the Porte to prevent his falling on the Russians subsequently to the conclusion of the treaty. The compromised chiefs then perceived that their only chance of escape, from the slow but sure vengeance of the Porte, was a united effort against it, under cloak of a difference with the Grand Vizir. The Pasha of Bagdad was joined in this league, so that the empire was at once threatened from the north, west, the east, and the south.   Mahomed Ali contributed towards the rising of Albania, the sacs of Egyptian coin; some of which I had received in change at Durazzo.

After allowing the Albanians to be singly over-powered, after having even assisted in their de-struction, he raised himself from his lethargy, and marched, at the head of thirty thousand Guegues, against the Grand Vizir, who was awaiting, at Monastir, the return of his troops from the south, to concentrate and direct his efforts against Scodra.

Monastir, or Bitolia, is the long-established seat of the chief Governor of Turkey in Europe, the centre of all the communications of Roumeli.   It commands, with Ochrida and the surrounding Der-vends, the lofty ridges, and the stronger passes of the chains which here bisect each other.   This was the position chosen by Mehemet Rechid, the Grand Vizir, for his head-quarters, menacing Il-lyria and the Pasha of Scodra to the north, Epirus and the Albanians to the south; and hence, with-out risking his person among these intricate passes, he could act on the turbulent and jealous con-federacy of his Albanian antagonists, while he secured a place of retreat in case of disaster; while he overawed the disaffected of Macedonia, kept open the communications with Constantinople, he kept in countenance the Pasha of Scodra, whom, by the possession of the Castle of Berat, he cut off from the Albanians; or, in the event of his march-

ing to their assistance, he could secure himself in
the adjoining fortresses of Ochrida Castoria and
Geortcha, and in the mountains to the south of
the Tomarus. The position, therefore, of Monastir was all-important, and, it will be readily
supposed, that every effort was made to strengthen
and provision it.

At the moment of Mustafa Pasha's expedition, the affairs of the Grand Vizir were as follows :—About eight thousand men (regulars) were
in Chamouria, completing its subjugation; about
as many more were employed in garrisoning the
different fortresses occupying the Dervends, and
securing the communications from Janina to Berat,
from Berat to Iscup, and from Iscup to Salonica.
The whole district contained within this pentagon
might be considered hostile country : he was himself at head-quarters, reduced to, at the very utmost, five thousand regulars (though disciplined,
they could not be called so), and about fifteen
hundred Albanians, whose fidelity could not but
be doubtful. With this handful of men he had to
garrison the neighbouring fortresses, and to over-
awe the inhabitants of Monastir itself; which,
without any fortification, contained an armed population that outnumbered this reserve, and who
but awaited the march of Mustafa Pasha, to rise
upon him. Add to these disheartening circumstances, want of provisions, deficiency of ammunition, and, at the most eventful juncture of all, a

military chief without a single para.   In this situation, the alarming intelligence of the march of Mustafa was almost immediately followed by that of his occupation of Perlipe, a town distant eight hours .only from Monastir.   Had he pushed on to Monastir, the secret confederates of the insurgents would have declared for them throughout Roumeli; perhaps in Asia, Daoud Pasha, of Scodra, and Mehemet Ali Pasha, would have seized the moment for action, and universal anarchy might have led to final dismemberment; but Mustafa Pasha, astonished at the facility of his first operation—totally deficient in military capacity, as in personal activity—deemed three days but a short respite from his fatigues, to enjoy his young conquering honours : these three days, devoted to festivity and the bath, were far differently employed by the genius of his antagonist.   Mehemet Rechid Pasha assembled a divan of the Monastir Beys, and delivered an address to them, which, as described to me by one of those present, " combined a prophet's truth, a martyr's firmness, with a woman's persuasion." He said to them, " I appeal neither to your allegiance as subjects, nor your faith as Mussulmans; I can hold out neither rewards to the obedient, nor threats to the refractory.   I have called you together, not to tell you what you ought to do, but to know from you what you intend to do.   As a private man amongst private men, I will tell you the state in which the empire is, and, as your determination shall be, I shall conquer or fall with you in a last effort, or I will quietly go my way, not uselessly waste our own and our fellow-creatures' blood." He concluded as follows :—" It is but a very few months since you allowed Russia to inflict an almost incurable wound on the empire, and an indelible stain on the Ottoman name. And how were you repaid? She despised you too much, to prolong the deception a moment beyond the completion of her immediate purpose. The man must be a fool, who does not see that Russia excites our mutual dissensions but for our common destruction: he amongst you must be mad, who does not see that, as chiefs of your race, all you possess will be lost by anarchy. The election you have to make, make it freely, but don't deceive yourselves ;—it is not between me and the Pasha of Scodra, it is between Turkey and Russia. If for the latter, there is no time for protestations: tell me at once, and within this hour, Shall the triumph of Mustafa Pasha and anarchy be complete? My horses are ready, and with those who are resolved to follow my fortunes, I shall soon be on the road to Constantinople." The dignity, the eloquence of the man, the memory and compunctions of the last campaign, the exposition of the pending crisis, filled the assembly with one spirit: a burst of enthusiasm interrupted his address; they fell at his feet, embraced his knees, called him their saviour and their father; conjured him not to abandon them; and declared their eagerness to shed the last drop of their blood in his defence.

He next assembled the Greek Primates. With them few words were necessary : in the impending prospect of anarchy from the success of the insurgents, all vague and distant thoughts of Russian protection were completely absorbed ; besides, new hopes had begun to dawn for them, and the even-handed justice of the Grand Vizir had already secured their affection and devotion. He merrily said, " Scodra Pasha is at Perlipe, and my chest is empty." Few in number, and exhausted by ten years of warfare, little assistance was to be expected from them ; but a crowning effort was now to be made, and it was nobly made ; the women collected their remaining ornaments ; the children cut from their hair and caps the gold coin that adorned them, and in a short time 250,000 piastres were collected, and presented to the Grand Vizir, of which he only accepted 100,000, six mules, with treasure, having just arrived from Constantinople. This sum was punctually repaid; and 80,000 piastres were presented to them subsequently, toward the building of their church. The Grand Vizir had only now to assume a bold countenance. Several guns were dragged up an eminence that commands the town; and he declared that he should lay it in ashes on the slightest movement of the inhabitants. The third day after

the arrival of Mustafa at Perlipe, and the eve
of his intended march on Monastir, the Vizir ordered the whole of his troops for a grand review.
They proceeded from plain to plain, forming, de-
filing; but the Vizir still continued to advance
until sunset, when he established himself on the
bank of a rivulet eight miles from Monastir. The
chiefs and soldiers now crowded round him, to
know what was to be done, and to inquire where
the review (atesh talim) was to take place. He
calmly answered, " My children, I will review you
at Perlipe." Such was the confidence inspired
into his followers by the firmness and talents of
this extraordinary man, that the intimation of a
struggle so disproportionate, and which left no
alternative between victory and destruction, was
received with a shout of exultation; and, strange
to say, not a man was found to carry the news of
his approach to Perlipe.

After two hours' rest, they were again in motion; and at dawn they were before Perlipe. The
Pashas were in the bath, where they had passed
the night; the troops were scattered through the
town. The news of the approach of the Grand
Vizir spread from street to street, like the news of
a conflagration. They hastily quitted the town,
and on the outside collected, in presence of the
handful of regulars. The Grand Vizir immediately
remarked the importance of some broken and
stony ground on his right, within musket-range

of the wings of both armies.   He despatched his
Albanians, above 1000, to occupy it, supported
by a regiment, to ensure their fidelity.   The
Guegues of Mustafa allowed them quietly to
occupy their ground, waving their handkerchiefs,
in token of friendship.   But, no sooner had the
Albanians opened their fire, than the Guegues, ex-
ásperated at the advantage they had suffered their
enemy to take, made a tumultuous rush towards
the eminence occupied by the Albanians.   A regiment (tambour) rapidly advanced from the front
of the Grand Vizir.   The Guegues, throwing away
their discharged muskets, now turned towards their
new antagonists with brandished yatagans and loud
yells.   The regulars, with astonishing firmness,
halted, reserved their fire, and received the charge
with a close and deadly discharge.   For a moment
the Guegues stood still—their shouts were silenced;
they then precipitately retreated to the main body.
Two partial charges were subsequently made, and
similarly received by this single regiment; and
then might be seen the crimson robes and glittering arms of this vast horde scattered over the
plain to the north, in full retreat.   But so weak
in numbers were the victors — so essential to their
preservation, amid their routed foes, was their
order and compactness — that the Grand Vizir
had to restrain the ardour of his men, and break
off a pursuit which, if continued to the passes of

Baboussa, might have irrevocably dispersed the
insurgent gathering.

In these strong defiles (Baboussa), the Guegues
halted, and immediately commenced to fortify themselves. The Grand Vizir had gained a victory, but
his position was not less precarious than before ;
difficulties and dangers multiplied around him ;
delay must be followed by a general insurrection ;
and an attack on Mustafa Pasha, with such odds
of numbers and position, he deemed a perfectly
desperate alternative,—but it was the only one.

Ten days after this brilliant affair, he led his
troops, flushed with their former easy success, and
full of contempt for their adversaries, to the foot
of the hill and gorge occupied by the Guegues. A
bold but ineffectual attack was made : new troops
succeeded to the first with no better success ; the
confidence of the regulars was gone ; many had
fallen, and the slightest demonstration of the
enemy would have struck them with panic. The
Grand Vizir gave up all for lost, raved in despair,
and tore his beard. A monastery overhanging
the pass had principally caused the failure of the
assailants. A Greek captain, from Chamouni,
offered, with 300 Christians, to carry it, or perish
in the attempt. The offer was joyfully accepted ;
and the small band, fetching a circuit to the left,
were soon seen scaling the rocks above the monastery. Cheered by the shouts from below, they

forced the monastery from above; while, at the same moment, the regulars made a general and desperate charge. Reserving their fire till they reached the summit, they knelt on the breastwork, and poured it, with dreadful effect, into the crowded tambour. A scene of carnage, frightful, but short, ensued. Hemmed in by the narrow gorge, retreat cut off by the masses behind, and the difficulty of the ground, they threw away their arms, and unresistingly submitted to their fate. Here the victors halted: their ranks had been thinned by a victory which had cost them more blood than it had cost the vanquished; indeed, they scarcely yet could believe the day their own, and commenced preparations for defence. Some time afterwards, seeing nothing of the enemy, a body was sent to reconnoitre their camp, and found it deserted.

The incapacity and inactivity of the rebel chief had already disgusted many of his followers. During this last affair, he had remained, several miles in the rear of his troops, at a Khan, where he had pitched a splendid tent, taken by his grandfather from a Vizir sent against Scodra. The tent had formerly belonged to the Sultan. When at length convinced that all was lost by the revilings of the fugitive Pashas—for six Pashas had espoused his cause,—he set fire to his tent, mounted his horse, and returned, quietly to shut himself up in one of the bomb-proof dungeons of his castle.

The Grand Vizir pushed on to Kiupreli, to gratify his troops with its plunder. It was deserted by the male Turkish inhabitants; but the women had ventured to remain, trusting to the sanctity of the harem. The Cadi also had remained, trusting to that of his office: those talismans had now lost their charm. The women—a sacrilege hitherto unheard of—were dragged from their retreats, and the mutilated body of the Cadi was thrown into the streets; affording another proof, in these unbridled moments, of the breaking up of the old barriers that contained and directed Turkish opinion. The Governor of Kiupreli, forming a reckoning with the Grand Vizir, took poison.

In concluding this rapid sketch of the last effort of Albania, I have no common satisfaction in having to record the following noble trait.

The Chamouriote captain, whose gallant conduct I have mentioned in the abandonment of Kiupreli to plunder, requested, as sole recompense for his services, the preservation of a neighbouring Greek village from the same doom. His request was granted, and he established himself in it with his men, while the rest of the troops were busied in collecting booty; and, in defending it from his fellow-soldiers, lost more men than he had lost in capturing the monastery.

Encouraged by success, the Grand Vizir seems to have imagined the subjugation of Bosnia as a result of his Albanian triumph, rather than a new and distinct enterprise; so, scarcely allowing his troops breathing time, and even before Scodra was invested, he led them to Iscup, from thence to commence operations against Bosnia.   The advanced guard, under Chor Ibrahim and Hadji Achmet Pashas, had penetrated into the defiles beyond Batac; and, with the main body, he followed them close.   The plan of the Bosnians was to allow him to engage himself amongst the mountains, retiring before him, and then to occupy the passes in his rear—notably, " the stone of Cachanic," fatal to Murad II.; then surround and starve, or cut him off in detail.   Want of combination frustrated this scheme, into which the Grand Vizir threw himself with headlong impetuosity.   Before the " stone" was occupied, the vanguard was attacked and dispersed; seven guns were taken.   The fugitives awoke even then the Grand Vizir with difficulty to a sense of his error and his danger; but, with his ordinary good fortune, by a precipitate flight he passed the defile before it was occupied, and reached Iscup, unattended and in the night, before the news of his disaster; which, in all probability, would have closed its gates against him.

The Grand Vizir now concentrated his forces against Scodra, and besieged it in form.   Mustafa Pasha, seeing his resources annihilated, and his expectations disappointed, opened communications with the Sultan, revealed the treasonable projects

of Mehemet Ali Pasha, and offered to open the
gates of his castle to Achmet Pasha, the private
secretary of the Sultan, if he were sent to Scodra;
and this surrender was accordingly made, about
the period of my landing in Albania. Mustafa
Pasha accompanied Achmet Pasha to Constantinople, was pardoned, and subsequently received
into favour.

CHAPTER XXIII.

RECHID MEHEMET PASHA—SADRAZEM.

To describe the person or the character of the Grand Vizir, Rechid Mehemet Pasha, is no easy task.   I shall commence with a few incidents of his life.

He is by birth a Christian, the son of a Georgian priest.   In his infancy, he became a slave of Hussef Pasha, the octogenarian Seraskier.   At an early period he embraced Islamism; his fiery spirit not brooking the exclusion from the higher career of arms and power.   The relationship which I have to express by the words "slave" and "master" is perfectly distinct from that which such would suggest to a Western reader.   The youthful foreigner from Circassia, Georgia, Yemen, or Abyssinia, purchased into the Turkish family, has no more menial offices to perform than the children of the house: he receives the same education that they do.   The Beiram sees him clothed in a new dress, as gay and gaudy as theirs; and the deference and attentions which the little, so termed, "slave," is taught to pay, from his tenderer

years, to his playmates and his masters, is scarcely
greater than the younger of these has to pay to his
elder.   The slave thus becomes the brother of his
master's children,—the husband, perchance, of his
daughter,—and, not unfrequently, the support of
his decaying years, and the prop of his house.
His slaves are invariably conducive to the success of every man who walks the higher career
of honours and distinction.   They are selected
with care—promoted after trial.   They increase
the numbers of his family; while, as devoted to
their chief, and as intimately connected in interest
as a son, they offer greater docility and pliability
of disposition, and may be displaced in case of
incapacity or error.

The Seraskier Pasha, to whom the Sultan himself applies the name of father, was originally a
Christian and a Georgian slave; and now the
highest dignitaries of the Empire, Halil Pasha
for instance, and Said Pasha, ·the sons-in-law of
the Sultan, have been slaves of the Seraskier.

There was nothing, therefore, in the designation of slave, then applied to the young, brave,
and handsome Rechid Mehemet, which barred
his approach to the highest dignities to which
his youthful imagination might aspire; nothing
degrading to that consciousness of superiority of
powers of mind and body which is of little avail,
if the oracular lispings of future greatness are
silenced in their pregnant promptings by the

sullen conviction of the impossibility of attainment. No such desponding hopelessness checks the young conceptions, not of the son of the Turkish freeman, but of the Turkish slave.   The consciousness of no impassable line or inaccessible elevation causes the prophetic fondness of the mother's vows to falter on her tongue.

Rechid Mehemet in the year 1820 had attained the rank of Pasha, and had been named Vali, or Governor of Bolu ; and, under the orders of Ismail Pasha, carried his contingent to the siege of Ali Tepedelene at Yanina.   Subsequently to the fall of that chief, he was promoted to the Pashalik of Kutayah, where it fell to his lot to put in execution the final decree of the Sultan against Veli Pasha, the son of Ali, and his family. Veli Pasha was executed ; but a timely intimation having been conveyed to his two fine boys, they took refuge in the harem of Reschid Pasha, who thus, from executioner, became their protector.

After the extirpation of the Pasha of Dama and his army, on the shores of the Gulf of Lepanto, Rechid Mehemet Pasha was called to the command of the war in Greece ; and then commenced that long interchange of wrong and treachery between him and the Albanians.   To him, however, surrendered Missolonghi ; to him surrendered Athens ; and to him was owing the salvation of the retiring garrison.   When the Greeks, after evacuating the citadel, were approaching the Piræus to embark, a body of

unruly Chaldoups shewed manifest signs of an intention to make a dash at them, when Rechid Mehemet Pasha struck his stirrups into his charger's
side, and, cutting across the path of the advancing
horde, levelled the foremost with his pistol, and
the second with his sabre.   On this very spot,
two years afterwards, three hundred Turks, marching forth under safe conduct from the cannonaded
convent of the Piræus, were suddenly fallen upon
and massacred by the Greeks.   Reshid Pasha
thus has figured in the histories of Greece under
three different names — Rechid Mehemet Pasha,
Kutayah Pasha, and Seraskier Pasha, or com-
mander-in-chief.

     After the battle of Navarin, the Porte, aroused
at once by exasperation and alarm, thought again
on Rechid Pasha : he received the rank of Roumeli Valessi, or superior governor of Southern
European Turkey, with the joint object of bring-
ing the strength of the remainder of Roumeli to
bear upon Albania, and of compelling the Albanians to a last effort to re-occupy that portion of
continental Greece which had been occupied by
the Greeks about the period of the battle of
Navarin, and the decision respecting which by
the conference of London was still uncertain.

     All his efforts, however, proved fruitless.   The
hostility of the Albanians had now become loud
and universal.   They were exasperated by the
emancipation of Greece, and they despised the
Sultan, whose authority throughout the whole

of European Turkey was next to annihilated by
the hostility of the great powers of Europe, added
to the lowering signs of another storm about to
burst from the north.   There were no elements of
any kind to work upon ; there were no cords to
touch, no means of producing effect, and every
door to action closed.   He totally failed in establishing order, was unable to move a single Albanian against Greece ;' and, bearded and insulted by
the Albanians, he was obliged, as I have already
stated, to make his escape by night in a fishing-
boat from Prevesa.   These circumstances overshadowed his fame, and rose up between him and
the memory of his brilliant services.   He was removed from his government, deprived of his rank,
and consigned to unwilling repose and obscurity
in a palace on the Bosphorus, till the battle of
Kovleftdja disturbed the dreams of Ramis Tchift-
lik with visions of Cossack lances and Baskir Pulks,
and Rechid Pasha was called to the Mabeyn, to
receive, from the hands of his old master, the
Seraskier Pasha, the Sable and the Balta, and was
the last Grand Vizir to issue from the gates of
bliss preceded by the Tartar horse-tails.

His rashness now completed the catastrophe
which the incapacity of his predecessor had well-
nigh rendered inevitable ; and the passage of the
Balkan and the treaty of Adrianople, events most
unaccountable and bewildering to those who were
most closely connected with them, ceased to be

considered amongst the ordinary events of humanity, or to bring responsibility and retribution on those who might have prevented their occurrence. Rechid Pasha's favour now grew in the common disaster, and strengthened in the downfal of older reputations. His old office of Roumeli Valessi was added to that of Grand Vizir; to that was annexed the charge of Dervend Pasha, or inspector of the defiles, which gave him the immediate command of the Greek Armatoles, together with the nomination to the Pashaliks of Yanina, Larissa, and some small Eyalets to the north, so that his followers and adherents might bask in his favour, and strengthen him in their strength.

How Rechid Pasha justified these anticipations, how he restored this loan of power, we have already seen ; and I now must introduce him personally to the reader.

It was early in the day when I arrived at Scodra. The Grand Vizir was busy, and could not receive me ; but, after dinner at twelve o'clock, he sent to tell me that, as I had arrived too late to see the capture of the castle, he intended to shew me that evening how it had been taken. The troops were collected from the surrounding positions ; and about three o'clock I was invited to join an old friend, Mahmoud Hamdi Pasha, formerly of Larissa, and now newly appointed Pasha of Scodra. We proceeded to a knoll overlooking the little plain in front of the hill, on which the castle was situated, where two or three regiments and some artillery were drawn up; while the lengthened battlements of the castle displayed a line of soldiers with their bayonets glittering in the sun, and we perceived the sponges and rammers of the guns in active employment. Presently the Grand Vizir came dashing into the little plain below, mounted on his white Persian charger, and accompanied by a gay and brilliant throng. He rode up to the edge of the water, on the opposite bank of which Mahmoud Pasha and I were seated on a carpet. His sabre was naked in his hand; and, after greeting us, he wheeled round, galloped from corps to corps, amidst a general discharge from the castle and artillery below, and set them all in motion; and, to my untutored eye, the celerity and compactness of the movements— the order and precision of the evolutions, were worthy of the heroes of Perlipe and the Derbend. The Grand Vizir rode about the field, directing every movement himself, and seemed to exult no less in the action of his steed than in the discipline of his troops. Several parties successively scaled the rocks, and reached the foot of the castle, and of course were successively repulsed; and finally, the whole body, forming on the bank of the stream which sweeps around the little plain, dashed into the water, and were soon scrambling up every portion of the opposite hill. But the Grand Vizir

was far ahead of them: his snow white steed was
seen bounding from rock to rock; and, as alone
he reached the battlement, the guardians vanished
from the walls, the blood-red flag displayed its
heavy fold from the highest tower, and a peal from
above and below, the music and effect of which
was heightened by the whizzing and the whirling
of the shot, proclaimed anew the fall of the bulwark
of Albania.

I hope the curiosity of the reader will not suffer
a severe disappointment if I decline to take him
with me to the divan khané and selamlik of the
Grand Vizir. Suffice it to say, that I found him
full of exultation in this hour of triumph, but his
spirit of adventure nothing quenched, and looking
to the successes obtained merely as furnishing
the means of wiping away the stains which the
war of Greece and the passage of the Balcan had
left on his reputation, and of repairing the misfor-
tunes which they had brought on the empire. His
first object was, of course, the subjugation of
Bosnia, which already was half effected, and presented little difficulty and danger. Then would it
have been easy to reduce Greece again under the
Turkish yoke; and the curb placed upon his ambition by European diplomacy, was far from appearing to him at that moment a check which might
not be removed, or a barrier which could not be
overcome.

That enterprise, however, being set aside, an-

other presented itself of much greater importance
—the reduction of Mehemet Ali. The attractions
of such an enterprise were incalculable for a mind
like that of the Grand Vizir, burning with the
memory of past failures, exulting in power, acquired almost solely by his individual prowess and
ability, and confident no less in his good fortune
than in his talents.

After the disgraceful Russian war, and the
treaty of Adrianople, under the ban of " civilised
and Christian Europe," while gloom and despair
hung over the whole Turkish empire, he alone had
broken the stubborn neck of the Albanians, and
established the authority of the Porte over these
countries, at this moment of its apparent dissolution, in a manner unknown before, and which
exceeded the power of Mohammed II. in the hour
of conquest. How could that conquest be secured,
save by enlisting these brave and turbulent spirits
in foreign adventure? and what an object of ambition was it not for him, who had surpassed the
conquests of Mohammed on the shores of the Adriatic, to emulate the glory of Selim on the banks of
the Nile!

But this new enemy was 2500 miles distant
from Scodra (as far as from St. Petersburg to
Herat); and that wary fox, to whom the thoughts
of Rechid Pasha were as well known as to himself, seeing the Porte now delivered from its war
with Greece, and therefore strengthened by its

loss — seeing Albania subdued, and that nursery
of soldiers placed at the disposal of the Porte, and
that state of anarchy and rebellion concluded in
spite of all the art and money he had employed to
prolong the exhausting struggle, soon felt that the
storm must now reach him, and sweep, to the very
foundations, the fabric of his hollow power :—unless
he anticipated and averted its coming by carrying
the field of conquest into the heart of Turkey, and
rallied round himself the discontent created by the
abuse of power and by the pressure of foreign war
and policy, which, with tenfold force, would have
hailed the standard of Rechid Pasha in the Delta,
and have overthrown, without a blow, the Gallic
dreams and Russian ends of an Arab empire.

The Grand Vizir required, at the very least,
twelve months to set Albania in order, after he
should be tranquil possessor of the whole country.
That time was absolutely requisite for the disposal
of those personal combinations on which alone
authority reposes; for the enlisting, organisation,
and disciplining of troops, and for the adjustment
of the civil administration, without which tranquillity could not exist, nor could the affections of
the people be conciliated, nor could pecuniary resources be drawn from it; indeed, time was requisite for sowing, harvesting, and repairing the effects
of the late devastations, and allaying with bread
the demons of anarchy and insurrection. Mehemet
Ali Pasha seized this interval: Syria was lost before

Rechid Pasha was enabled to march a single detachment.   The desultory hordes of Hussein Pasha
had already been sacrificed by his incapacity; and,
before he was half prepared, he was called to the
command of beaten and dispirited troops, and to
meet a practised, confident, and victorious enemy.
His banner, however, was followed into Asia by
thousands of the so lately subdued Albanians, and
a finer army never marched under Turkish colours.
It is not the event of the war that would astonish
any one who had seen Albania at the period I saw
it; it is the fact of Albania remaining tranquil under
the excitement of Ibrahim Pasha's march; it is the
fact of Rechid Pasha having quitted it without his
departure giving rise to a fresh revolt; it is the
fact of his having been able to carry along with
him, I will not say an army, but a single regiment.
When he appeared at Constantinople at the head
of so gallant and unexpected an array, hope and
confidence again revived; but new complications
and dangers attended the sudden change: the
Ottoman star shone brightly for a moment, and
then its light was eclipsed, and Rechid Pasha
became a prisoner in the tent of the Egyptian.*

* There are mysterious circumstances connected with the
battle of Conieh that time may perhaps clear up. As Rechid
Pasha is now no more, I may mention that he is suspected of
having made overtures to Ibrahim before the battle, perhaps
with the view of joining forces, marching on Constantinople,
and displacing the Seraskier. He miscalculated, not under-

The features of the Grand Vizir are prominent and distinct, and extremely intellectual and
variable. Wherever seen, they could not fail to
impress the beholder with the idea of great powers
of mind, and of a consciousness of superiority above
the display of it. His expression, when not irritated, is benignant. Such a disposition seems little
to accord with many facts of his life, and those
facts, too, with which I was most conversant; but
there must be a solid substratum of benevolence in
his character to have prevented him from becoming a monster of ferocity, amidst the exasperating
circumstances which had crowded the last twenty
years of his life. True, he has ordered executions
ruthless in their severity. He had caused the heads
of the guilty to fall, and had made use alike of
treachery and wholesale execution; but he had
never shed blood wantonly, and his purple vengeance
had fallen without partiality. He is at that period
of life when feature is most expressive; when,
without having lost its expanse, plumpness, or fire,
it is pencilled and defined by character. A spreading black beard covers the half of his breast; but
the gray hairs scattered through it, and which in
the centre have triumphed over the black, have
more than once been pointed out to me by the

standing the connexion of Ibrahim's movements with foreign
diplomacy. Rechid Pasha, before marching on Conieh, sent
back the signet of Grand Vizir — a most strange, and, without
the above explanation, a most unaccountable occurrence.

mournful solicitude of his " children." He is the
idol of the troops—he is kind and coaxing in his
daily intercourse with them—dreadful in his wrath,
and a hero in the field.

He is familiarly termed their " Baba :" they
speak of their affection for him as of a thing per-
sonified under the name of " Babalik." He is
indefatigable in his application to business—he has
no less quickness of perception than industry; but
is destitute of method, and does every thing, great
and small, himself. However, his strong sense and
indefatigability free him from that bane of Eastern
power — favouritism. Superior to his age and
nation in powers and frame of mind and body, he
is also superior to their vices. Twenty hours a
day has he been known to apply himself unre-
mittingly to business. In the field, his activity is
such that no servants or secretaries can follow him.
He seems equally proof against hunger, thirst,
fatigue, heat, cold, wine, woman, and flattery.
What would this man be with caution, moderation,
and a more enlarged view of the word justice?

This sketch of the character of Rechid Pasha
was written at Scodra; since then it has been more
fully illustrated in the extensive Asiatic command
combined in his person. To him has the conduct
of the war against the Koords been intrusted; and
the forces for the long-menaced rupture between
the Porte and Mehemet Ali have been placed at his
disposal. In Europe and Asia has he already

played a more important part than any **Turkish**
Satrap since the days of the Kiuprili.   He has
fought and triumphed, and created the elements of
his successes amidst populations so diversified,—on
fields so remote from each other, that a traveller
would have gained fame and reputation by following the tracts along which he has led armies, and
by exposing the condition of the people whom he
has handled or subdued.

CHAPTER XXIV.

DURING my stay at Scodra, the very interesting circumstance occurred to me of visits from the common soldiers.   One of them came one evening,
and brought me an apple; and then, instead of
sitting down beside me in that unceremonious and
patronising manner with which travellers are familiar, he retired, and stood as if forming the
circle which commonly surround their own chiefs.
Luckily, I improved this opening, and soon had
levees that might have vied with those of the Albanian Odjacks.   My journal would be endless, if I
were to enter into the many occurrences characteristic of these populations, because every day was
a drama.

But I must not pass over in silence my amiable
and interesting host, the Imaum, whose attentions
to me were unremitting, notwithstanding the complete disturbance of all his domestic habits by my
sojourn in his house.   Though one of the best,
because it had suffered the least, still one or two

shots had passed through it, and it was but small; he gave up to me the whole of the Selamlik, and retired into his Harem, with the inmates of which I was very soon on friendly terms. I was surprised one evening on returning home, and my room being cold and without a fire, when the Mollah invited me into the Harem to warm myself. The women tucked up the loose handkerchiefs hanging over their heads, so as partly to cover the face; and the Imaum's wife did not scruple to present me with a cup of coffee, while an old slave approached with a pipe. When in the midst of this family scene, the visit of an Albanian Bey was announced; his suite was already in the court, ascending the ladder that led to the corridor in front of the house. The Imaum rushed to secure the door of the Harem; and, as retreat for me through the door was now become impossible, because I must have been seen by the attendants of the stranger, I had to make my exit by a small back window into the garden.

I cannot describe the feelings that rose in my mind when this invitation was given me. I trembled lest the expression of surprise on my countenance would alarm my host into a retractation of his offer. It was not till I crossed the threshold that I believed in its reality; and no sooner was I seated by the fire, than I asked myself, what is all this mystery about? The veil at once was rent, and the mystery had vanished.

After the departure of my visitor, I had a conversation with my host, prolonged nearly till morning, on the subject of religion. What an influence over Turkey does not the joint character of Christian, Protestant, and Englishman afford? As Christian, you are the depositary of their differences amongst themselves; as Protestant, you are an object of interest, by an affinity of religious simplicity and worship, and even of dogma; while distinct from the Greek and the Romish Churches, idolatrous and sacrilegious through their forms, in the eyes of the Turks: as Englishman, you are the depositary of all their political and national hopes and alarms. These characters, however, are of no avail, unless you know their feelings sufficiently to touch the chords that interest them, unless you know their manners sufficiently to make them bear you respect, unless you appreciate their merits sufficiently to awaken their sympathies, and unless you know their errors and their failings sufficiently to give weight to your words and value to your opinions.

The reader may be surprised that I should have ventured to entertain my Imaum with a disquisition on the Wahab tenets, for which he expressed, as in duty bound, his perfect condemnation and absolute horror. But as the Mollah did not exactly know what the Wahab tenets were, I got him into the admission of several of the principal tenets before informing him that they were the

Wahab doctrines; which, however, he no sooner ascertained, than his adhesion was retracted; and, on the other hand, he endeavoured to establish the Mussulman doctrines at variance with Christianity. He quoted Christ's prediction of the coming of the Holy Ghost, on which they seek to establish the prophetic character of Mahomet; adduced the symbolical designation of Mahomet in the Old Testament, by his synonyme of " Treasure," or " Achmet," corresponding with Mahomet; and referred to the passage which they allege we have expunged from the Gospel of Matthew, indicating the advent of Mahomet as the accomplishment of the prophecies.   I had replied by the general tone of the Gospels, as affecting the character of Christ, which are completely in contradiction with this interpretation, and by the absence of any revelation of new dogma by Mahomet, and by endeavouring to shew that the true character of Christianity was not less hostile than Islamism to the idol worship practised of that Christianity which exists in the East.   How far his previous convictions were shaken respecting Wahabeeism and Christianity, I discovered the next day, when I found him in deep discussion on the subject, with six old men of his congregation.

We went over a great portion of the conversation of the previous evening. About the Wahabees, indeed, they seemed to care little; but, with regard to the doctrines and dogmas of Pro-

testantism, deep interest was evinced. But the
Mussulman, here standing between the limits of
the Greek and the Latin Churches, has been led to
reflect more on the characters of Christianity, than
where the Greek rite alone prevails, and where,
consequently, they only know Christianity as the
Greek Church. I was called upon by the Imaum,
to repeat to them that we did not adore the Virgin
Mary, that we said no prayers to saints, that we
had no images, no cross, and no crossings, that we
had no confession, and that we did believe nothing
but what was in the Gospel. I then asked them,
what their worship consisted in ? They answered,
in the belief of the unity of the Godhead, constant
adoration of God, almsgiving, and the belief in the
holy writings (the Pentateuch, the Psalms, the
Gospels, and the Koran). The difference, I then
said, between us is merely, that you have the
Koran more than we have. But the Koran, in all
its dogmas, is but a repetition of the Gospels.
No, said they, there is another difference between
us, or else you would pronounce the words, " La
illahe, hillallah, Mahomet resoul Allah." I answered, that a flag was useful in time of war,
because it prevented those of the enemy's camp
from mingling as friends; and when Mahomet
enjoined on his followers the use of that phrase, a
watchword was necessary to separate the Moslems
from those with whom they fought, and to imprint
upon them an indelible character, as contrasted

with the barbarian Pagans to the East, and the idolatrous Greeks on the West. But that if Mahomet lived at the present time, I could not conceive that a man who, as a legislator, had produced so wholly unparalleled an effect on the state of the world, should now suffer to exist a symbol, which, instead of uniting them in victory, excluded them from sympathy, and which became a barrier between them and a nation, who had every interest to support their nation, and to improve their condition. To these observations, which were more of a political than a religious character, no answer was made ; when I ceased, the silence was unbroken, until I proceeded again in the same strain ; referred to the contrast of their present with their former habits, and shewed them how many practices, at present introduced into their religion, were not only not enjoined by their faith, but condemned by it ; and had been imitated from the faith they so much despised, namely, the Greek Church. The use of the word " Giaour," for instance, which is an offence punishable by the Mussulman law, and the absence of all forms of respect towards the subjects of other courts, and the professors of other creeds, immediately derived from the practice of the Greek empire, and with which the national habits of the Turks were so much at variance. At length, one of the company said :—" Your words are all true, and you are a better Mussulman than we are :" and another repeated an old prophecy, which said, that the time would come, when the cleverest and the greatest of the kingdoms of Frangistan should become the elder brother of the Ali Osman douvlet (the Ottoman empire).

The Imaum, my host, was not a wealthy man; he had no fields to cultivate, but he worked his garden himself, and had only one male attendant, a little ragged boy. From his office of priest he derived no emolument, except the fees for washing the dead. He subsisted on the small proceeds which accrued to him from the direction of a Vakouf, the property having been rendered vakouf by one of his ancestors, who had stipulated by will, that the " Metevelli," or Inspector, should always be selected from amongst his descendants.

In cities and villages of importance, there is always a choice for the priesthood amongst men of substance, or at least of easy means of existence. In the poorer villages, however, the office of Schoolmaster, which is remunerated, is very commonly added to that of Imaum; or, if the Imaum is a peasant like the rest, some advantage is given him in the way of assistance or presents. There is no ordination amongst the priesthood, and no organisation, the election depends entirely on the congregation; and as there is neither exclusion nor restriction, public opinion acts in so equable and peaceable a manner, that it is very difficult to ascertain the principle in the forms, or indeed to perceive any forms at all.

The strong devotional character of Islamism, the power which that faith displays, in influencing and moulding habits in every stage of social advancement, the hold which it takes of their minds, the unity of faith, and equality of dispositions established amongst its professors, are things which have excited the wonder and astonishment of those who have directed their attention to this subject. And that astonishment is still further increased by the absence, in their worship, of all appeal to the senses or the imagination, and the absence, in their Church Government, of those bonds which we look to alone for strength, and of those interests which appear to us necessary to give permanency or uniformity to a system. I am inclined to think that the absence of a clergy, instead of increasing the difficulty of accounting for the facts we see, goes a great way to account for them. The service of the altar, and the influence of the pulpit being open to all, makes this career of honour and distinction a national career, and associates men's honour with piety, and public spirit with religious devotion. The absence of walls of separation between the doctors and the professors of the faith, gives a uniformity to their ideas respecting it, whence springs unity; not from the power which the State can direct against the non-conformist, but because radical grounds of difference have been removed. Thus the union of Church and State, instead of endangering political rights and religious dogma, serves reciprocally to check the excesses of each, through the necessity which the State feels of the sanction of the Church, and through the desire ever present in the Church or nation, of controlling the government. The Sultan is chief of the religion, but he is not the chief of a clerical body ; he is the dispenser of no benefices, he is the expounder of no dogmas, he is the arbitrator of no church discipline; he is but the first un-beneficed sayer of prayers of the congregation of Islam. There is no feeling of irritation produced, or tendency to scepticism instilled, by the payment of money for religious duties. Faith is not distracted by the struggles of clerical bodies; religion is not scandalised by the failings or errors of professed representatives.

CHAPTER XXV.

THE LIFE OF THE HAREM.

THE smile of beauty, amidst the gathered throng, is wanting throughout the East, to grace the honours of the wise, and to gild the laurels of the brave. The hymeneal ring is not there the great and visible source of the activity and the energy of man's early years. The influence of women is different in manner, unobtrusive on observation, and not so exclusively concentrated on a single relationship, but it certainly is not less than among Western nations. How much of the thirst of power, and therefore of energy and action, is prompted by the calm satisfaction and applause of the secret Gyneceum? How much of the respect for the recognised principles of honour, faith, and loyalty, amidst slippery circumstances, are not to be traced to the every where powerful and identical influence exercised over the men by the invisible Harem :—whence, from generation to generation, is derived, unchanged, the same early domestic habits; and through which the domestic type of the race has been spread, where its limits extend, or its population been dispersed; by which the character of the individual has been preserved unchanged, after the glory of the race has faded, and the power of the nation has passed away.

In Turkey, individual character, such as it was in the days of conquest, remains the same in these times, when every external circumstance, and every foreign opinion and influence, coincide to place it in the last stage of dissolution. This unexampled circumstance ought particularly to be borne in mind, in looking at, or in endeavouring to render to ourselves, an account of that half of the population—women—who are too commonly neglected in our reasonings on all nations, but who have been wholly omitted in our estimate of the Turks; among whom, however, they have a more distinct existence, a more special and definable character, greater influence on education, morals, and habits, than with us; and where, consequently, they form a much more important part of the political body.

Can I dare to cross the threshold of that Harem, that mysterious and invisible home of Eastern life, which fixes every family, like a standard tree, by itself, yet exactly resembling all its neighbours, distinct in bearing, one and the same in substance and in character;—without the knowledge of which, events the most familiar are often without their key, and lessons the most instructive without their fruit? In the domestic and social state of the

female sex in the East, varieties are moreover presented to us, interesting and curious in themselves,
but not less so from their affording counterparts of
ourselves, sufficiently resembling us to bring the
differences into evidence, and collecting, in one
point, two separate and most attractive classes of
interest now exhausted in Europe; viz., new manners in other men, new ideas respecting our own,
derivable from the contrast. Whether I can convey to others the subject-matter of that interest, or
whether such a degree of interest may be legitimately attached to these subjects, it is not for me
to determine; I feel it only incumbent on me to
anticipate the question, how a male traveller can
in Turkey know any thing of the women. Without seeing or conversing with a single Turkish
woman, it is no very difficult thing to form an idea
of their state. You must commence by knowing
the men; in them, and through them, it is easy to
know the women. There is no reason to be surprised at our ignorance of the life of the Harem,
when we are equally ignorant of the habits and
ideas of the Selamlik. I hold it to be utterly impossible to form a correct estimate of any portion
of the Eastern mind, and consequently of Eastern
existence, unless you are thoroughly master of the
whole; even as it is impossible to pronounce a
single phrase of a language correctly, unless you
are completely in possession of the language itself.
So the habits of the Harem, the manners of the

Selamlik, can neither of them be understood, excepting after being fully in possession of Eastern thought and character.

It is universally believed, that the Turks never speak of their women, and that, to inquire for a Turk's wife, is an affront and an insult; so it is amongst themselves: but a stranger has, in every country, if he chooses to employ them, greater means of information than the natives themselves. He has the inestimable advantage of being familiar with an infinitely greater number of facts and ideas. He can draw contrasts, seize upon the salient and important points, which a man, familiar with himself and his own, never can. His mind is ever on the alert, his presence excites discussion, the deference that is paid him allows him to lead it to the objects which interest him; and his character of foreigner opens up trains of thought which countrymen and co-religionists conceal from each other, and enables him to overstep the limits which habits or prejudice may have prescribed to inquiry and discussion. Thus it is that I have always found the state of women, and the comparison of the condition and manners, education and ideas, of their women with those of Europe, an object of deep interest, and a never-failing subject of conversation; and, with Turkish women, whom I have never seen, I have entertained an intercourse of messages and inquiries through their male relations.

Boys and girls are brought up together; they go to school together, the boys are constantly in the Harem, nor are the girls excluded from the Selamlik. Now, if it is these first years that stamp the character of man, they equally mould the character of woman; that mould is here identical for both. From the period when we assume an active part on the stage of life, the male character takes new colours from external things; its bearing and its manners become such as " the court, camp, church, the vessel, and the mart," inculcate or require. The women have no such obligations or distractions to change the course of their infantine habits and duties; the forms and observances which I have pointed out as the curb of childhood, become the rule and occupation of their future lives; and even a Sultan's Harem, composed of elements so diversified, and of numbers of hearts and dispositions so perplexing, where nothing exists according to our notions, to occupy their thoughts or to restrain their passions, will exhibit a scene of the most picturelike representation, where courtly forms are never for a moment violated, and which yet possesses so much of enjoyment, that deliverance and liberty, with a dower and a husband, is considered, and often felt, a punishment and disgrace.

In endeavouring to describe the character of the children, I have asked the reader to picture to himself a child in all the amiability and attractive-

ness of its nature, but without shyness and without
rudeness. To picture a Turkish woman, I would
beg him, if possible, to fancy to himself woman
without vanity and without affectation, perfectly
simple and natural, and preserving the manners
and the type of her childhood, in the full blossom
or fructification of her passions and her charms.
Turkish women are the slaves of habit, but that
servitude leaves thought unshackled and fancy
free ; and there is amongst them a striking ori-
ginality of mind, which is rendered the more remarkable by the uniformity of their habits, and the
more vivid by the concentration, within a narrow
circle, of the energies which we expend on external
things.

Love between the sexes is by no means the
important affair in the East that it is amongst us.
With us it stands alone, the deity or the idol, at
whose shrine all other affections are sacrificed, to
whose law all other duties give way. Marriage is,
generally speaking, the excitement to distinction,
the reward of success, and stands an epoch pre-
eminent in our existence. But " thou shalt leave
thy father and thy mother, and cleave unto thy
wife," has not been transcribed from the Gospel to
the Koran. The facility of divorce, the faculty of
having more wives than one, are not the causes,
but the effects, of the existing difference of national
habits. Where the affections are so strongly in-

volved in the other relationships, and where, from habit and the consequent structure of their houses, the family lives so constantly in common, the wife cannot acquire that exclusive affection, or that domestic power, which she derives in Europe from the force of habit,* as well as from the comparative weakness of other, and especially of filial and parental ties.   The wife in the East is not the mistress of the household, she is the daughter of her husband's mother.   If they were told of a country where the mother has to remove from the family roof to make room for the son's wife, they would consider the tale as a trial of their credulity, or as a satire on human nature.

When a Turk, in his domestic or his political character, breaks through the bonds of habit, his passions then have no further restraint.   But the general tenour of the life of the Harem is, as far as I have been able to judge, one of tranquil, but contented and happy equanimity; excepting the case,

---

* Principally from the separation of families on marriage, and from the precedence which the daughter-in-law takes of her husband's widowed mother.   The absence of family etiquette, and the confusion of ideas respecting it, is, to an Eastern, quite sufficient to account for, to him, the strange state of society in which families separate, to avoid contradictory pretensions between mothers and daughters-in-law, between sisters-in-law, &c., or indeed between these degrees of blood relationship.

by no means common, when more than one wife divides its authority and prerogatives.

In talking one evening to a Turk, of a trip I proposed to take of a couple of weeks, he offered to accompany me. Next morning, however, I found him entirely changed; after attempting various excuses, he said, " I will not be ashamed to tell you the real cause of my disinclination to fulfil my promise of last night. When I began to think how I could tell my wife, I could not find the way to do it. For so long an absence I had no reason to assign that would satisfy her; and could she think that I would run away uselessly from my home, unless I did not care about it? Now, my wife is of a rich house, and a Constantinopolitan (Sheherli), yet she has lived with me, in this poor village, for fifteen years, and I have never heard yok! or ah! from her lips," (that is, an expression of discontent, or a word of opposition.) This instance, which I do not quote as an exception, of the feelings which we might suppose not capable of surviving the honeymoon, after fifteen years of matrimony, will, I trust, not be lost on my married readers: and the same tone of harmony and attachment I have invariably perceived, when I have had opportunities of judging of the feelings of Turks towards their homes.

In a country where forms are of such paramount importance, not only in the intercourse, but in the very constitution, of society; where they not

only are scrupulously observed in their infinite
modifications between the various ranks and relationships, but where they form and establish those
ranks, and almost relationship itself:—it is clear,
that from them may be gathered the most decisive
evidence of the consideration in which one sex
holds the other, and of the duty and respect which
one relation is considered to owe to another. It
is probably because we never have had any opportunities of seeing men and women together, that
we have so generally, and during so many ages,
admitted the doctrine of the inferior, moral, and
social position of women in the East. It strikes
me, that a sketch of the mode of address and
intercourse in the interior of the Harem, will prove
the erroneousness of that opinion, and, moreover,
be the most acceptable details which I could give.

Let us suppose a Harem of distinction, where the
return of the master is announced, and the wife is
seated beside the mother-in-law, surrounded by their
attendants, such as the Keleri ustah, Cafiji ustah,
Sazende bashi, the Kalfahs and Alaïcs; corresponding with the Tcheboukji, Cafiji, Ibrikji, the
Ushaks and the Kulehs of the Selamlik. An
Alaïc announces, by the regular sign, the arrival
of the *Paterfamilias;* the slipper-shod and light-
footed crowd disperses in an instant; the young
Alaïcs of the wife are not suffered to be seen by
the husband, but others await him at the door of
the Harem, ranged on both sides. He salutes them

with " Selam aleikum ;" they hold up the flowing parts of his dress, his sabre, if he wears one,
and lift him, as it were, by the elbows. His wife
meets him before the door of her chamber, and
after he has saluted her, in the same manner, she
kisses his hand, raising it to her lips and forehead;
and, as we will suppose the visit to his mother,
follows him into the room. His mother gets up;
he, now suddenly dropping his stateliness, steps
forward, and, bending down to the ground, attempts to take his mother's hand, to carry it in
like manner to his lips and forehead; she does the
same. She then reseats herself in her corner, and
says, " Otourun evlatum," Sit down, my child: he
respectfully acknowledges the invitation, and perhaps it has again to be repeated before he com-
plies with it, and then places himself in a respectful attitude, and at a distance, or on the shilté
on the floor. The attendants have ranged themselves along the lower portion of the room below
the divan, the wife alone stands in the middle of
the floor, the mother not making free to ask her
to be seated in the presence of her son, the son
not taking such a liberty in the presence of his
mother; and, in all their intercourse, it is thus left
undecided which is the host; and thus, each performing towards the other the ceremonies practised by the guest to the host: I need not repeat
that, in the Eastern ceremonial, the guest of superior rank becomes the host of his host. But while

c c 2

these forms are rigidly observed at each period of meeting, they in no way interfere with the natural flow of spirits, or the display of affection.

But as in the Harem every person has her own apartment and establishment, it never happens that a son enters thus abruptly the presence of his mother. A message is first sent to her favourite attendant, to know if his mother is dressed or visible. On the affirmative answer, a message is sent to herself, to say that her son desires to kiss her feet; and, on permission being granted, he presents himself at her door.

The wife appears to be treated very differently from our notions, but she is treated by her husband as a younger sister is, and that in nowise differs from the treatment of a younger brother. There is no difference as regards sex. On the other hand, the treatment of a mother by her son or daughter, shews a much greater degree of authority in woman than is to be found in Europe.*

Nor can the great and the powerful emancipate themselves from the control which these habits and forms shew to reside in the mother over her children. Imagine Ibrahim Pasha staying a

* I was first made acquainted with the feelings of respect which Turks entertain for the sex by entering, with some Mussulman friends, the apartment of one who was laid up, and attended by his mother: the whole party saluted the lady by kissing her hand.

whole week in the Harem of his mother, waiting
to find a favourable opportunity of pressing a
request upon her; and, when admitted, kissing
her feet, refusing to be seated, and standing an
hour and a half with his arms crossed before her.
The subject of his earnestness is no less instructive.
Mehemet Ali, several years before, with that indifference to the prejudices and habits of his country
which characterises him, had had some intercourse
with a slave of his wife, the mother of Ibrahim
Pasha. This the old lady had resented in a very
decided manner; Mehemet Ali, not submitting as
he ought to have done to the decision of the
Cadun, she abandoned his house, and since then
has resided by herself in the castle. This scene of
family scandal was, however, too great for Mehemet Ali Pasha not to feel its effects, and to
desire a reconciliation. All his attempts were,
however, ineffectual; in her contempt for the man
who had put this affront upon her, who had borne
him " not only sons but heroes," she persisted in
refusing even to notice his attempts, to which she
gave but one invariable reply, " I don't know who
Mehemet Ali Pasha is." In the meantime, however, he lost his son, Toussoun Pasha; he was so
affected by this loss, that he fell into fits of raving
and delirium, which occasioned serious apprehensions for his life, and which left him, for some time,
in a state of insensibility. On this occasion his
wife went to him, and never quitted his pillow

while there was danger; she then retired again to her own establishment. This led to a fresh attempt at reconciliation; her answer was, that though Mehemet Ali Pasha neglected his duties, she could not, therefore, neglect hers; she had done her duty, he was now well again, required no assistance from her, and therefore she ceased to recollect that he was in existence. It was on this occasion that Ibrahim Pasha observed the etiquette which led me to mention the circumstance, while he, the conqueror of Syria, and the victor of Koniah, humbly sued, from an aged woman, for the pardon of the Viceroy of Egypt, and had his suit rejected.

It is singular to observe the extraordinary resemblance of the general features of female existence, and of the minutest details of habits, at the remotest periods of Eastern history, and at the present day; and yet, strange to say, the Europeans, the most familiar with the East, seem all to have been equally unconscious of the feelings of Easterns respecting women, and of their conduct and manners towards them.

Sir John Malcolm is of opinion that women, in a former age in Persia, occupied an "honourable station" in society; since Quintus Curtius relates, that Alexander did not venture to sit down in the presence of the mother of Darius, until desired to do so: because, among the Persians, it was not the custom for sons to sit before their mothers. The reader, after the perusal of the foregoing anecdote, will perceive that the habits of the Harem of Mehemet Ali Pasha, exactly coincide in this, as probably in every other respect, with the manners of the Harem of Darius; and here do we see in the East of antiquity, as in the present day, family ties overlying reasons of state, and domestic rank superseding social rank. This incident will forcibly strike whoever has employed his time or his mind in examining the East, as throwing light on the character and the triumphs of that greatest of men—Alexander.

Lord Byron, in "Sardanapalus," makes the monarch, his queen, and her brother, equally admit, although they variously treat the indignity offered by Sardanapalus to his legitimate spouse, by his intercourse with the fair Greek slave. The sentiment is perfectly Eastern; and, indeed, it is the only point in the Harem portion of the tragedy that has any touch of the East about it. Bishop Heber, however, reproves this poetic license as follows :—" We are not sure whether there is not a considerable violation of costume, in the sense of degradation with which Myrrha seems to regard her situation in the Harem, no less than in the resentment of Salemenes, and the remorse of Sardanapalus, on the score of his infidelity to Zarina. Little as we know of the domestic habits of Assyria, *we have reason to conclude, from the habits of contemporary nations, and from the manners of the*

East in every age, that polygamy was neither accounted a crime in itself, nor as a measure of
which the principal wife was justified in complaining." Myrrha was not a wife, but a mistress.

It is well known, that the sovereigns of the
house of Ottoman have, since the time of Baya-
zid II., been debarred from the privileges of matrimony. The pretence of this restriction was the
dread of seeing again the wife of a Sultan exposed
to misfortune or indignity; but the real reasons
were, the private liberty which the Sultan himself
acquired, and the emancipation of the powerful influences of the Court, and even the Janissaries,
from the preponderance and power of a regal con-
sort, whose person would be inviolable. It is not,
therefore, to be expected that, in the Seraglio of
Constantinople, the same restraint should be placed
over the fancy of the monarch, that the relationship to his wife of a powerful chief placed over the
betrothed lord of the Harem of Nineveh. Nevertheless, Sultan Mahmoud, with his Harems and
Odalisks, is far from enjoying, in this respect, the
range of fancy, and the faculty of selection, enjoyed by his Christian peers. Inexorable custom,
and the settled notions of right and wrong, (which
are the only laws in the world, let legislators and
parliaments write and talk their worst,) oppose an
insuperable barrier to his supposed omnipotence.
The present Sultan is said to have been once
deeply in love; his suit, as a lover, was admitted,

but the " Sultan" was compelled to sever ties deemed inconsistent with the dignity of his station, and the honour of the imperial Harem. He himself was the child of romantic love. His mother, dressed as one of the officers of the palace, used invariably to attend her lord; and when he went to the Divan, whither she could not accompany him, he carried her slipper in his breast, that, as he said, he might ever be under the influence of his good genius.

Having spoken of the Sultan, in connexion with this subject, I linger ere I turn away:—the time is not yet come; but when it does, what an interesting field will not his character and times present! There is in him such a fund of benevolence and of kindliness of feeling, so much extravagance and caprice, so much art and dexterity in the management of the detail of Turkish politics and events, so much vanity, and so little pride : such a love of the eccentric and of novelty, and such a mixture, in his times, of great events, great disasters, great successes, strange ideas, and curious incidents.

When combating an idea so universally established in Europe, as that of the licentiousness of the Harem, I am tempted to quote incidents that have occurred in the families of men of notoriety and distinction, because the accuracy of such examples would not be doubted, or at least their inaccuracy could be easily exposed. If I do not do so, it is not for want of materials, but the delicacy of the subject will sufficiently account for my reserve. I may, however, say, without telling any secrets, that, with the exception of two or three, the men filling the highest dignities of the empire have only one wife; and the anecdotes I am sorry not to quote go to prove, that the treasures which their Harems may contain are strictly locked out of sight of their nominal masters.

What I have already said of their manners will shew that the domestic occupations of the women, independently of those avocations which women have in Europe, are numerous enough to occupy a great deal of their time; I mean even in the Harems of the rich! for, as to the mass of the population, it is needless to say that there is pretty nearly here as much drudgery as in the rest of the world, and that time is wanting for that which is necessary, instead of its superabundance requiring the distraction of novels, or the " idle business" of fashionable existence. A Turkish lady, in the midst of her suite, is such as Electra was in the midst of her handmaidens. Almost every thing that is requisite for the household is prepared at home; a great deal of embroidery is used in their dresses, or in the ornaments of their household: but it is not only the putting together of the most tasteful parts of their furniture or attire which demands their care, the various materials are themselves of home produce. The cotton that grows in their fields, the silk nurtured under their roof, is spun by their own hands; the dyes are prepared in the kitchen; the silk is plaited into braid and lace, the loom and the shuttle are driven by fair hands.* A household is thus a domestic manufactory of all that is requisite. Even heavier labours fall to the lot of the female servants: grinding of corn with hand-mills, pounding of coffee, and the like. The habitual state and numbers of retinue are thus combined with economy, and that almost St. Simonian community of worldly goods which characterises the general habits of the East, as a natural consequence of their domestic manners; and, while thus numerous and diversified occupations fill the time and occupy the thoughts of the apparently secluded inmates, they receive a species of worldly instruction, and a knowledge diversified and practical, which, perhaps, gives a real culture to the mind, as solid, and far more interesting than the commonplace book-learning of many of those who would set down the information of Turkish women as ignorance — their ignorance is that of our great-

* In the Harem is generally made that delicate stuff of silk, or silk and cotton, which looks like crape, with brilliant stripes of soft satin, and which is worn by men and women for their inner clothing, and is used for sheets. This stuff, by the delicacy of its texture, the harmonising softness of its colour, and its light transparency, gives an elegance and a chaste richness to the person and the night costume which singularly contrast with the stiff form and glaring whiteness of our blue-starched canezous and jabots, and the ludicrousness of our dishabille.

grandmothers.   In consequence of these habits, one seldom is able to get in the market, or bazaar, any of those things that may be considered the luxuries or the elegancies of the East.   But, on the other hand, a stranger may apply to a Harem to have such work done for him as he cannot procure elsewhere; for instance, any portion of the national or provincial costume of a Harem which resides in the capital; the request, instead of an insult, will be taken as a compliment.   It is no uncommon thing to hear, " Such or such a Harem works well;" " Such another Harem works better;" " Such a thing can only be made in such a Harem."

In the capital, of course, these patriarchal habits have, to a certain degree, been obliterated, but the type remains; and in nothing can the depth of its impress be more clearly visible than in the superiority assumed by the ladies of the distant provinces over those of the capital.   And here, again, may an analogy be traced with the habits of our own country at a former period, when the lady of the distant castle despised the life of the court, and considered those who basked in its favour as the mere satellites of a prince who eclipsed them by the splendour he cast over them.

Another source of domestic occupation, which may seem rather extraordinary, are religious duties.   Prayers, short, it is true, but repeated five times a-day, and each time preceded by the abdest, or religious ablution of hands, feet, arms, legs,

head, and neck.* Before each of the two meals
there is a dipping of the fingers in water, and a
copious ablution after each, not by plashing in
filthy water in a basin, but by having pure water
poured from a vase over a wide basin. Nothing
can exceed the cleanliness of the whole establishment, that is to say, the interior; for the outside
may have the air of an old barn, and the environs
be choked up with filth and dirt. In the inside the
aspect is very different. The constant use of soap
and water will attest the cleanliness of their persons; and yet, in the East, one gets an idea of
cleanliness beyond the reach of washing, and which
is the result of three or four hours spent in the
vapour bath, and which you leave with a sensation
of cleanliness so perfect, that it seems impossible
that any thing can soil you.

The habit of leaving boots, shoes, and slippers
at the door, and wearing leather buskins, made to
fit tight to the feet, and without thick soles, or,
indeed, of going about barefoot while it is necessary, for the noiselessness in which the Turks
rejoice is also a habit most essentially conducive
to cleanliness. The floor is as clean as any other
part of the dwelling; a spot on the hand is instantly washed off; the accidental ruffle of a curtain
or a sofa immediately smoothed down; a shred on

* But, in the interval between two washings, should they not
have touched any thing which soils, there is no necessity for
repeating the abdest.

the floor is ńo sooner observed than picked off.
The habits of order are thus carried to what would
be with us a fatiguing excess.

It is a common observation, that cleanliness of
the person coincides with order and integrity of
mind.   May not cleanliness have much to do
with the characteristic integrity of the Turks?   It
certainly forms among them an essential portion of
education, and begets those feelings of self-respect
that so remarkably distinguish them from the
masses of other people.   You are perfectly sure
that a Turk is always unsoiled by the contact of
any thing uncleanly or disagreeable.   So with
regard to every thing that is presented at their
table.   Washing amongst them, even if not enjoined,
would assume the character of a religious duty, and
cleanliness the importance of an article of faith.
The slightest impurity weighs on the conscience,
because it irritates the nerves.   This feeling is
carried so far, that the water itself must be perfectly pure ; and, having once touched the person,
must not touch it again.   Water, used in ablution,
must always have the character of a running
stream : it is poured, by one attendant, from a jar
with a long and narrow spout, while another holds
a basin with a pierced cover below.   About their
houses there are numerous fountains, where a
slender stream may be turned over a marble basin
for washing.   At the mosques, close to public
charitable institutions (of a description unknown in

Europe), and in the lanes and streets, numerous water-cocks of this description are placed low down, with a step of marble before them, to afford to the public the convenient means of washing their feet and legs, as well as their arms and head. After getting accustomed to their mode of washing, ours has something very revolting in it; and one can easily conceive the disgust which a traveller sometimes unconsciously excites while fancying he is acting in perfect conformity with the rage for ablutions of the people among whom he is residing.

The life of the women is not, however, confined to the Harem: they go regularly to the bath; which, like the Thermæ of the Romans, is a place of recreation and of merriment, of public meeting and of family mirth. The Khanum is accompanied by her slaves and children: she there meets her friends, similarly attended. Their gorgeous apparel is laid aside; and, wrapped in easy and statuelike drapery, they assemble in a middle chamber, where the marble floor is gently heated, and into which is suffered to enter a portion of the steam from the warmer apartment of the bath beyond it. Here they sit, chatting about their children, their sons, their husbands, and perchance, at times, approach, and even opine on, the graver matters of ministerial changes and European policy. While pipes and coffee are served by their attendants, and girls, sitting at their back or at their feet,

knead them with their little hands, and gently perform a complicated service of slight shampooing,
patting, and dressing of the hair. All this time the
children and attendants, rejoicing in the habitual
liberty of the place, are within washing, chatting,
singing, and throwing water about. When the
multiplied operations of the bath are over, and
when they are again attired as before, and previously to their customary dresses being put on,
a repast is not uncommonly served; and this
recreation, which lasts nearly a whole day, recurs
once a week.*

Visiting and shopping are no less the delight of
the fair of the East than of the West; and to these
out-door occupations have to be added excursions
on the water, and drives, which lately have become
the vogue since the stately pace of the gilded Araba,
drawn by buffaloes or oxen, has been superseded
by light carriages on springs, like the cars of whirli-
gigs for children at fairs, drawn by one or two
horses, and dashing along the new roads that have
been lately made on all sides of the capital.†

The women are generally far more observant
than the men of religious practices; but, among

---

* Every house of distinction has got a private bath.

† There is a different drive fixed for every day in the week
in various suburbs of the wide-spread capital, so as to give the
fashionable of all quarters an equal chance. There are, in like
manner, seven market-places, one day of the week being
appointed for each.

the former, there is none of that religious pride and exclusiveness that is found amongst the latter. With the men, religion has been mixed up with political differences; and thus political causes have given a haughtiness and a stubbornness to their intercourse with the subjects of the Christian powers; and thus has arisen a strange opposition between their personal and their national character. Amongst the women, the former class of feelings is less brought into play: they have no pride, and little vanity; and, although strictly observant of the practices of religion, they do not shew their piety by contempt for others. There is here no class of persons to take advantage of devotional feelings for their own private interest: there are no ceremonies of religion for which money is to be paid or received, no auricular confession, no absolution, and no ghostly visits of family priests to excite lucrative devotion.

The affection that reigns between the slaves of the Harem and their Cadun differs little from filial regard, while they are treated as children by their mistress. It is no extraordinary thing to see one of the Sultan's sisters going to sup at the lowly dwelling of one of her Cheracks or Alaïcs, who has been married out of her Harem, not to a Pasha, or a governor, but to a common shopkeeper, or a petty officer. When an Alaïc is told by her mistress that she is going to give her away in marriage, the answer is, " What have I done, that this should happen to me ?"

In a household, wages are not the bond between the master or mistress and the servant. The servant may have a small allowance, which is considered as his wages; but that sum generally does not, perhaps, amount to a twentieth or a hundredth part of that which in reality he or she receives, which comes in the form of presents and of recompenses from the master or mistress; and by presents from without, in proportion to the grade of the family, or the elevation of the influence of its master.

The habit of irregular remuneration, in lieu of fixed, invariable, and *actionable* wages, produces a difference of mental habits, as regards servants and masters, that I am sure is not to be understood through description; and yet every day you see Europeans, those men who affect such comprehensive views and such powers of logic, reviling the habit of giving presents, not perceiving that this practice leads to the preservation of those interesting domestic relations which I conceive to be the greatest lesson, political and moral, which is presented to us by the Eastern world.*

* The bacshish, or present, becomes a mark of approbation (and no feeling is so prominent in an Eastern's mind as the desire of approbation), so that, in a hard-driven bargain for services, you will not be unfrequently called on to specify what the

The slave, being bought young, being educated
in the house, being the object of peculiar regard
and a source of distinction, may be considered at
once as a member of the family; and slaves in
after life, when separated from their patron, designate their first patron as their father.* The
constant intermarriages between slaves and daughters of a family, and female slaves and sons of the
family, give to their domestic position something
more interesting than natural family ties. But
hired servants also may aspire to some share in
these privileges and advantages; there is no idea
of degradation attached to their position; they may
rise to any grade in the state, and each immediately
feels, in his own position and in his own circumstances, the effect of any change, whether of elevation or depression, in the station or position of
their master; and each, again, depends for his
position in the household, for his prospects in life,

bacshish will amount to. An Englishman, bargaining for a
boat, had fixed 600 piasters. The men then inquired what the
bacshish would be. The Englishman did not understand this
at all, and the bargain was nearly broken off, when some one
suggested, " Make your bargain for 500, and give the remaining 100 as bacshish." This arrangement satisfied every body.

* At a meeting of reconciliation between Ibrahim Pasha and
Rechid Pasha, at Missolonghi, the former addressed the latter
in these words :—" It is not written that sons shall always hate
because their fathers quarrelled : " alluding to the schism between
Mehemet Ali Pasha and the Seraskier Pasha, whose slave
Rechid Pasha had been.

D D 2

on conciliating the master's good-will, which thus of itself alone, and without reference to consequence, becomes a subject of pride and an object of emulation. I have heard it remarked by Europeans, who have had opportunities of judging of the interior of Turkish establishments, that great jealousy reigns among the household respecting the favour of their master or their mistress. But this is not a result of any peculiar jealousy of individual disposition, but of fundamental differences of institutions and ideas. By the absence of fictitious lines of separation between the classes of mankind, individual character becomes more important, is more developed, and the affections of men acquire an immediate and decisive influence over state, station, and fortune.

The European servant with his fixed wage, in the impossibility of aspiring to any thing higher, and treated as a menial, coalesces with his fellows against his master, because he has nothing particular to expect from his devotedness or his master's regard, and his only chance of improving his circumstances is through peculation. No friendly or affectionate intercourse takes place between them; their position has rendered them heartless or dishonest; and the character thence accruing contributes still further to lower their station, and obliterates every trace of mental intercourse between the class of masters and those who form the larger portion of our household, who are present with us during the greater portion of our time, and on whose services all our comforts depend. Hence we are deprived of a great source of enjoyment, and are unconscious of that species of domestic happiness which is a chief source of gratification to every individual throughout the vast regions, where unnatural feelings have not been inspired into the mind of man respecting his fellow-creatures.

From this separation arises, also, a difference of style and manner of education, ideas, pursuits, and modes of expression, which establish so strong a distinction between the class of masters and the class of servants, that we can scarcely conceive a state of society in which they can co-exist on friendly affectionate terms, sympathise without loss of respect, and fraternise without prejudice to duty or infraction of custom. This facility of domestic intercourse in the East depends also, in a great degree, on the equality of the mental state, and of the manners of the various grades of society. The ideas of every class are much the same, and the effect which is produced in every man's house by his elevation in the scale of political influence, or even by pursuits of an intellectual character, is equally sensible in them; while, as to manner, the porter and the tradesman know equally well how to conduct themselves as the Vizir and the General. The combined effect of these various dispositions and circumstances is, that the Harem of the East resembles less a European

family than a European court—if in a court
simplicity and affection were to take the place of
vanity and interest. The master of the family is
treated like a little sovereign; and no wonder that
he despises, that he disregards, the attractions and
the throngings of external society, and that, absorbed in his family and his home, he regards as
indifferent, if not as foreign, many of those principles and combinations which constitute our national
feelings and our ideas of patriotism.

It is not to be overlooked, in a country where
the recollections and the apprehensions of war and
warfare can never be wholly withdrawn from the
feelings and habits of the family circle, that woman
is respected amid the catastrophes of war, her
abode unmolested in the sack of a city—a result of
the early impressed respect for the family hearth.
Here is a singular term of comparison, which those
only, who have witnessed both Europeans and
Asiatics during such fearful suspensions of discipline
and law, can justly appreciate.*

* The Indian government, about twenty-five years ago,
found itself under the necessity of fitting out an expedition
against the pirates who infested the coasts of Arabia. When
the British force had broken their power, the opinion of the brave
leader, and of his professionally judging veterans and other
officers, was loudly pronounced for measures of the extremest
kind, which, by one fearful example, should strike terror into
the minds of those ungovernable tribes which inhabited several
hundred miles of the Arabian coast. But, fortunately, in the
English camp there were three young men who had caught the
genius of the East. Their voice prevailed; mercy and kindness

It must not, however, be thought, that the observances and ceremonials which I have attempted to describe interfere with the spontaneous prompting of mind and feelings, and cast a net of form and stiffness over the common practices of life. When you have become accustomed to them, you forget that they exist quite as much as we ourselves forget that the habits of our own daily intercourse would be curious or surprising to a stranger; such as the impossibility of speaking to persons to whom you have not been introduced, the wearing of tight stays, boots, or collars, by a whole people, from the hour of rising to that of going to bed, the sitting a couple of hours at a dinner-table, or any one of those habits which, unless one has chanced to see something different, appear the ordinary course of nature.

The society of Turks is neither sombre nor formal, and nowhere is affection or regard expressed with less constraint; but intimacy never degenerates into familiarity, hilarity into boisterousness, or kindness into vulgarity.

The nearest relatives, as the most intimate

was the policy which has secured, during the long interval between that expedition and the present day, the total cessation of piracy throughout these seas. It was stipulated, however, by these young men, that, in the occupation of the fortress of the pirates, the native, and not the English, troops should be used, from the conviction that the excesses, of which the English troops would be guilty, would frustrate the objects in view.

friends, never are familiar.   On the other hand,
the servant or the slave, that treats his master with
the most profound humility and respect, would
feel shocked and insulted by the exhibition of
want of confidence, or by restraint put upon the
use of speech.   What difficulties do not, therefore,
attend our intercourse with a people so dissimilar?
And is it surprising that such contradictory impressions should be produced upon the strangers who
have seen and attempted to describe them?   The
Turks remind one of a porcupine : grate their feelings or their prejudices, and every where a sharp
and hostile point is presented to your hand ; know
them, and be known by them, and they are as
smooth and pliable as down.   Having experienced
each of these effects, I can connect both with the
cause, which was in myself, and not in them.
When I first quitted the confines of Turkey, it
was with hatred in my heart and contempt on my
lips—the necessary consequence of the treatment I
had received from them, and which was again the
necessary result of my position as a European,
and my ignorance as an observer.   Chance and
perseverance led me to other conclusions ; and
thence an experience of another kind.

Words are but the representatives of impressions and of feelings.   When between two men
there is a difference of original impressions, they
cannot be said to have a common language, because the ideas represented in the speech of the

one is not conveyed to the intelligence of the other; and in nothing is this absence of a common language more sensibly felt than in our estimate of the domestic state and feelings of the East. A European derives his principal social gratification from mixing in society; a Turk derives his from existence in his family. A Turk would be punished by exclusion from his home, in the same way that an European, moving in the higher or middling ranks of life, would be punished by confinement to his home. These facts being ascertained, the conclusion is evident — that there is a greater degree of family enjoyment in the one country than in the other; but it is a very difficult thing to arrive at these facts; because a European, seeing the Turk incapable of enjoying what to him are principal sources of enjoyments, will conclude that he is dull and insensible, and not that his enjoyments are derived from other sources. Perceiving in them no desire to enjoy themselves in modes similar to ours, such as rushing about from one place to another, congregating together in throngs, he will suppose them deprived of so many mental faculties or qualifications.

Seeing them preferring to stay at home, and, instead of enjoying such things as the theatre, opera, concert-room, or ball-room, confining themselves to slothful and ignoble indolence behind the walls and lattices of the Harem, he will conclude that the Harem contains attractions suited to the low moral level which must coincide with the supposed incapacity to enjoy what is refined or estimable. Forgetting, or not knowing, that " Harem " is " home," and unconscious of the associations connected with it — of the concentration in one spot of security, protection, filial duties, paternal authority, love, delicacy of manners, and of intercourse ; of a combination, in fact, which it might be considered a successful effort of the imagination to create. Wholly unconscious of those claims, duties, attractions, and occupations, we can account for the Turk's attachment to his Harem only by supposing that sensual gratifications are concealed behind the mystery that envelopes it; and we therefore distrust any observations, and disregard any fact, that tends to an opposite conclusion.

CHAPTER XXVI.

STATE OF WOMEN — THEIR INFLUENCE ON DOMESTIC MANNERS
AND NATIONAL CHARACTER — COMPARATIVE MORALITY OF
THE EAST AND THE WEST.

WE believe women in the East to exist in fear and
trembling of their lords and masters. I, however,
have been convinced of the reverse : on the best,
in this case, of all testimonies — that of the ladies
themselves.

I shall allow a Turkish lady to speak for herself, and expose, in her own words, her opinions
on that subject.

"In what," says Fatmé Hanum, "is our position inferior to that of men ? If we do not mix
in their common society, they do not mix in ours ;
and the loss is assuredly on their side. A husband
labours to gain his fortune, his wife to spend it. A
woman shares in all the advantages, privileges, and
honours of her husband's state, and even with more
splendour than that which he himself enjoys. Is
he rich, and has he his Selamlik crowded with
attendants ? Her apartments are no less thronged,
and she is no less observed and waited upon. Is

he a Vizir? does he receive the visits of the
grandees of the empire? His wife receives the
ladies of the grandees, and his patronage is dispensed by her through her female friends. Does a
husband attend the levee of his sovereign? so does
his wife;* and, moreover, she pays her court to
the various Sultans† and Caduns of the palace,
whose favour a grandee can only arrive at through
his wife.

" A Turkish lady is independent of the political
dangers that assail her husband, except through
him.‡ Her life, her person, her property, even
her establishment, is sacred and secure. Her
tongue is free and uncontrolled; and neither
husband, pasha, nor sultan, could dare to interfere
with its use.

" If the husband has the faculty of divorcing
his wife, the wife also can divorce the husband;§
and the mother of a son is absolute mistress.

* At the Sultan's levee of ladies, they are all unveiled.

† The Sultans (not Sultanas), of the female sex, are the
daughters, sisters, and aunts of the sovereign. It is the common title of every member of the family. The chief of the
state is termed Padischah; but the holder of the office, in the
title attached to his name, is not distinguished from the rest of
his family.

‡ The wife of a Mollah was, however, recently exiled to
Boussa; but she was a most notorious politician and intriguer.
Every body laughed; but every body said, " It is well done!"

§ The occupier of the highest legal post in the empire lives
at present in disconsolate widowhood, being abandoned by his

" In all the practices of religion, there is a perfect equality between men and women : prayers are the same for both ; the title of Chodga is common to both ; so is that of Hadji. The privileges of the pilgrimage are common to both.

" The women have as much freedom as the men, and much more enjoyment in excursions, parties of pleasure, visiting, shopping, and going to the bath.

" A woman's property is as secure as that of a man. A wife's fortune is her own, and does not, as amongst you, become the property of her husband.

" The women receive as much, and the same education as the men.*

" The women are treated by the men with a respect which still they do not always shew in return ;† and when a woman addresses a man, he reverently casts his eyes on the ground.

wife, said to be the most lovely person in Constantinople. He was most distractedly attached to her ; but, taking a dislike to him, she left him ; and all the power of the law and of passion could not bring her back.

* The number of girls attending the public schools is hardly inferior to that of the boys. Among the names of the most celebrated living poets figure those of three Khanums. One of them, Perishek Khanum, during the reign of Sultan Mustafa acted as his private secretary. Mehemet Ali Pasha's secret correspondence is carried on by two female secretaries.

† The Seraskier Pasha, the first man in the empire, and the patron (or father, they having been his slaves), of the two sons-

" In what, then, are we the slaves of our husbands ?   In what are we inferior to the women of Europe ?   Is it because the men do not stare at us impudently in the face, and through quizzing-glasses ?   You talk of your great advantages in the selection of husbands and wives ; but are your marriages happier than ours, and have you the means of separating if you do not agree ?   And who would care for a husband who goes, giving his arm, and giggling and laughing, with the women ? and what husbands can love a wife that other men can finger and twirl about ?"

It is an old story, that there is no disputing tastes.   But from this inquiry one result appears as nearly certain—that the female sex in this, as in other parts of the world, carry the sceptre in their hands, though it is called a distaff.*

In this *plaidoyer*, every allusion to polygamy has been artfully excluded ; and certainly the Harem presents a very scene when its authority, and the heart of its master, is divided by two or

in-law of the Sultan, sits not in the presence of Gules Khanum, until told to do so.   She is the sister of the celebrated Hassan Pasha, the patron of the Seraskier.   This proof of the superior sway which family relationships, even when only fictitious, exercise on the most elevated positions of the state, indicates the weight and power of home and family—of that circle of which woman is the centre.

* It is no trifling prerogative of the sex, that the servant or the slave can marry the master or his son, without exciting animadversion or entailing reproach on her helpmate or his family.

more rival queens.   But, even then, the scenes
of discord and the storms of passion are not
such as our fancies would portray, or our manners warrant. The general habits, the constraining
presence of a numerous retinue, which can never
be excluded, prevents the throbbing of the heart
from glowing on the cheek, and the tempest of the
breast from escaping by the tongue. The passions,
it is said, ,that are suppressed are half subdued;
and the Turkish wife, who could not tolerate the
slightest wanderings of her spouse if the object of
it is illegitimate, and whose rage in that case
knows neither bounds nor moderation, is obliged
quietly to submit to share all her prerogatives with
a legitimate rival.

On the subject of polygamy, a European has
all the advantage in discussion with a Turkish
woman, because her feelings are decidedly on
the side of her antagonists; but then she has
a tremendous power of reply, in the comparison
of the practical effects of the two systems, and
in the widely spread rumours of the heartless-
ness and the profligacy of Europe.*

All the convictions of our habits and laws stand
in hostile array against the country where the principle of polygamy is admitted into the laws of the

* In European Turkey, in Asia Minor, in Central Asia,
Bokhara, Persia, and even in dissolute Egypt, the Foundling
Hospitals of Europe are invariably a subject of inquiry and
astonishment.

state. But yet, while we reproach Islamism with polygamy, Islamism may reproach us with practical polygamy, which, unsanctioned by law, and reproved by custom, adds degradation of the mind to dissoluteness of morals.

Although polygamy is permitted by the laws of Mahomet, that permission does not alter the proportions of men and women. While, therefore, the law of nature renders this practice an impossibility as regards the community, it is here still further restrained among the few who have the means of indulging in it, both by the domestic unquiet that results from it, and by the public censure and reprobation of which it is the object.*

The morality of the East results from many causes. The easy circumstances of the people—the simplicity of their minds—the attractions and the ties of their peculiar domestic habits; and it may in part be due, as I have heard it argued by men of the law, to the permission to marry more wives than one, and to the faculty of divorce on the plea of aversion.† They reason thus : Among the wealthy, and the more indifferent to public opinion, who constitute the higher portions of every society, is not to be found the constancy and the unity of affections which result in the

---

* A case of polygamy was unknown in Candia, amidst a population of 40,000 Mussulmans.

† The Protestants of Hungary admit the plea of " irrevocabile odium."

mass of a nation from the difficulties and the toils, and, consequently, from the moderation and virtue of humble life. If the law, therefore, is so severe and prohibitive, that the higher and wealthier classes will overstep it, they infringe, as regards themselves, their feelings of duty, and exhibit a theme for scandal, and an example for imitation. But if the law enables, in some degree, those passions to be gratified which it does not succeed in restraining, it leaves the power of conscience intact, and the authority of law supreme. In Russia, you have by law strict and irrevocable monogamy; the wealthy break the law — the law loses its moral power, the people, in this respect, their conscientiousness.* In Turkey, some hundreds, or, at the utmost, throughout the Empire, some thousands of men, have more than one wife. There is no scandal thence resulting, and constancy to a single mate is the general character.

Some may be startled by the mere mention of the word polygamy; but polygamy is not denounced by the inspired writings — the patriarchs practised it.

* The general morality of the Greeks in Turkey (those of the Fouar, and of the higher orders, excepted), is not less remarkable than that of the Turks, and their ecclesiastical laws are the same as those of Russia: the practice, however, is different. If the bishop in Turkey refuses to grant a divorce when sought by both parties, because contrary to the canon, he is very soon informed that, if he does not, the parties will apply to the Cadi.

Have those who speak of the triumphs of Islamism, as resulting from the unbounded gratification
of sensual lusts, which, if offered to its followers,
and who denounce polygamy as the source of de-
population and weakness in the Turkish empire,
ever dreamt of comparing the moral statistics of this
country and of Europe?   Have they compared the
amount of sensual gratification indulged in in London and Constantinople?   Have they estimated
the frightful mass of misery and degradation pressing so directly on the sources of population in the
former capital?   Have they compared, in the two
cities, the numbers of females reduced to the most
abject state of human misery, and rendered useless
to society; and of unknown beings, cast in helpless infancy on the charity of strangers, and bearing, through life, an indelible stigma of reproach
and infamy; themselves a witness to the corruption, or the faulty legislation of the country in
which it was their misfortune to see the day?
England, we believe, is the most moral country in
Europe; and we every day hear the revolting exhibition which our public places present, quoted as
a proof of that superior morality.   We may find
enough in M. Dumont's Tables to satisfy us, for
any practical purpose, as to the morality of France.
Italy, Spain, Germany, have only to be mentioned,
to make us turn elsewhere for samples of domestic
virtue· or public morality.   And yet, throughout
the whole of these countries, you hear the Turks

reproached and denounced as immoral and profligate!

If I were required to state that which struck me in Turkey as its most salient character, I should unquestionably answer—morality; and I think that, if not the importance of the difference, at least the fact of the contrast, will be admitted by any one who will take the trouble of comparing the impressions received by a Turk in Europe, and by a European in Turkey. The first will not be a week in any of our towns, without coming to the knowledge of, if not brought into contact with, dissoluteness and vice of every description. The European will be twenty years in a Turkish town, without seeing any thing of the kind, and he will find it impossible, if so disposed, to have his curiosity gratified.* It may be, as it has been so often said, that as regards the intercourse between the sexes, this is the result of the constraint put upon both parties; but still the restraint is of a moral, never of a physical nature. There are no Duennas appointed by jealous husbands; no men in Turkey lock up their

---

* I restrict this, of course, to *Turkish* towns. The stranger will, God knows, find vice and corruption enough, of every description, at Pera and Galata; but these are *Frank* quarters. Let him go to the Turkish quarters of Constantinople, and he will seek in vain for any abode which it would be disgraceful to enter. Nor will he perceive any instance or indication of the street vices, or of the coarse and boisterous enjoyments of continental rabble, and of insular gentlemen.

E E 2

wives; indeed, locks for any purpose are rare.
Daughters are not placed in boarding-schools surrounded by high walls. The restraint in question,
is that of continual existence in the presence of
the family. Among the higher orders, no man can
do any thing in secret, or frequent, in private,
places where he would be ashamed to be seen in
public. It is the same with the women. The
general feelings of integrity tend to maintain morality. It is further protected by the public censure, which attaches no less to men than to women.
Indeed, it falls on the former in a heavier degree;
for they say, " He should have known better." No
honour is to be derived from triumphing over
female weakness. But what virtue can be compared to that which, without precepts or struggle,
rises spontaneously from the simplicity of the affections? And such I conceive to be the virtue of
the Turks. The men see no women but their
wives, and think of no others. The women only
know their husbands, and are wholly occupied with
them. Their affections are, therefore, more fully
set on each other, and there is neither distraction
nor suspicion.

Again, the intercourse between the various
grades of society is friendly and affectionate. The
domestic and the social existence equally develope
the affections; and man's happiness resides in his
affections.

Women stand higher by the Mussulman law

than they do in the Roman, and, consequently, in the European codes and customs derived from that great mother of Western legislation. The privileges and advantages of a class of society depend chiefly on the laws regarding property, which imperceptibly, but steadily, from century to century, confer influence and power to those favoured in the distribution. It is most essential to the comprehending of the relative position of Mussulman and Christian women, to compare their legal rights as regards property.

Islamism admits of no rights of primogeniture, and distributes (deducting one-third, of which the father is allowed freely to dispose,) the fortune of the parent equally among all the children; two shares to the males, and one to the females; and in every remove of kindred the same proportion is observed. Here, then, is a difference made against women. But it will be observed, that as there are no rights of primogeniture by which the eldest male absorbs the whole fortune, the Eastern daughter stands in a position relatively higher than the European daughter of an ancient family. This distribution of the property is a great prop to the domestic union and happiness of Eastern families.

It is, however, with respect to marriage, that the Mussulman woman is especially favoured. The husband, instead of expecting a dowry, has to give one. She also receives a portion from her father,

which goes to the husband, one-third being set
aside for the use of the wife. Thus are husband
and father mutually obliged to contribute to secure, for the woman who becomes a wife, an independence, over which neither are allowed to retain
subsequent control; although, by this copartner-
ship, the interest of both is kept alive, and combined in the object they are bound to cherish.
Here is revealed that depth of thought which
bursts upon one, when pondering over the laws of
Mahomet: invariably do you find them directed
to the formation of the character. It is to a
similar effect produced on the minds of his followers, that is to be attributed that unbounded
devotion to the man who never *explained* himself;
and who has won and retained the convictions of
so many millions, during so many centuries, in
religion, custom, law, and politics, without using a
syllogism, or pretending to a miracle!

The property of married women remains under
their own control; their husbands cannot touch it,
nor is it liable for their debts. The widow, in the
partition at her husband's death, receives the third
of the dowry given by her father, the whole of the
dowry given by her husband, and, from the fortune of her husband, from a fourth to an eighth,
according to the relationship of the remaining
heirs. Any property that was hers before, or that
may have fallen to her during her husband's life-
time, remains her own.

As regards divorce, women have, by law, nearly equal facilities as their husbands, in relieving themselves from ties which they do not cherish; and practically, as regards the Turks, I should say, that women (when of rank and fortune equal to their husbands) do exercise that power more than the men, and hold it over their husbands as a check on polygamy. This faculty of divorce may appear to us prejudicial to morals; but I have no hesitation in saying, that if you withdraw from Eastern society, as at present constituted, the faculty of divorce, morals and happiness would suffer in an incalculable degree. Where intercourse between the sexes is so much restricted before marriage, the faculty of separation afterwards, should reciprocal antipathies arise, becomes indispensable. It is so more particularly in the domestic circle of the East, because the family lives so entirely within itself, with so few enjoyments beyond those which its mutual relations and common sympathies afford, that disagreement between its principal members would annihilate, to them, a great portion of the value of life. A third, and conclusive reason, for the facility of divorce, is the prevention of polygamy. No woman will willingly share her conjugal rights with a partner; and while the law gives her husband the power of giving her one or more partners, it secures to her an independent fortune and position, and the facility of quitting him; which, combined with the opinions of society, and the ties and sympathies of kindred, place in the hands of the wife, when a woman of rank, the means of controlling her husband's acts, when her charms have ceased to possess over him the despotism which the fair of every region, and of every sect, seem to have alike the power and the will to exercise.

Men who are fearful of submitting themselves to this control, marry slaves, or women much below themselves. Such cases are, of course, by no means common.

Barrenness, however, greatly changes the lot and position of women. The contempt in which it is held, in public estimation, deprives of consideration a woman so situated. The Eastern's chief enjoyment is children; a childless home is a curse; a childless wife a disgrace; a childless old age, a prospect of loneliness and contempt. A childless woman, therefore, loses her prerogatives; and, however connected, she has to submit, without murmur, to the introduction of another wife into the Harem, or makes a compromise with her husband, such as that which Sarah made with Abraham.

Such is the general position of women, as regards possessions and civil rights in the eye of the Mussulman law, the principles of which I have endeavoured concisely to sketch in their practical and moral bearings. I have yet to notice that portion of the penal code which bears on the social position of women—the proof and punishment of infidelity.

The basis of all Mussulman institutions, ideas, and customs, is the hearth, the home—that is, the Harem—the one spot on earth, which each man holds his own—secret and " forbidden." It is his wife, in whose behalf this sanctuary is created, it exists only in her, and it *is* whithersoever she goes. The honour of woman—the centre of this homestead, and constituting the chief element of Eastern society, must naturally be guarded by the severest penalties of the law, as of public opinion ; and it is so. The punishment for adultery is death—not the death that is inflicted by a single, and a salaried executioner, but death at the hands of an indignant people, inflicted—not with the sword or the axe, instruments ennobled by associations with national honour and glory, and with civil power and justice—but by a multitude, a rabble—her own sex—children—her relatives—her former playmates — who gather the stones from the wayside, to cast at the adulteress !

But while a doom, thus appalling, is pronounced—a doom, tragic and poetic—so illustrative of the scope and character of Eastern legislation, speaking to the imagination, rather than acting on the fears, of men, and effective, by the character it creates, rather than by the restraint it imposes — while this doom is recorded against infidelity, it stands rather as the expression of public

abhorrence, than as a law which is to be carried
into execution.   The testimony required is such
as in scarcely any supposable case can be obtained; and the punishment decreed against an
unsuccessful accuser, such as effectually to deter
from accusation.   The annals of the Ottoman empire record but a single instance of punishment for
adultery, which occurred ten centuries after the
promulgation of the law; and which so aroused
public indignation against the judge by whom it
was pronounced, that he fell a victim himself to a
similar fate to that he had awarded, inflicted upon
him by popular vengeance!

We daily observe the deteriorating effects, on
young minds, of the mixture in promiscuous society.   The best results of education on the mind
are thus endangered at all times—often sacrificed;
and generally impaired by that thronging together,
which has become a necessity of our existence.
The absence, in a nation, of such assemblages,
proves a sufficiency in itself, without these external
and dangerous expedients; and entirely removes
the evil that there exists, and the contamination
that thence proceeds.

All these causes, and others besides—in their
direct tendency—in their reaction on each other,
in the restraint imposed by the national character
they produce, would lead one to suppose great morality in this people, if the fact were unascertained,
and suffice to account, on very plain and intel-

ligible grounds, for that which is known to exist.
But all these are intimately associated with the
home of the East—that home which, to them, is
more than country; and has given, to the patriotism that includes it, though deprived of external
props or visible bonds, so energetic a calmness, and
so long a life.

This domestic happiness and virtue is, however,
not common to all parts of the East. It is peculiarly Turkish; and the deep root which the
love of home (not the spot of birth, but the hearth,
wherever placed) has struck into that people, cannot be better demonstrated than by its capacity to
overcome the effects of the continual introduction,
as slaves, or wives, of perhaps the most dissolute
races on the face of the earth — the Georgian and
the Arab. Love of home could not survive the
loss of simplicity of mind, and of singleness of
affections. The Georgians bring neither with
them; and if, with the Africans, they have not
corrupted the Turkish character, it is only because
the combined effect of education, manners, custom,
and religion, are concentrated in that one focus, so
strongly as to preserve its character unchanged
from the remotest period of history down to the
present day, under a greater variety of circumstances, vicissitudes, and temptations, than any
other people has ever been exposed to.

These characters of the Turkish mind and morals
are not only striking in comparing them with the

other races that inhabit the same soil, but also in the immediate change that is visible in those that attach themselves to the same stock, admit the same opinions, and adopt the same manners, by their conversion to the faith which the Turks at the present day profess. To this fact I can bear unequivocal testimony; and, though the change may in part be owing to the municipal character of Islamism, I should be principally inclined to account for it by the assimilation of these populations to the domestic morals of the Turks.

I may here appear to be attributing events of magnitude to very insignificant and insufficient causes; but what can be so important in any mass as the unit — in any combination, as the element? Is not the nation an aggregate of families? — the national character, is it not that which is common to each individual? — public opinion, the aggregate of those opinions which each member of the community entertains? But national character and public opinion, are they not the basis of all laws, institutions, and events? And yet how relatively inactive are they not amongst us; seeing that, in all public matters, the energy of each man's mind is exerted against the convictions of his brother, his neighbour, and his fellow-citizen? In Turkey, family and nation differ but in numbers; character and opinion know no distinction of public and individual: they are one and the same. The character of the family and the opinions of the man

are the character and the opinions of the nation;
and no one who has looked steadily into their minds,
can disregard the minutest circumstance that affects
one man; for it affects all; and all in the same
degree and in the same manner.

In expressing the admiration with which the
Turkish character inspires me, I must restrict that
praise entirely to its domestic and passive existence
— to the Turk — son, husband, father, master,
neighbour; whatever qualities he may possess
flow from these characters. He is brave, because he defends his home; he is docile, because
he had a father; he is not factious, because the
unity of the state includes and represents that of
the family; he is faithful to treaties, because he
lives well with his friends; he has retained for
centuries, by means invisible, dominion over extensive regions and populations, different in character, strange in tongue, and opposed in interests,
because he sought to interfere with their customs
no more than he would constrain the individual
disposition of his family, and because they have
been taught uniformity of demeanour towards him
without prejudice to their diversity of nature, and
because he did not treat as a judge, or resent as a
partisan, the differences of opinion, or the violence
of acts, which would have rendered, if so treated,
hatred irrevocable, and opposition systematic.

The Turk — agriculturist, seaman, general,
mechanic, or professor — is as far below other

European nations as he is above any of them in his domestic virtues or his social integrity. He exists, therefore, he has a place among nations, only in consequence of these which, again, are not the result of principle, but of habit; and of habits — the impress of which is derived from the Harem. This empire has resisted overwhelming power and wrong; but now a more fearful trial awaits it; that is, not so much the fact of adopting other manners, as the fact change. The change of habits will not lead, supposing it were desirable, to the introduction of those of Europe, but merely to the destruction of their own. A reaction against Europe may finally be the result of hopes disappointed and of imitation unsuccessful — when they will no longer possess a national character to fall back upon.

The only changes, that can be beneficial to Turkey, must come invisibly and slowly; and such benefits reside solely in individual instruction, in rendering literature popular and useful, in the extension of the principles, and in the application of the results of science. Wherever manners, customs, laws, institutions, are touched, evil is done, and danger created. It is only after *they* have become acquainted thoroughly with Europe, that they can know what to imitate. The changes which affect the manners of a people, when produced by external causes, must be destructive of its moral and domestic qualities. Those trivial modes and habits which are the language of morality, becoming confused, a confusion of ideas takes place which lowers the tone of the mind. The old habits are lost; the new ones, be they perfection itself, are mere ineffective forms. And thus, wherever Easterns and Europeans come into contact in numbers, the degradation of both ensues. The Europeans, being possessed of greater military and political power, the Easterns have suffered most from this contact. The standard of morality among the Europeans being lower, the tendency of their superiority is naturally towards the extinction of Eastern character, and with it institutions and independence.*

A work, the fruit of thirty years' labour, has recently appeared on the Ottoman empire. It is from the pen of the most popular of Oriental scholars; has been, or is now being, translated into all European languages; and is, and will be, considered the standard authority on all Eastern matters. I allude to M. Von Hammer's " History of the Ottoman Empire."

The reader, who has taken an interest in the subject of these pages, or in the opinions they express, may naturally inquire how far these views are borne out by the opinions of M. Von Hammer; and on no point, probably, will that desire be so likely to arise as in respect of the state of women

* Of this, Greece is a melancholy example.

in Turkey, and in the East. I am sorry to say that the opinions of M. Von Hammer do not support those I have expressed; indeed, his are the very reverse; and, since I have the disadvantage of differing from M. Von Hammer, my only resource is to avow the difference, and to meet it.

M. Von Hammer gives the Arabs credit for chivalrous devotion to the fair sex;* but reproaches the Turks with reducing women to the lowest state, denying to them privileges, distinction, and respect, and considering them, in some degree, as domestic animals. He does not conceive, however, that Islamism has degraded the female character, since he admits of high chivalrous feeling in the propagators of Islamism; but he believes that Turkish character and opinion have reduced the weaker sex to that humble and lowly condition; and this opinion he confirms by the etymology of the title Cadun — which he derives from a term connected with the household.

Having stated my own opinions, and, I may add, my positive knowledge, respecting the social station occupied by women in Turkey, I leave to the reader to weigh what I have advanced against the statements and opinions of M. Von Hammer; but I cannot allow the argument which he draws

* The respect paid by Turks to women is not, nowadays, to be found among the Arabs. The Arabian population inhabiting towns is dissolute and licentious; among such a people no respect for women can exist.

from a supposed etymology to pass without refutation.

It would be supposed, by the reader unacquainted with Turkey, that Cadun was equivalent to Madame, and was the term of respect generally coupled with feminine names. This is not the case. Cadun is " *The* Lady of the House." The term synonymous to Madame is Hanum (Khanum), derived from Khan, or Lord. Among the Turks, from time immemorial, this peculiarity is to be found — a peculiarity which ought not to have escaped the research of the learned and amiable orientalist— that there is no distinction of gender, that men and women are addressed in precisely the same forms of speech and manner, nor is there even distinction in the terms or pronouns. The original lordly title of Aga was common to men and women. Timour's wife, one of the most celebrated characters of Tartar story, was Touman *Aga.* Subsequently, this title became common— was applied in the same extent as " Monsieur"— and, in consequence, the Turks sought a more respectful designation for the sex, and adopted that of Beg, or Bey; and at this day, in India, this title remains appropriated to women—Begum (my lord). Bey, amongst the Turks who spread westward beyond the Caspian, sunk to a lower station, when they adopted, as the loftiest designation, the title Khan, which they found in these regions; and from that time the word Hanum (My

Lord), came to be conferred on all women, without distinction of grade, or of married or single. Thus, the style of address is Perischek Hanum, Gulis Hanum, &c. The possessive pronoun *My*, added to the title when applied to women, is as *Mon*-sieur, *Mon*-signore; so also, in English, in this incipient stage of courtliness, though we have not yet framed a word to convey the same feeling of respect, we do say *My* Lord. The title Khan is given only to men of very distinguished birth, or in the very highest style of Eastern composition; whilst it is given at all times to all women above the grades of those engaged in manual labour.

In conversation, the title joined to a name is not used : you do not, for instance, render " Yes, Madam," by " evet Hanum," but by " evet Effendim " — the title, Effendi, derived from the Greeks, being used indiscriminately to men and women, although it has become the specific designation of men who, while being instructed in letters, are not of the rank of Beys.

Thus, it would appear that the social title applied to women, and the equality used in the common forms of speech, far from bearing out M. Von Hammer's assertion, distinctly prove the reverse. They shew, that among the Turks doubts have not been entertained of absolute equality of personal consideration between the two sexes, and that the differences that are made imply special honour and respect paid to the fair.

M. Von Hammer ought also not to have forgotten,
that, in the first collision between the *chivalrous*
Arabs and the Turks, so contemptuous, as he as-
sumes, in their treatment of women, the latter
were commanded by *a Queen !*

Differing so completely on such a fundamental
question as the relative state of one half of the
population, it may naturally be expected that on
most other points our opinions are not identical.
I deeply deplore, what I consider, so unfortunate
a bias in the mind of the historian of Turkey : because it necessarily follows that, in treating of facts,
those circumstances assume a more prominent position, which appear to confirm the writer's precon-
ceptions, and are also more readily credited.   On
such grave questions as religion, administration,
constitutional principles, national opinion, prospects, and means of restoration of that Empire,
there is not an opinion of M. Von Hammer's
to which I would subscribe, with, perhaps, the
single exception of the Dragomans ;   but there
M. Von Hammer was practically acquainted with
his subject, having been a Dragoman himself.

A knowledge of the East is, I conceive, at the
present time, a necessary element in the study
of Europe ; and, in illustration of the importance
of such knowledge, I would instance the facility
afforded to a man conversant with the East of estimating the powers of mind of the European states-
men who have had to judge or to act with

reference to it.   The following quotation is interesting, no less as affording new means of judging
of the mind of Napoleon, as from the light his
opinions throw on this subject.

" Mahomet* restricted the number of wives
to four; no Eastern legislator had allowed so few.
One may well inquire why he did. not suppress
polygamy, as Christianity had done (?); for it is
very certain that no where in the East is the
number of women superior to that of men.   *   *
*   *   *   These countries, being inhabited by
men of various colours, polygamy may have been
the only means to have prevented persecution.
The legislator may have thought that, to prevent
the white from becoming enemies of the black,
the black of the white, and the copper-coloured
of both, it was necessary to make them all members of the same family, and thus to struggle
against the disposition of man to hate all that
is not himself.   If ever we intend to give liberty
to the black, and establish perfect equality in our
colonies, we must authorise polygamy.   Then will
the different colours, forming a portion of the same
family, be confounded in the opinion of each.
Without this, satisfactory results will never be
obtained."

It certainly is a very strange thing to observe,
and a very difficult thing to account for, that in

* Memoirs of Napoleon, Vol. V., p. 99, note.

the East neither difference of colour, nor of rank,
class, or station, creates difference of feeling or
aversion between man and man, in opposition to
the universal experience of European nations,
who speak so much of philanthropy and liberty.
It comes also singularly to countenance this idea
of Napoleon, that the distinctions of rank are
externally marked, by attributing to the persons so
distinguished the character of " brother," " father,"
&c.; in fact, some *family* character or tie.

One of the greatest contrasts that strikes me,
between the West and the East, is the absence of
the slights and heart-burnings which occupy so
large a portion of our existence, and which are,
indeed, the shadows of our life. They beset us in
our early childhood; they invade our family circle;
they rule our social meetings; prosperity is not free
from them, and adversity owes to them its sting.
Now in the East, you never see a man slighted;
every individual has a fixed position; the child as
well as the grown man, in the school-room as well
as in public society. There are none of those
public throngings, where distinction of the one is
only gained by the slighting of the many; which
assemblages are the result of a great amount of
vanity and *amour propre* in a nation, and tend to
reproduce their causes. It is from these causes
that the greater part of our restlessness, and of our
activity, proceed. That activity has produced
manifold effects, both good and bad,—effects, in

either character, unknown in Turkey. On the
one hand, the progress of science; which, however, I take to be by no means incompatible
with the domestic existence of the East; on the
other, the complication of laws, the oppositions of
opinion, and the accidents and necessities of the
material and political state of the Western world,
which necessitate, in the individual, an immense
amount of activity, expended uselessly in counteracting the effects of the activity of other men.
The Turk never gets up, but when he has some-
where to go; never works, but when he has something to do; never speaks, but when he has something to say: he entertains no opinion without a
reason, and pronounces no judgment without a
necessity and a right; he is, therefore, the very
antithesis of a modern European. He can sit still,
hold his tongue, and sit by himself, without suffering from irritation, and without affecting to despise
his fellow-creatures. If he is careless of the mis-
fortunes of the morrow, he enjoys the existence of
to-day; and though no man so pugnaciously defends that which he does possess, yet he never
puts himself in the alternative of endangering what
he has, for the chance of obtaining something
better. His domestic — his Harem existence forms
his mind; and in that mind is to be found his
social and his political character; and the words
(however correct) that may be applied to the description of the political state, without the com-

prehension of his domestic character, are forms
without substance.

It may be very reasonably supposed, that the
seclusion of women from male society would give
to the latter that coarseness which, in Europe, is
felt to be counteracted by the mixture of the
sexes. But this proceeds from the peculiar circumstance, that we make a difference in our social
intercourse between men and women, which the
Easterns do not, while they pay as much deference to men as we do to the fair sex. Women
and men are addressed by the same title—the
same modes of salutation; and a gentleman com-
ports himself towards another gentleman, as in
Europe he would comport himself towards a lady.

But although men and women do not mix in
general society, the sexes live in the constant presence of each other in the Harem; and, in the
most intimate family circles, a greater degree of
decorum is observed there than in the public meetings of Europe. These are the ties which have
held together their empire so long against all
hope and all belief. The patriotism of this people
is to be found in their domesticity, which the seclusion of the Harem has veiled from the sight,
which has been preserved from that very circumstance, and has given rise to the belief that it did
not exist.

In conclusion, I must not omit that the home

of the Turk is, in the eye of the law, like the castle of the Englishman; that no officer of justice can enter it, even should the door stand ajar, without express permission; and its inner portion, the Harem, he must not enter at all. While the habitation of the family is thus held sacred, the rights, prerogatives, and authority, which custom, from time immemorial, has granted to it, and which we designate by the term patriarchal, are no less rigidly maintained; but if you never hear of justice interfering between members of a family, in the event of domestic violence or wrong, it is not because the law *sanctions* an authority in relationship superior to the public tribunals, but that, in Eastern jurisprudence, there is no public *accuser*. The injured party alone has a right to seek justice, and has equally the faculty of dispensing with its decisions. The law does not proclaim an abstract principle of justice, but lends assistance to the injured, when called upon to do so. Should, therefore, the father of a family exceed the bounds of moderation or justice in punishing a son, servant, or slave, the idea of judicial interference would never present itself to any one; not that the injured would not receive support, but because the law could not take its course unless on the demand of the injured, who would be prevented by public opinion, if not by habit and feeling, from appealing against his own blood.

Napoleon, in Egypt, was struck and puzzled by this state of things: he confounded two very distinct points — paternal authority, and security of a man's house from the intrusion of officers of police. The father of a·family, according to the code of Islamism, has no judicial authority of any kind whatever: he can retain neither wife, child, servant, nor slave, except by free consent; and yet in reality he possesses a power which, to those who do not feel as they do, appears the result of despotism in the parent, sanctioned by the laws.

The explanation which I have here given, will, I think, suffice to shew, that if the agents of authority are refused access to the house of a Mussulman, or of the Christian and other inhabitants of Mussulman countries, it is not because their control would interfere with any judicial authority exercised by the head of the family over its inmates.

" Every father of a family in the East (*Mémoires de Napoleon*, t. v. p. 103) possesses over his wife, his children, and his slaves, an absolute power, which the public authority cannot modify. There is no example of a Pasha, or an officer of any description, penetrating into the interior of a family, to trouble the chief in the exercise of his authority. It is a thing that would shock the national customs, manners, and character. The Easterns consider themselves masters in their houses; and every

agent of government, who has to put in execution
a decree against them, waits until they quit their
homes, or sends for them."

This inviolability of the homestead, treated as a
species of despotism, the Englishman will probably
understand in another light. Indeed, this principle
and practice is one of the most remarkable points of
resemblance between the English and the Turkish
character and institutions. The Turkish is the only
European language which possesses, in the word
" Harem," a synonyme for the English " Home,"
and, in fact, implies a great deal more.

CHAPTER XXVII.

CONCLUSION.

I MUST now conclude this journal, leaving the reader at Scodra, although I intended carrying him to Constantinople; but the subjects I have touched on have grown under my pen; and, in reconsidering what I have said, I have to regret the necessity of excluding much that appears to me important, or the inability to convey more in the space allotted to me.

I intended, in commencing these volumes, to have restricted them to matters of fact, and have referred, at the opening of the first volume, to an Appendix, such matters as required too much detail to be woven into the narrative; but the same reason which has curtailed the journey, has excluded the Appendix, which itself would have nearly equalled in size the work.

If the reader is so far satisfied, we may resume together, at a future period, the thread of this discourse, now cut short.

THE END.

Ingram Content Group UK Ltd.
Milton Keynes UK
UKHW021948270323
419267UK00005B/133